Mike Meyers' Certification
Passport ✶

MSCE Windows®
2000 Professional

**EXAM
70-210**

Brian Culp

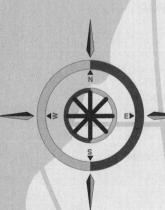

Osborne

New York • Chicago • San Francisco
Lisbon • London • Madrid • Mexico City
Milan • New Delhi • San Juan
Seoul • Singapore • Sydney • Toronto

McGraw-Hill/Osborne
2600 Tenth Street
Berkeley, California 94710
U.S.A.

To arrange bulk purchase discounts for sales promotions, premiums, or fund-raisers, please contact McGraw-Hill/Osborne at the above address. For information on translations or book distributors outside the U.S.A., please see the International Contact Information page immediately following the index of this book.

Mike Meyers' MCSE Windows 2000 Professional Certification Passport

1 2 3 4 5 6 7 8 9 0 DOC DOC 0 1 9 8 7 6 5 4 3 2 1

Book p/n 0-07-219593-2 and CD p/n 0-07-219592-4
parts of
ISBN 0-07-219367-0

Publisher	**Project Editor**	**Indexer**
Brandon A. Nordin	Lisa Theobald	Karin Arrigoni
Vice President &	**Acquisitions Coordinator**	**Design and Production**
Associate Publisher	Jessica Wilson	epic
Scott Rogers		
	Technical Editor	**Illustrators**
Editorial Director	Glen Clarke	Michael Mueller
Gareth Hancock		Jackie Sieben
	Copy Editor	Kelly Stanton-Scott
Acquisitions Editor	Lisa Theobald	Lyssa Wald
Nancy Maragioglio		Beth Young
	Proofreader	
	Dave Nash	**Cover Design**
		Ted Holladay

This book was composed with QuarkXPress™.

Information has been obtained by McGraw-Hill/Osborne from sources believed to be reliable. However, because of the possibility of human or mechanical error by our sources, McGraw-Hill/Osborne, or others, McGraw-Hill/Osborne does not guarantee the accuracy, adequacy, or completeness of any information and is not responsible for any errors or omissions or the results obtained from use of such information.

About the Author

Brian Culp cut his teeth in the IT world in a small networking outfit called IBM before gaining his MCSE certification and stepping into the classroom. He is currently President and CEO of LANscape, Inc., and no, they won't trim your shrubbery or build you a berm. LANscape provides training services to companies big and small, and also provides network administration.

About the Technical Editor

Glen E. Clarke is a Microsoft Certified Systems Engineer (MCSE), Microsoft Certified Solution Developer (MCSD), and Microsoft Certified Trainer (MCT). Glen also holds Prosoft's Certified Internet Webmaster–Certified Instructor (CIW CI) certification and is an A+ certified technician. Glen currently works as a technical trainer for PBSC, one of Canada's largest technical training centers, where he spends most of his time delivering the MCSE and MCSD curriculum. When he's not working, Glen loves to spend quality time with his wife, Tanya, and their two children, Sara and Brendon. He is an active member of the martial arts community, where he currently holds his first-degree black belt in Tae Kwon Do. You can contact Glen at gleneclarke@hotmail.com.

Dedication

For my grandfather Roy, who fixed Philco radios—not for people who owned them, but for the Philco company engineers—and never charged a dime. He would have done something like this, only a lot better.

And for Griffin, my three-year-old son, who thinks I should be writing stories about snow monsters and swords.

Acknowledgments

This project would not have reached completion without the support and hard work of many, many people. I would like to specifically thank Nancy Maragioglio at McGraw-Hill for her encouragement, patience, and most of all old-fashioned, roll-up-the-sleeves hard work. I would like to thank technical editor Glen Clarke for his efforts hiding blemishes in my first drafts, and for his many suggestions that improved the book. Any technical errors that remain are mine and mine alone. (Except for any really big ones. Those are still Glen's fault.) I also need to thank Lisa Theobald for her weekends and evenings making the text readable and for accommodating my last-minute changes. I would also like specifically to mention the efforts of John Nicholson at Johnson County Community College, who helped get me started on the path to authoring this book, and David Fugate for his guidance and support. Thanks are also in order to the IBM people in Seattle who took a green IT guy under their wing, specifically Rich, Michael, and Pat. I also want to thank my family for their support. My brother Matt is essential if you need to remember the names of movie characters. And thanks to every Starbucks in Kansas City for supplying me with enough caffeine during this project to kill most livestock.

Contents at a Glance

Contents

4 Configuring and Customizing the End User Experience

Objective 4.01

Objective 4.02

Objective 4.03

Manage Applications by Using Windows

Check-In

May I See Your Passport?

What do you mean you don't have a passport? Why, it's sitting right in your hands, even as you read! This book is your passport to a very special place. You're about to begin a journey, my friend, toward that magical place called CERTIFICATION! You don't need a ticket, you don't need a suitcase—just snuggle up and read this Passport—it's all you need to get there. Are you ready? Let's Go!

Your Travel Agent—Mike Meyers

Hello! My name's Mike Meyers. I've written a number of popular certification books and I'm the president of Total Seminars, LLC. On any given day, you'll find me replacing a hard drive, setting up a Web site, or writing code. I love every aspect of this book you hold in your hands. It's part of a powerful new book series called the *Mike Meyers' Certification Passport*. Every book in this series combines easy readability with a condensed format. In other words, they're the kind of books I always wanted when I prepared for my certifications. Putting this much information in an accessible format is an enormous challenge, but I think we have achieved our goal and I am confident you'll agree.

I designed this series to do one thing and only one thing: to get you the information you need to achieve your certification. You won't find any fluff in here—the author, Brian Culp, has packed every page with nothing but the real nitty gritty of the certification exam. Every page is packed with 100 percent pure concentrate of certification knowledge! But we didn't forget to make the book readable. I hope you enjoy the casual, friendly style. I want you to feel as though the author is speaking right to you, discussing the certification—not just spewing facts at you.

My personal e-mail address is mikem@totalsem.com. Please feel free to contact me directly if you have any questions, complaints, or compliments.

Your Destination: Windows 2000 Professional Exam 70-210

If a journey of a thousand miles begins with a single step, this is that step. Although you don't have to take the Windows 2000 MCSE exams in any particular order, it is generally accepted practice that this one will be your first. The Windows 2000 Professional exam is a good starting point for your journey, as the knowledge that you gain here will provide a good conceptual base upon which you will build for the rest of your MCSE certification. This test will measure your ability to implement, administer, and troubleshoot information systems that incorporate Microsoft Windows 2000 Professional.

You can expect to be tested on topics such as installing Windows 2000 Professional, configuring hardware such as network cards and disks, configuring the desktop environment for end users, implementing the networking protocols, establishing connectivity between computers, and troubleshooting security settings. In addition, MCSE candidates are expected to have at least one year of experience implementing and administering network operating systems.

The MCSE certification is one of the industry's most powerful certifications—always has been. Now that the exams have been updated to incorporate the Windows 2000 operating system, some significant changes have been made to their difficulty level. Microsoft has changed test questions to reduce the emphasis on learning facts to instead require synthesis of information in real-world scenarios. Nearly half the items in the core exams demand that the candidate have troubleshooting skills acquired through hands-on experience and working knowledge. Because of this new difficulty, the MCSE will carry more clout than ever, as the numbers of people who achieve certification will surely be fewer.

The MCSE certification is *the* certification that demonstrates a mastery over the Microsoft Windows operating system. And unless you think that Microsoft will be out of the network operating system business anytime soon, it will remain a valuable certification for years to come, well worth the investment of your time and resources.

Your Guide, Brian Culp

Brian Culp is one of those people who just have to buck trends. Unlike the majority of his fellow nerds, Brian is also a certified jock! Let's first point out his major nerdish accomplishments. Before teaching computers, Brian learned the IT ropes in Seattle, Washington, at a small outfit called IBM. (He also remember another big computer name up there as well, maybe in Redmond…can't think of it right now.) Brian currently holds three certifications: the MCSE and MCT, and he's also A+ certified.

He has been teaching the Windows 2000 MCSE track to students far and wide since the operating system hit the shelves. Along with the standard core MCSE track and design courses, he has taught and written courseware for Microsoft Systems Management Server 2.0. Today, Brian's students' scores of his conversational teaching style and technical knowledge consistently rank him as one of the Midwest region's top technical instructors.

He now is president of LANscape, Inc., a firm that provides technical training and administrative expertise to small and medium-sized businesses.

Prior to his life in front of a computer, Brian played baseball in the Colorado Rockies organization, where four knee surgeries and general lack of talent (*his* words, *not mine*) conspired to force his retirement in 1996. Brian has also been paid to write non-computer texts, as he was a sports columnist for the *Roanoke Times* in Roanoke, Virginia, and the *Overland Park Sun* in Overland Park, Kansas, during his baseball career.

Brian graduated from Kansas State University, where he set the school's all-time home run record with the last swing of his college career (those turned into doubles with a wooden bat, by the way), and now he competes in sprint-distance triathlons during the summer months. (The knee has been fixed up enough to allow him to run 3 to 5 miles or so.)

Brian is always eager to hear feedback and comments from readers in an effort to improve the style and content of this and future projects. You can contact Brian at one of two e-mail addresses to discuss any issues or questions relating to the book: bculp@lanscapecomputer.com, or bculp23@hotmail.com.

Why the Travel Theme?

One of my favorite topics is the metaphor of gaining a certification to a taking a trip. Many of the elements are the same: preparation, an itinerary, a route—even mishaps along the way. Let me show you how it all works.

This book is divided into eight chapters. Each chapter begins with an Itinerary that provides objectives to be covered in the chapter and an ETA to give you an idea of the time involved in learning the skills in that chapter. Each chapter is broken down by real exam objectives, either those officially stated by the certifying body, or if the vendor doesn't provide these, our expert take on the best way to approach the topics. Also, each chapter contains a number of helpful items to bring out points of interest.

Exam Tip

Points out critical topics you're likely to see on the actual exam.

Travel Assistance

Shows you additional sources such as books and Web sites to give you more information.

Local Lingo

Special terms   Describes terms in detail in a way you can easily understand.

Travel Advisory

Warns you of common pitfalls, misconceptions, and downright physical perils!

CHECKPOINT

The end of the chapter gives you two handy tools. The "Checkpoint" reviews each objective covered in the chapter with a handy synopsis—a great way to review quickly. Plus, you'll find end-of-chapter "Review Questions" (and "Review Answers") to test your newly acquired knowledge.

But the fun doesn't stop there! After you've read the book, pull out the CD and take advantage of the free practice questions! Use the full practice exam to hone your skills, and keep the book handy to check answers. When you're passing the practice questions, you're ready to take the exam—go get certified!

The End of the Trail

The IT industry changes and grows constantly, and so should you. Finishing one certification is just a step in an ongoing process of gaining more and more certifications to match your constantly changing and growing skills. Read the "Career Flight Path" at the end of the book to see where this certification fits into your personal certification goals. Remember, in the IT business, if you're not moving forward, you are way behind!

Good Luck on your certification! Stay in touch!

Mike Meyers
Series Editor
Mike Meyers' Certification Passport

Introduction

What About XP?

As Microsoft puts it, "The MCSE certification is the premier certification for IT professionals who design and implement the infrastructure for software solutions based on the Windows 2000 platform and Microsoft server software."

But certifications are like Michael Jordan's retirements—they don't last forever. Because Microsoft's certification strategy allows more than one track of certifications to be valid at any one time, it's especially important that you be certified in the product that you'll be working with the most. Of course, holding certifications in other tracks is always a bonus.

If you're holding this book, XP has shipped and is available. It's also likely that by the time you read this, the tests for the XP Professional/ Windows .NET Server platform have been released out of beta and count toward MCSE certification. So what should you do? Isn't it just better to wait and study XP when more reference material becomes available? When will the Windows 2000 certification go away?

The answer to this last question is "not anytime soon." To quote directly from Microsoft's training and certification Web site, "MCSEs who are on the Windows 2000 track *will not be required to pass Windows XP Professional/Windows .NET Server exams to retain MCSE certification.* The Windows 2000 exams and the Windows XP/Windows .NET Server exams of the MCSE certification are expected to remain available concurrently."

So the XP exams will not be replacing the Windows 2000 exams; they'll exist alongside the Windows 2000 tests, with both counting towards the MCSE. Or, as Microsoft puts it, "The Windows 2000 exams and the Windows XP/.NET Server exams are expected to remain available concurrently. Retirement schedules for all exams are affected by a number of factors, including the needs of the industry and release of the next version of the Windows operating system." (This next version of Windows is code-named "Blackcomb" and its release has just been pushed back at least a year.) Candidates who have earned the MCSE credential by passing either the Windows 2000 to Windows XP/.NET Server exams, or a combination of both, *will remain certified until the same date.* After an exam retires, candidates have at least 12 months to fulfill any upgrade policy.

Your Windows 2000 MCSE certification is safe, and it will be for the foreseeable future. There's no need to worry about the XP certification "taking over" anytime soon. Will the 2000 certification tests ever be retired like the NT 4 tests just were? That you can count on, just as surely as the XP certification tests will also be retired at some point. We will outlive the Windows 2000 and XP operating systems. The skills and knowledge you acquire in your Windows 2000 training will provide a solid foundation as you learn about future Microsoft operating systems, whatever they be.

The Author's Take on Why Certify?

I get asked this once in a while by students who obviously aren't planning on taking any certification tests anytime soon: "What's the big deal if I certify? I know how to do what I need to do. Experience is a lot more important anyway." Fair enough. Here's how I respond:

Yes, experience counts; it always has in every walk of life, and there is no argument about that. But experience and certification are two completely different things. The certification is simply a demonstration of aptitude; it is not and never has been a substitute for real-world experience.

Moreover, how do you think you get experience in the first place? You first demonstrate that you can do a few things—that you can walk and chew gum at the same time—and then you are turned loose on the world. MCSE certification will open doors for you that otherwise would not be open. It's when you reach the point at which you can combine a few years of experience *and* certification that you are a force to be reckoned with in the workplace. That's when you can command a bidding war for your services. And even if you intend to stay put in your current job, employers will often provide incentives for certification. (Even the implied value of certification can be good for your bottom line. An employer that knows your value in the marketplace will be more likely to reward your certification efforts with pay raises come review time.)

If you are still waffling, compare yourself, certified or uncertified, in terms of a car mechanic or, better yet, your dentist. If you know nothing about a mechanic and he or she is not ASC certified, would you feel comfortable taking in your car for a major overhaul? Or would you choose the mechanic with the certification? And there's no way you'd be more impressed with a dentist who hangs his Leroy Neiman paintings on the wall rather than his dental school credentials, right?

Now consider this: If you're looking to hire a computer professional with two years of field experience, would you first interview the applicant with the MCSE or without it?

Don't be influenced by the myth of the "paper MCSE." There is no such thing. I hear that load of (insert explicative here) referenced all the time and it makes me ill. You know what? *All* MSCEs are paper MSCEs. That's what the certification is: a piece of paper that certifies that you have passed a series of very difficult tests. It's not an easy thing to do. It also says many things about you.

For starters, it shows that you have made a commitment of time. Certain book titles notwithstanding, you cannot "cram" for the MCSE tests and expect to do well. You must *study* for them, and that's going to take a considerable investment of your time. This is one of the shortest books you will ever pick up on the subject—and it still is almost 400 pages. To me, that's a lot to read. So you can expect to spend a good deal of your life over the next couple of weeks curled up with this yarn.

The MCSE certification also demonstrates that you have put in the effort, dedication, and discipline necessary, and that you have an propensity for understanding how computers work—something not all people possess. So good luck on getting the piece of paper that says all these things. It's one of the most valuable pieces of paper you will even earn.

Now, don't get me wrong: A certification is what it is—it doesn't replace attitude, work ethic, or professionalism. And it's *not* a get-rich-quick scheme, although you probably have heard ads in the marketplace that make it sound as though it were. I am not Don Lapre, and I am not selling you a voucher to a life of Hawaiian vacations, helicopter rides, and Barbra Streisand concert tickets. And I can assure you that there will not be teeming hordes of employers waiting outside the testing center waving *carte blanches* in your face like you were a free agent quarterback visiting the home of Redskins owner Daniel Snyder. You will still have to bust your chops, like in any walk of life.

It also helps if you enjoy what you do. My advice is that if you like computers— if you are fascinated, like I am, in finding out more about how these silly machines work—jump in with both feet. You'll have a lot of fun, and every day you'll find out something new.

So go on and pass the 70-210 Windows 2000 Professional exam and then give yourself a big pat on the back when you're done. Have a beer; send me one while you're at it. Just don't let others tell you that your investment of time and energy wasn't worth it. They didn't do the work. They won't reap the benefits.

There's my short answer to the "Why certify?" question. A lot of students in my classes stop asking questions by the third day. I'm not sure why.

Installing Windows 2000 Professional

	NEWBIE	SOME EXPERIENCE	EXPERT
ETA	4 hours	2 hours	1 hour

You don't have to be a card-carrying Rhodes scholar to realize that the Windows 2000 Professional operating system is of little use unless it is first installed on a computer.

Steps involved in the setup process include preparing for installation by making sure that your computer meets the minimum hardware requirements and that Windows 2000 Professional will support all the hardware you intend to use. You also will need to consider whether you should install a clean copy or upgrade from your current operating system. Other tasks in the preparation process include the important choices of a file system and partitioning scheme on the hard disks where you will be performing the installation.

This chapter includes issues regarding upgrading to Windows 2000 Professional, applying updates to installed applications, and deploying service packs. For the exam, you will be expected to understand the troubleshooting of failed installations as well.

Even though many installations won't require the depth of knowledge presented in this chapter, installing is a task that you will be performing dozens, or hundreds, of times over the course of your administrative career.

When you install Windows 2000 Professional, you should also consider whether the computer you are setting up requires *dual-boot support,* which is the ability of a single computer to run operating systems other than Windows 2000 Professional.

For test preparation (as well as real-life) purposes, you need to be especially aware of what to do if problems arise during installation and what to do should they be encountered. You can expect to be peppered with questions regarding what steps to take to recover troubleshoot a failed installation. The questions you will come across on the Windows 2000 Professional exam will likely be case-study based and will test your ability to choose the best possible installation method given the details of a particular environment.

Perform an Attended Installation of Windows 2000 Professional

Objective 1.01

To make a more informed choice about installing the Windows 2000 Professional operating system (OS), it is useful to know some of Microsoft's stated design goals. A familiarity with these goals can help you make a better business case for Windows 2000 installation and sets the backdrop against which you will begin your understanding of the OS. Windows 2000 programmers had the following goals in mind when they developed their code:

1. Integration of the best features of Windows 98
2. Integration of the best features of Windows NT 4 Workstation
3. Lower Total Cost of Ownership (TCO)

Windows 2000 Professional borrows from a host of features that were integrated into Windows 98 but were not present on Windows NT 4.0 systems. The features brought over from the Windows 98 platform mostly focus on ease of use and compatibility with existing hardware. These features include *Plug and Play* support, which allows the operating system to automatically recognize and install hardware devices; support for the *Advanced Configuration and Power Management Interface (ACPI)*; use of the *Active Desktop*; and support for the *Universal Serial Bus* and *Institute of Electrical and Electronics Engineers (IEEE) 1394* standard, which defines ways to connect peripheral devices to computers.

The emphasis of design goal 2 is ease of use and hardware compatibility. Windows 2000 Professional includes a number of features that were not available with Windows NT 4 Workstation. These features included support for technologies such as Plug and Play, universal serial bus (USB), IEEE 1394 (FireWire), and Advanced Configuration Power Interface (ACPI).

The transition from previous versions of Windows should go smoothly. While the user interface has changed slightly from the Windows 9*x* and NT 4 environment, it was designed so that users of those OSs would be able to accomplish tasks with little to no additional training and so that new users would be able to intuit how to perform a specific function, such as open a program or add a printer. Additionally, the installation process has been designed to be much simpler than that of Window NT Workstation 4.0 installations, with greatly reduced user input.

Travel Advisory

Most of the technologies mentioned here are given further attention throughout the course of this book and are mentioned here to set the milieu. For a quick reference of these technologies, check out a great Web site that dispenses concise definitions: it's called Webopedia, and you can find it at **http://www.webopedia.com.**

The best features of Windows NT 4 Workstation were integrated into Windows 2000, for design goal 2. Windows NT Workstation 4.0 actually serves as the foundation upon which Windows 2000 Professional was built. In fact, you can think of Windows 2000 as NT version 5. The features carried forward from Windows NT 4 into Windows 2000 include those that make Windows NT the choice for business desktops worldwide. These features include a higher degree of OS stability. Put simply, Windows 2000 Professional crashes less often than Windows 98. Another important feature, especially to business users, is the local security built into the OS. A valid user name and password are required to interact with Windows 2000 Professional, and local security can be set on files and folders with the NTFS (NT file system).

A main design goal of Windows 2000 Professional is design goal 3: to reduce the cost of owning, maintaining, and upgrading the operating system. Windows 2000 includes easy-to-use administrative interfaces through the Microsoft Management Console (MMC) snap-ins, and it provides multiple deployment options, including the use of unattended installations and the Remote Installation Service (RIS).

What's New in Windows 2000

Windows 2000 offers many new features that were not available on previous versions of Windows, and that works to give Windows 2000 a competitive edge in the OS market. This book, and the Windows 2000 core exams, focus heavily on these new features:

- Disk quota support (on NTFS partitions)
- Internet printing support
- Encrypting File System (EFS) support (on NTFS partitions)
- Wizard-based administration and configuration
- Enhanced virtual private networking (VPN) support
- Offline file support
- Slipstreaming of service packs

Exam Tip

As a rule of thumb, any time a new feature of Windows 2000 is mentioned, you can bet that it will be the subject of a test question or two. Microsoft has really emphasized tougher tests for the Windows 2000 track, and testing on concepts that apply to NT 4, even though they may be critical for real-world administration, wouldn't make the exams very hard for NT veterans.

Preparing to Install

The first order of business when performing an installation of Windows 2000 Professional is to make sure it will play nicely with your existing hardware and software. Windows 2000 Professional can be a little finicky about who gets let into the game.

To help you determine what software and hardware components Windows 2000 Professional will and won't work with, Microsoft publishes and continually updates its Hardware Compatibility List (HCL), a directory of the currently tested hardware components on which Windows 2000 Professional will run. A copy (HCL.txt) is kept in the \Support folder right there on the installation CD-ROM, and you can always see the latest copy on the Web at **http://www.microsoft.com/hcl**.

The good folks in Redmond recommend that you check the HCL prior to performing an installation of Windows 2000 Professional; they might even think that most people actually do. The best rule of thumb is that a check of the HCL is warranted if you're considering an upgrade of an older computer. Most modern computers will support Windows 2000 Professional quite nicely (see the list of minimum hardware requirements in Table 1-1), regardless of whether or not hardware components exist on the HCL. And not every piece of hardware will appear on the HCL, even though it might get along with Windows 2000 just fine.

Of course, this brings us to the other method of verifying whether or not the hardware you are considering will support Windows 2000 Professional: just install the darned thing on the intended computer. If it works, that's right—the hardware is supported. If not, well, you can always try to find new drivers or wait for a service pack release. This will be a problem, however, if you don't have the luxury of a test computer or a removable hard drive on which to perform an install.

> **Travel Advisory**
>
> Here's a quick note about removable hard drives: get them. Removable drives allow you to experiment with multiple configurations without fear of messing something up. You can keep a "'production" hard drive for storing all your work and critical data and a "test" hard drive where you can try out all the features of Windows 2000.

So again, the caveat emptor here is, be careful on older hardware. Installation "issues" have been known to arise. For example, I have an older printer that is great for laptops because it is easily moved. Actually, it's great on laptops running Windows 98, because no driver for it exists on the Windows 2000 installation media and the manufacturer won't bother to write one. I have seen numerous other problems with older hardware, from network cards to scanners, which flat out won't work on Windows 2000.

Travel Advisory

New computers and peripherals are usually just fine with Windows 2000, but you should be prepared to shell out some extra money to upgrade hardware if you are using older stuff.

To determine software compatibility, you will need to check with the application vendor, check the Microsoft compatibility list, or check both. You can find the software compatibility list by searching the keywords "software compatibility" at **http://www.microsoft.com/windows2000/**. But, as with hardware, probably the best way to check application compatibility is just through old-fashioned trial and error, and of course away from a production environment.

Travel Advisory

Windows 16-bit applications that use virtual device drivers (VxDs) will not run properly in Windows 2000.

Microsoft likes to test your knowledge of two tools on its exams—tools that further aid an administrator in the task of determining whether hardware is up to snuff. One is the Windows 2000 Readiness Analyzer, and the other is the installation utility itself, run with a special switch from the command line. The syntax of the command is

```
winnt32 /checkupgradeonly
```

Both of these tools accomplish essentially the same thing—namely, checking for hardware and software compatibility. Either of these two utilities checks your computer for upgrade compatibility with Windows 2000. On a computer running Windows 9x, an upgrade report generated by the /checkupgradeonly tool will be created in the %systemroot% (usually \WINDOWS) folder as upgrade.txt.

Local Lingo

%systemroot%   This variable denotes the Windows installation directory. If you accept the defaults, it will be \WINDOWS on 9x computers and \WINNT on Windows NT 4 and Windows 2000 computers.

For Windows NT 3.51 or 4.0 upgrades, the report is saved to the Winnt32.log in the %systemroot% folder. We will discuss the syntax of the `winnt` command in Table 1-2.

Exam Tip

Microsoft loves to test on the use of the /checkupgradeonly switch.

Table 1-1 shows the minimum and recommended requirements for an installation of Windows 2000 Professional.

TABLE 1.1	Minimum Installation Requirements	
Component	**Minimum Requirement**	**Recommended Requirement**
Processor	Pentium-class 133MHz processor	Pentium-class 133MHz processor
Memory	32MB RAM	64MB RAM
Hard drive space	2GB boot partition with 650MB free space	2GB boot partition with 1GB or more free space
Network	None required	Network card as required by your network topology (usually a card on the PCI bus)
Display	Video adapter and monitor with VGA resolution	Video adapter with VGA or higher resolution

Travel Advisory

Windows 2000 installations also require a boot and system partition that has not been compressed by technologies such as Windows 9*x* DriveSpace or DoubleSpace.

As mentioned, these installation requirements leave plenty of breathing room on any new system, and Windows 2000 Professional will run beautifully on modern computers.

Starting an Attended Installation

After you've ironed out compatibility issues, you can start the attended installation by using one of several methods. Probably the easiest way is to boot the computer from the CD-ROM. You may need to adjust the BIOS settings of the computer, but most computers robust enough to handle Windows 2000 can be set to boot from the CD. Other methods of attended installation include installing over the network, which means connecting to a share that includes the contents of the \i386 directory, and launching the Setup program, winnt32.exe, if you are already running a 32-bit operating system such as Windows 98 or Windows NT Workstation 4.0. If you are running a 16-bit operating system, such as DOS, you will have to run the winnt.exe installation program instead. The winnt.exe and the winnt32.exe installation programs support a number of switches that can save some time during the installation process.

The `winnt.exe` Setup switches supported by the Windows 2000 installation are listed in Table 1-2.

TABLE 1.2	Setup Switches Supported by the Windows 2000 Installation
Switch	**Description**
`/s: [path]`	Specifies the location to the i386 folder, which contains the Windows 2000 Setup source files; usually used with unattended installations. If you do not supply the /s switch with the winnt.exe, it will ask where the source files are.

(Continued)

TABLE 1.2	*CONTINUED*
Switch	**Description**
`/u: [filename]`	Specifies an unattend file, which contains all the answers to questions you are asked during installation. You can put the answers in the unattend file and tell Setup to use the answers from this file with the `/u` switch.
`/udf: [id],[filename]`	Some Windows 2000 install settings must be unique—for example, computer ID. You can configure a "uniqueness database file" (udf) and tell Setup to use this file with the `/udf` switch. You will also pass it the ID for the computer and the name of the file that has the unique settings. Setup will search the udf file for the ID and apply settings associated with it.
`/r: [foldername]`	To install an additional folder to the system with setup, you specify the `/r` switch. The folder remains on the system after installation is complete.
`/rx: [foldername]`	To install an additional folder to the system with setup, specify the `/rx` switch. The folder is removed from the system after the installation is complete.
`/e: [command]`	To execute a command after the graphical portion of Setup has completed.

To use any of these switches, you pass the switch to the winnt.exe program, like so:

```
winnt.exe /s:d:\i386 /u:acct.inf
```

Setup will then begin copying the necessary files for the Windows 2000 installation to a temporary folder on your hard drive. Once the files are copied to the hard disk, you are prompted to remove any floppy disks and reboot the computer.

Travel Advisory

It is good computing practice to disable virus-scanning software prior to beginning a Windows 2000 Professional upgrade. This is because the Setup program will access the Partition table of the hard disk, something which most anti-virus software programs get riled about.

Windows 2000 Setup then launches the text-based portion of the installation, where you can repair an installation by pressing R or continue with the installation by pressing ENTER. This portion is shown in Figure 1-1.

After you have selected to continue the installation, you should read the Windows 2000 License Agreement. At the end of the agreement, press F8 to acknowledge that you've read it.

Next select the partition where you want to install Windows 2000. Note that when you're presented with the partition screen, you can not only select a partition for installation, but you can delete and create new partitions. To create a partition, you press C on your keyboard (as shown in Figure 1-2), and to delete a partition, you press D.

To install Windows 2000 on all the free space as one partition, highlight that free space and press ENTER. Windows 2000 will automatically make a single partition out of all the selected free space and install the operating system to the WINNT folder. After you have selected a partition, you can select the file system that will be used. Windows 2000 supports FAT, FAT32, and NTFS for the installation partition. For more information on these file systems, refer to Chapter 2.

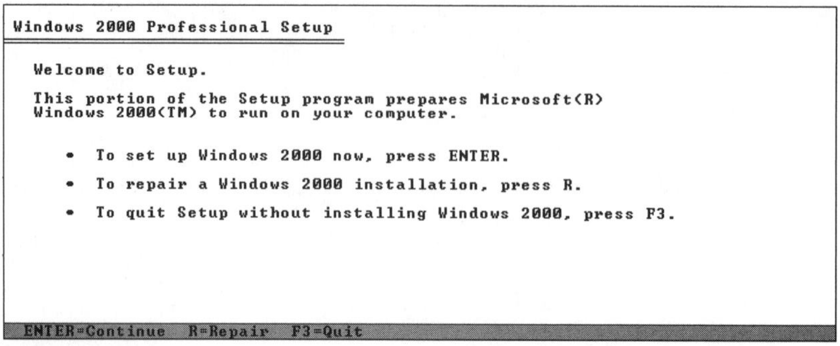

```
Windows 2000 Professional Setup

  Welcome to Setup.
  This portion of the Setup program prepares Microsoft(R)
  Windows 2000(TM) to run on your computer.

     •  To set up Windows 2000 now, press ENTER.
     •  To repair a Windows 2000 installation, press R.
     •  To quit Setup without installing Windows 2000, press F3.




  ENTER=Continue   R=Repair   F3=Quit
```

FIGURE 1-1   Starting the Windows 2000 installation

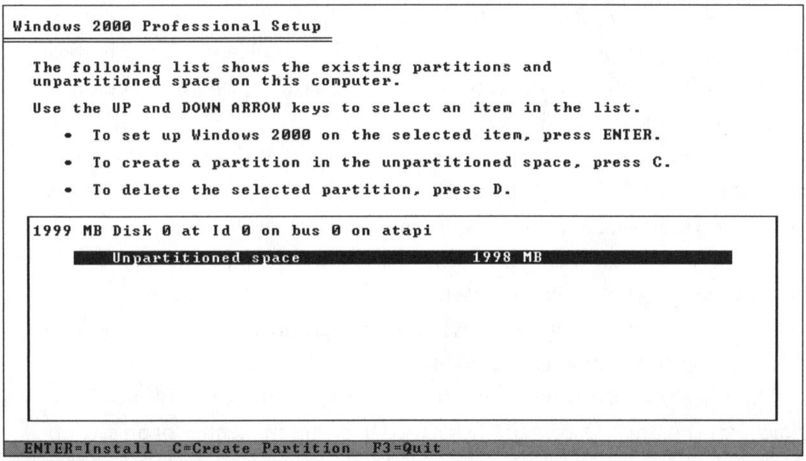

Windows 2000 Professional Setup
The following list shows the existing partitions and unpartitioned space on this computer.
Use the UP and DOWN ARROW keys to select an item in the list.
• To set up Windows 2000 on the selected item, press ENTER.
• To create a partition in the unpartitioned space, press C.
• To delete the selected partition, press D.
1999 MB Disk 0 at Id 0 on bus 0 on atapi
Unpartitioned space 1998 MB
ENTER=Install C=Create Partition F3=Quit

FIGURE 1-2 Selecting a partition

After these decisions are made, the Setup program will copy more files, reboot your computer, and then the Setup Wizard (shown in Figure 1-3) will start. From the Setup Wizard, you will be asked to supply user and computer names, product ID, network settings, and other information.

Windows 2000 Professional Setup
Welcome to the Windows 2000 Setup Wizard
This wizard installs Windows 2000 Professional on your computer. The wizard needs to gather some information about you and your computer to set up Windows 2000 properly.
Click Next to continue with Setup.
Windows 2000
< Back
Next >

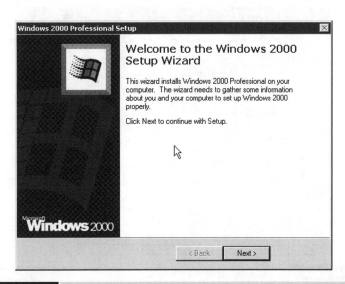

FIGURE 1-3 The Windows 2000 Setup Wizard

The Setup Wizard begins by detecting the hardware in the system and installing the appropriate device drivers. After the installation of your hardware is complete, Setup will ask you to make regional settings, where you change your locale and your keyboard layout.

If you decide not to change your locale settings at this point, you may later make the change through Regional Options in the Control Panel. After you select locales, you are asked to provide your name and organization.

The Product Key dialog box, shown in Figure 1-4 appears next. This is an important dialog box, because it's where you type your 25-character product key, located on the back of the Windows 2000 Professional Setup CD case. Without this key code, installation is impossible.

Another vital dialog box, the Computer Name and Administrator Password dialog box (Figure 1-5), contains fields used to create an identity, or an account, for the computer. In a Workgroup environment, computer names must be unique to the specific Workgroup. Furthermore, the computer account can be added to a Windows 2000 domain. Computer accounts represent a significant level of participation in a domain and are used for application of Group Policies. For example, they can be used to restrict which computers a domain user can log on to. Don't forget the Administrator Password that you type in here; you will need it to log on to Windows 2000 Professional for the first time.

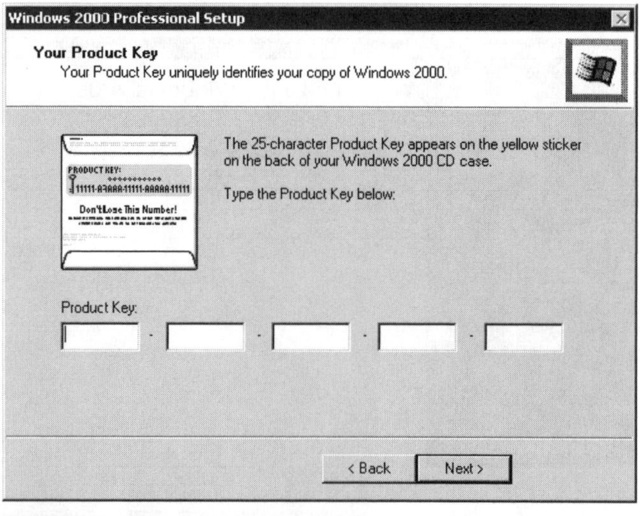

FIGURE 1-4 The Product Key dialog box

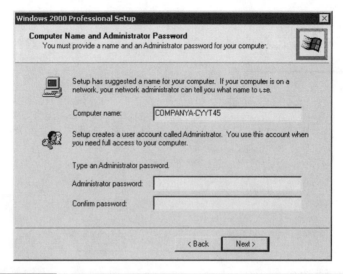

FIGURE 1-5 The Computer Name and Administrator Password dialog box

If a Plug and Play modem is installed, the Modem Dialing Information dialog box will appear. If not, the Date and Time Settings dialog box appears, where you configure the time zone and ensure that the correct time is set.

The Network Settings dialog box, shown in Figure 1-6, is where you specify how you want to connect to other computers. Choose Typical Settings to install network connections and the Workstation and Server components. It also sets up TCP/IP with the addressing information to be assigned automatically. Choosing Custom Settings allows you to install and configure each of these networking components separately, as well as install others.

The Workgroup or Computer Domain dialog box, shown in Figure 1-7, asks whether your system is part of a workgroup or domain. This dialog box is another "biggie" if your computer is to behave as you want. You will, however, be able to go back later on and change workgroup or domain membership, and the computer name too, so don't panic if you mess up this step.

The Windows 2000 Setup program then progresses by installing the necessary Windows components; this will take some time. After it has installed the components it then performs "Final Tasks." The Setup Wizard creates the Start menu, registers components into the system Registry, and removes any temporary files created by the Setup Wizard.

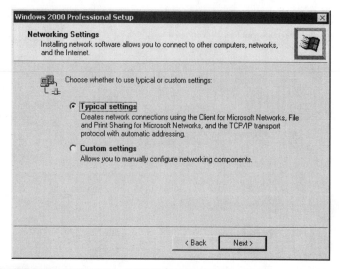

FIGURE 1-6 Network Settings dialog box

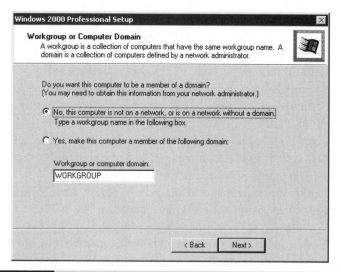

FIGURE 1-7 The Workgroup or Computer Domain dialog box

The Setup Wizard will inform you when the installation of Windows 2000 is complete, and it will ask you to remove the CD and click Finish.

The system restarts with the Network Identification Wizard, shown in Figure 1-8, which helps you set up the computer for networking by asking whether the

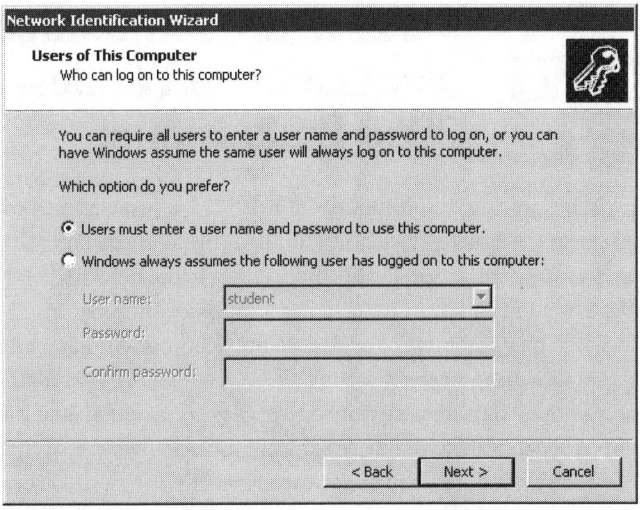

Network Identification Wizard

Users of This Computer
Who can log on to this computer?

You can require all users to enter a user name and password to log on, or you can have Windows assume the same user will always log on to this computer.

Which option do you prefer?

⦿ Users must enter a user name and password to use this computer.

○ Windows always assumes the following user has logged on to this computer:

User name: [student ▾]

Password: [   ]

Confirm password: [   ]

[< Back]   [Next >]   [Cancel]

FIGURE 1-8   The Network Identification Wizard

system should log in the same user every time, or whether each user must provide a valid user name and password to access the system.

For networks with security concerns, it is recommended that you not log on to the system as the same user account each time. Better to choose User Must Enter A Username And Password To Use This Computer. After the Network Identification Wizard is finished, the installation of Windows 2000 is complete.

Exam Tip

Even though it's not specifically mentioned as a test objective, Microsoft expects you to be familiar with the Setup of Windows 2000 Professional (though you aren't expected to memorize every setup screen). Several questions require knowledge of this process.

Travel Advisory

For exhaustive information about the installation process, see the *Microsoft Windows 2000 Professional Resource Kit*, Chapter 4, from Microsoft Press.

Perform an Unattended Installation of Windows 2000 Professional

You should be familiar with four areas of unattended installation: how to plan for an automated install, prepare the automatic install environment, customize the answer files, and deploy the OS and applications to the network computers.

An unattended installation involves setting up a computer with Windows 2000 Professional and potentially any desired applications without a user's intervention. If you have been performing installs in the field for any length of time, you probably know of a third-party software package or two that does this as well. Most admins will continue to use these software packages because of their ease of use, but Microsoft loves to test you on *its* way to install Windows 2000 on multiple computers at once. You can bank on at least two questions on this subject matter, even if it does not necessarily map to real-world use of the OS.

Creating an Answer File with Setup Manager

That being said, the automation of the installation process is one of the most significant improvements made to Windows 2000. To automate installation, answer files are needed. An answer file's job is to answer the questions that Setup poses during an attended installation. Pulling off the scripting of an install is now easier and more flexible than ever through the use of the Setup Manager. This wizard-based interface leads you through a series of questions (as all wizards do) that let you quickly create a script for a customized installation of Windows 2000. This is a big improvement over the way it had to be done in Windows NT 4, where knowledge of cryptic script-file syntax was required (unless cryptic script syntax is your bag).

And, if you're into that kind of masochistic torture, you can still create the script files the old-fashioned way by editing the unattend.txt file that installs with Windows. You can find it in the \i386 directory on the installation CD-ROM. The Setup Manager makes this much easier though, and eliminates errors in syntax.

Here's how to use the Setup Manager.

1. Extract the Windows 2000 deployment tools from the deploy.cab file that is found in the \Support\Tools folder on the Windows 2000 Professional

CD-ROM (it's on the Server CD as well). Right click the files you want to extract, and then select Extract from the context menu. It is a good idea to have the destination folder already created before the Extract procedure, as the extract utility does not let you create folders.

2. After you have extracted the Windows 2000 deployment tools, you can run the Setup Manager to do one of three things, as shown in Figure 1-9: create a new answer file, create an answer file that will duplicate the current computer's configuration, or edit an existing answer file.

3. Click the Next button. For this example, it is assumed that you want to create a new answer file. The Product to Install dialog box appears next. You can select a Windows 2000 Unattended Installation, a Sysprep Install (discussed later), or a Remote Installation Services install, as shown in Figure 1-10. For this example, choose Remote Installation Services.

4. In the User Interaction dialog box that appears next, select one of five levels of user interaction during the install. Each option is described when you select its respective radio button. Assume that the Provide Defaults options is selected and click Next.

5. The Administrator password dialog box appears, as shown in Figure 1-11. You can have the user prompted for the Administrator password, specify an account and password, or choose to log on automatically as Administrator when the computer starts. Make a choice and click Next.

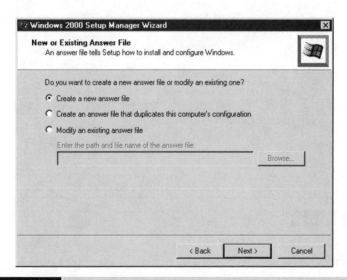

FIGURE 1-9   The answer file options

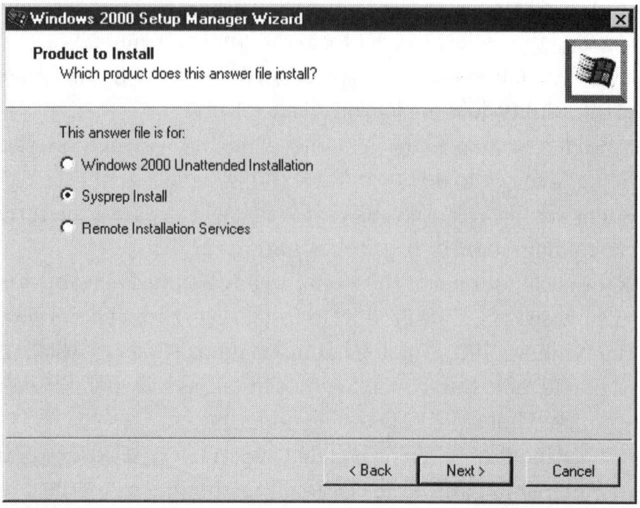

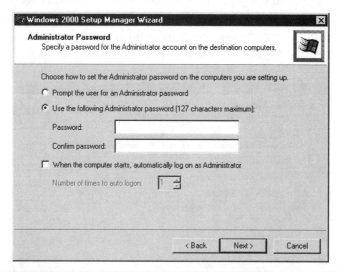

FIGURE 1-10   The Product to Install dialog box

FIGURE 1-11   The Administrator Password dialog box

6. In the Display Settings dialog box , configure your display settings. Each of the drop-down boxes will configure the user's display without the user having to change settings through the Display applet of the Control Panel.

7. In the Network Settings dialog box, you provide answer file information about how the computer will interact with the network. Notice that you are

essentially going through Windows 2000 Professional Setup, except rather than configuring the computer on the spot, these answers are used to generate a file that can be used in configuration.

8. Click Next to configure the Time Zone. Then click Next. The Additional Settings dialog box then lets you edit settings like these:

- Telephony settings
- Regional settings
- Languages
- Browser administrator shell settings
- The location of the installation folder
- Any installed printers
- A command (if any) that will be run the first time a user logs on

9. The default selection is No, Do Not Edit the Additional Settings, which we'll select. Click Next to continue.

10. In the Setup Information File Text dialog box, provide the answer file with a descriptive name and any other text that might be helpful. You might want to include information here that would let you quickly recognize what kinds of information are contained in the file. After entering this information, click Next.

11. The Answer File Name dialog box appears, as shown in Figure 1-12. This is the file name and storage location that will be saved to the hard disk. The default name for the file is remboot.sif. Click Save and then click the Next button.

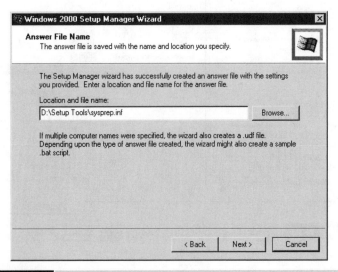

FIGURE 1-12 The Answer File Name dialog box

12. After completing the Windows 2000 Setup Manager Wizard, a dialog box appears to verify the successful creation of the answer file. Click the Finish button after you have reviewed this information.

Disk Duplication Using the SysPrep Tool

If your goal is to install Windows 2000 Professional with identical configurations on several computers, the most efficient installation method is to use *disk dupli-cation*. You may have heard this called *ghosting, cloning,* or *imaging* in the field. The image refers to the snapshot of the computer configuration that will be copied to other systems on the network, giving each system a consistent configuration. Windows 2000 includes a slick little utility that will help create these images, called SysPrep. It is extracted from the \Support\Tools folder in the same way that the Setup Manager is, as shown in Figure 1-13.

The main job of SysPrep is to remove the security identifier (SID) of the source computer, which is essentially the thumbprint of the computer. When you

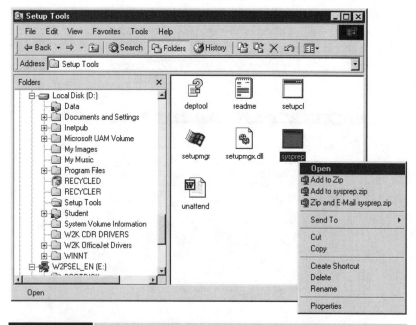

FIGURE 1-13   Launching the SysPrep tool for disk imaging

delete an account, you are deleting the SID, which is why if you delete an account and then create another account with the same name, you must reset all permissions for that account—to the computer, the new account is a *different* account. Without getting too technical about it, if you have a network in which computers' SIDs are the same, you have problems.

Local Lingo

SID A unique number that identifies user, group, and computer accounts. Internal processes used by Windows 2000 refer to the SID of the computer account, not its name.

After you've used SysPrep to create the image, you can then copy it to destination computers through third-party software or through disk duplication.

SysPrep is also responsible for generating a mini-Setup wizard that is added to the master image of the operating system. After you have installed the image on the target computer, this mini-Setup wizard guides the user through the process of entering user-specific information during setup, such as

- Product ID
- Regional settings
- User name
- Company name
- Network configuration

What's key about the use of the SysPrep tool is that you have an understanding of the required components on the clients who want to use the master copy of the operating system. For a client using this SysPrep image to do an install, the hard disk controller and hardware abstraction layer (HAL) must be identical to the source computer. The other stuff, such as the video card and the network adapter, do not need to be the same because the SysPrep tool will cause all the clients using the master image to run a full Plug and Play detection as a part of the OS setup.

The four switches shown next can be used to modify how SysPrep behaves, and knowing them is a good idea as you prepare for the exam.

Switch	Description
`/quiet`	Runs with no user interaction
`/pnp`	Forces Setup to detect Plug and Play devices on the destination computer
`/reboot`	Restarts the source computer
`/nosidgen`	Doesn't regenerate SIDs on the destination computers

We've talked quite a bit about using SysPrep and *preparing* a computer for the creation of the master image. To make sure you understand this technology, let's review the steps:

1. Install Windows 2000 Professional on a source computer. Extract the deploy.cab file from the CD-ROM as described previously.
2. Log on to the source computer as the Administrator to install any other applications as desired.
3. Run the SysPrep utility from the extraction folder.
4. The Windows 2000 Professional System Preparation Tool dialog box appears, warning you that security parameters will be modified. Click OK, and you will be prompted to shut down your system.

Now the image is ready for use. Copy the image to a shared folder or CD-ROM for distribution computers.

Local Lingo

Shared folder   A place on a network computer that other computers can connect to and get stuff, like image files. A more thorough discussion of shared folders can be found in Chapter 2.

Once this image has made it to the destination computers, your end users can start up their computers. The mini-Setup wizard will prompt each user for the variables mentioned, and the install is on its way. You can also automate the completion of the mini-Setup wizard by creating a sysprep.inf file with the Setup Manager Wizard.

Exam Tip

You should know that the Setup Manager creates a file called
sysprep.inf for use with SysPrep-imaged installations.

 **Objective 1.03**

Upgrade From a Previous Version

You will have three options after assessing the compatibility of the hardware to receive a Windows 2000 Professional installation:

- Perform a clean install of Windows 2000 Professional.
- Upgrade a previous installation.
- Preserve the existing installation of whatever by installing Windows 2000 Professional in a separate folder.

Objective 1.01 assumes that you are performing a clean install, although the options will be similar to upgrading. This section covers the last two parts of these three options, which are outlined in the splash screen when you insert the Windows 2000 Professional Setup CD-ROM into a computer with a preexisting operating system like Windows 98.

Configuring Dual Boot

When you install Windows 2000 Professional into a different folder than the current OS, you will have configured a computer that is *multiboot*, or *dual-boot*, capable. This second OS folder can be located on the same partition as the current OS or on a different one. Be mindful, however, of your file system considerations when configuring a system for dual-boot. For example, remember that Windows 9*x* cannot read any data locally from an NTFS partition without the addition of a third-party utility. Also, NTFS version 4, the file system native to NT 4.0, is not fully compatible with NTFS version 5. Here are some other important considerations when setting up a dual-boot configuration:

- If you will be dual-booting to Windows NT 4, make sure that disk compression is turned off. Windows 2000 will not be able to read the drive properly if it is on.

- Never upgrade to dynamic disks. Dynamic disks are seen only by Windows 2000 Professional computers and are not recognized by other operating systems.
- Perform the install of Windows 9x or DOS before installing Windows 2000. If you install Windows 2000 first, you can't install a previous OS without trashing the Windows 2000 installation.
- Make sure you have enough disk space. Two OSs will take up a lot of room, and you will have to install applications twice to be used with both OSs.

Travel Advisory

When setting up a dual-boot computer, if Windows NT 4.0 contains no service pack or a version prior to SP4, the Windows 2000 Setup routine will warn you not to continue the installation. If you plow ahead anyway, you will not be able to boot into Windows NT 4.0 after Windows 2000 is installed. Just desserts for your stubbornness, if you ask me.

Upgrading to Windows 2000 Professional

When you think about it, the computer's OS is nothing more than another piece of software installed on a computer, just like any other application. And just like other applications, the OS has an installation directory where the bulk of the files are placed. When you install over the current folder holding the computer's OS, you are performing an upgrade. You will be able to perform an upgrade to Windows 2000 Professional on the following operating systems: Windows 95, 98, Me, NT Workstation 3.51, and NT Workstation 4.0. Conceptually, it's like going from Office 97 to Office 2000—out with the old, in with the new. The data and applications on the computer should be unaffected (that is, unless they are incompatible with Windows 2000 Professional, which you should have found out beforehand if you had done your homework!).

Travel Advisory

As mentioned, installation order is important when configuring a multiboot computer. You will have to use the Emergency Repair Disk (ERD) to repair the system partition for a return to Windows 2000 functionality if you install Windows 2000 Professional first.

Want to upgrade from DOS or Windows 3.1? Tough. In the first place, such a computer's hardware probably won't suffice. There is no upgrade from DOS or Windows 3.1, but if you want to install Windows 2000 on a computer running DOS, you may run the 16-bit version of the Windows 2000 Setup program, winnt.exe.

Exam Tip

If a computer running Windows 9*x* that lives in an NT 4.0 or Windows 2000 domain will be upgraded to Windows 2000 Professional, make sure that you create an account for the computer object in that domain. This can be done either prior to or during the upgrade of the OS.

Use Windows 2000 Server Remote Installation Service to Automate Installations

Another way that automated installations of Windows 2000 Professional can be performed is through the Remote Installation Service (RIS). This area of expertise is one that you will be tested on throughout your MCSE track, so it is in your best interest to get familiar with this technology as quickly as possible. You are likely to see questions covering this topic on all four of your core exams, because the technology crosses so many disciplines. You will see a few questions on the 70-210, a few more on the 70-215 (Server), a couple on the 70-217 (Network), and it will especially be a part of the 70-217 (Active Directory) test.

RIS installations work by letting a client computer simply boot up and find an image of the OS that is then downloaded and installed. This client-server technology includes a RIS server, which must have the RIS software installed and house the Windows 2000 Professional installation images. The RIS client requires a Pre-Boot Execution Environment (PXE) network card v.99c or greater or a RIS boot disk.

Properly configured, there is little, if any, need for user interaction. However, several procedural steps need to be completed when performing an installation using RIS. Some of these procedures will involve preparing a Windows 2000 Server to house the RIS image. Some involve the correct authorization of the

DHCP and RIS services in Active Directory, and others involve making sure the client computer can boot up and locate a RIS server.

As the purpose of this book is to give you the basics of what you need to prepare for an exam, the discussion will not be a blow-by-blow account of everything that needs to be done. Instead, we will hit many of the high points, with an eye toward what needs to be done from the perspective of the Windows 2000 Professional computer to be set up. In other words, this is an overview, not a lesson, in RIS.

Travel Advisory

For more detailed information on RIS, see Osborne/McGraw-Hill's *Windows 2000: The Complete Reference,* Chapter 3, "Unattended Installations," by Kathy Ivens and Kenton Gardner.

As mentioned, the RIS server is the computer running 2000 Server that will also be running the RIS service and hold the images that will be used for client installation. Two kinds of images can be stored on a RIS server: CD-based images and RIPrep images. CD-based images contain the Windows 2000 Professional OS files (it's possible to do Windows 2000 Server images, but it wouldn't be worth the trouble) and can be customized through the use of answer files. RIPrep images are based on a preconfigured computer and can contain application installations as well. RIS with a RIPrep image is Microsoft's version of a cloning program, like Symantec's Ghost.

To prepare the RIS server, the following must occur:

1. The RIS service must be installed. This can be done with the Add/Remove Windows Components section of the Add/Remove Programs applet in the Control Panel. The RIS server must then be authorized in Active Directory through DHCP Manager.
2. After RIS is installed, you will configure RIS by typing **RISETUP** in the Run dialog box. The Remote Installation Services Setup Wizard starts. After clicking the Next button from the Welcome screen, the Remote Installation Folder Location dialog box appears. This is just the folder that holds the RIS images.
3. The Initial Settings dialog box appears next, allowing you to configure the RIS server to respond to client requests. Notice that the server does not respond to client requests until you tell it to do so. It is enabled with a check box, as seen in Figure 1-14.

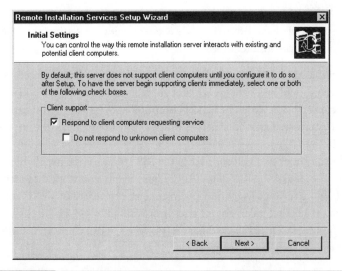

FIGURE 1-14   Configuring the RIS server to respond to image requests

4. The next steps will depend on what type of image you are setting up on the RIS server. You will be prompted in the next few screens for the installation files location, the image folder name, and the friendly name. When you are finished, a Review Settings dialog box gathers all your choices for review.

5. The installation files will be copied at this time, a process that can take several minutes to complete. Click the Done button when through.

6. Next, users who will perform RIS installations must be granted the right to create computer accounts. These users must also have the right to Log On As A Batch Job user. (The details of how to grant user accounts rights to perform system tasks are covered in Chapter 8.)

Exam Tip

The Remote Installation Folder in step 2 must reside on a separate partition than the operating system, and it must use NTFS version 5.

RIS relies on the following network services to be in place:

- DCHP, which is used to assign IP addresses to RIS clients
- A Domain Name Service (DNS) server, which is used to locate Active Directory

- Active Directory, which is used to find the authorized RIS servers and RIS clients, as well as to manage RIS configuration settings and client installation options

All right, enough acronyms already. (As an aside, regarding accepted social etiquette, you should know that you're not going to get many dates if you start peppering conversation with a bunch of computer acronyms.) As you can see, this technology crosses many boundaries, which is why this won't be the last you hear from RIS.

The computer that will connect to the RIS server for the install of Windows 2000 Professional is the RIS client. RIS clients rely on a network card technology called PXE—Pre-Boot Execution Environment. The magic of a PXE-compliant network card is that it can go out and find an IP address without the use of an operating system. Once this card has an IP address, it can connect to a RIS server and be sent an installation image.

Exam Tip

You can also create and use a RIS boot disk to start your client computer. The utility used for the generation of the RIS boot disk is called rbfg.exe, and it can be found on the RIS server. You just might see a question that requires you to identify this tool.

After the PXE-compliant system has been started, you will take the following steps to install the RIS image:

1. Press F12 to start a network service boot on the client computer. The RIS server will be found, and the Client Installation Wizard will start.
2. After pressing ENTER, the Windows 2000 Logon dialog box appears. You will be prompted for the user name and password and a valid domain name.
3. A menu will appear showing you the setup options available. These options include Automatic Setup, Custom Setup, and Restart a Previous Setup Attempt. You will most likely choose the Automatic Setup option.
4. After selecting which setup option to run, the image on the RIS server will be installed if only one image is available. If multiple images are available on the RIS server, you will be able to choose which one to apply to your machine.
5. The remote installation will now begin. What happens next during setup depends on whether or not you have configured the use of unattended installation files.

Objective 1.05   Deploy Service Packs

The first thing you need to understand about Service Packs is that their name—Service Packs—is misleading. When Microsoft hires me to run the company, I am going to start calling them Operating System Updates, because that's what they are. You can locate them on the Windows Update Web site, a centralized, online resource for Windows updates that is just one of the smartest, easiest to use, greatest little things that Microsoft has ever put together. On this site, you can find hot fixes, drivers, and service packs for all kinds of Windows products, and the interface even suggests the best ones to download and install automatically.

Local Lingo

Hot fix   An operating system update that is meant to address a specific feature; something Microsoft recommends be installed right away rather than being included in a service pack release. A recent example of this was the hot fix that was released for IIS 4, which fixed an issue that left the Web Server vulnerable to attack.

In earlier versions of Windows, 32-bit operating systems like NT 4.0 (Windows 2000 is essentially NT 5, by the way), the application of service packs was a pain in the ASCII. Veteran NT administrators can sit around telling service pack war stories like the crew of the fishing boat in *Jaws*. That's because every time a change was made from the operating system's CD-ROM or distribution point, the service pack had to be reapplied.

Local Lingo

Distribution point   A folder where the installation files for the operating system are stored and shared. For example, if you copied the contents of the \i386 directory to a shared folder called \W2K Pro, you would have just set up a distribution point.

Figure 1-15 demonstrates the relationship between a client and a distribution point.

Now for the big improvement. In Windows 2000 Professional, a technology called *slipstreaming* avoids the administrative overhead of service pack reapplication. With slipstreaming, you can just apply the service pack update to the source files in the Windows 2000 Professional distribution point. Any installations made from this distribution point also include the application of the service pack. Further, any services or drivers added to the local installation come from the distribution point, again avoiding the need to reapply the service pack to the local machine.

A demonstration of the slipstreaming technology has brought tears to the eyes of many an NT admin.

Exam Tip

The important thing to remember, and the thing about service packs that you are likely to be tested on, is that you need to apply the service pack to a distribution point, even if the distribution point is the local machine, to take advantage of slipstreaming.

To implement slipstreaming, you must modify the default behavior of update.exe, the service pack installation utility. From the command line, type

```
update -s: distribution folder
```

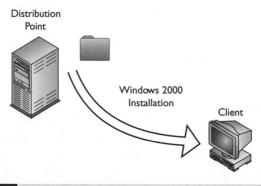

FIGURE 1-15   Client and distribution point

where *distribution folder* is the location of the OS files. This command will execute slipstreaming. From then on, use the distribution point to perform any changes to services or drivers on the local installation.

Exam Tip

Even though most administrative tasks can be accomplished from Windows' graphical interface, Microsoft loves to ask you questions about the times when it cannot. You are expected to know the commands and important switches used for many of these command-line utilities.

Remember, without following the steps of slipstreaming, you will have to revert to the Dark Age method of reapplying service packs after making changes from the Windows 2000 Professional installation CD-ROM.

Objective 1.06

Troubleshoot Failed Installations

To borrow a phrase from Austin Powers, "This organization will not tolerate failure!" The same can be said for the setup of Windows 2000 Professional. Following are a few guidelines that will help you overcome many installation pitfalls.

First, make sure all of the hardware is supported. Most technicians start to look at the HCL after a failed install. And at the risk of repeating the obvious, Microsoft recommends that you remove or upgrade the components not on the HCL *before* attempting installation again.

Another important task is to make sure that the computer's basic input/output system (the BIOS) is up to date. Vendor-provided BIOS updates can resolve many installation failures. One example of this: disabling the Plug and Play Operation System setting in the BIOS is important before installing Windows 2000 Professional on computers that don't support the Advanced Configuration and Power Interface (ACPI) specification. (Most newer computers will support ACPI.)

Your next step in troubleshooting installation failures is to determine at which point of the setup process the failure is occurring. Three distinct installation phases can be evaluated, as shown next.

- In the *Setup Loader phase,* some of the installation files are copied from the source to the local disk that is to receive the OS.
- In the *Text-Mode setup phase,* you see white text against a blue background. Installation and configuration of hardware drivers continues. Minimum system requirements are verified here before setup continues.
- The *GUI-Mode Setup phase* is the conclusion of the setup process. Additional device drivers are detected, installed, and configured.

If installation fails at the last phase, restarting the computer may resolve the problem, allowing setup to continue. However, rebooting to resolve installation failure isn't an option during the first two phases of setup. If installation fails during either of these phases, rebooting the computer will just bring you back to the same error.

A couple of information log files are created during setup that can be of assistance in troubleshooting the installation process. These files are a record of all the essential setup information:

- **setupact.log**   Includes a listing of all the actions that were performed during installation and a description of each. The actions will be listed in chronological order.
- **setuperr.log**   Includes any errors encountered by Windows 2000 Setup. For each error, an indication of the severity of the error along with its description is included.

Several device-specific or component-specific log files also may be generated during the setup process or when a new Plug and Play device is added. These log files are stored in the %systemroot% directory (it's usually \WINNT). Here is a listing of a few you will want to be familiar with:

- **Comsetup.log**   Logs the COM setup routines
- **Mmdet.log**   Logs multimedia installation and resource definition
- **Netsetup.log**   Logs network computer name, workgroup, and domain validation
- **Iis5.log**   Logs the installation and configuration of Internet Information Services 5

CHECKPOINT

✔ **Objective 1.01   Perform an Attended Installation of Windows 2000 Professional.** This objective presented an overview of the attended installation options. We looked at some of the preparation tasks, such as using the HCL to ensure that all installation hardware is supported under Windows 2000. We also examined important setup decisions such as installing into a workgroup or domain, choosing the language and locale settings, and partitioning your disk.

✔ **Objective 1.02   Perform an Unattended Installation of Windows 2000 Professional.** This objective focused on some of the unattended installation options. We looked at how to generate script files to be used in conjunction with unattended installations. These script files can be used to provide answers to the common installation questions that are asked during attended installations.

✔ **Objective 1.03   Upgrade from a Previous Version.** We looked at some of the upgrade paths available for upgrading installations of Windows 2000 Professional from previous operating systems. We also identified potential problems that can be encountered while upgrading the OS.

✔ **Objective 1.04   Use Windows 2000 Server Remote Installation Service to Automate Installations.** We looked here at the Remote Installation technologies available to get Windows 2000 Professional on many computers with a minimum of administrative effort. We learned the basics of how to set up and configure RIS, and we looked at some of the RIS client requirements.

✔ **Objective 1.05   Deploy Service Packs.** In this objective, we examined the process for applying service pack updates to the Windows 2000 operating system. We also looked at some new features that make the application of service packs much easier.

✔ **Objective 1.06   Troubleshoot Failed Installations.** This objective identified a few of the common problems that can occur during installations, and what to do should these problems occur. We looked at some of the resources, such as log files created during installation, that can help us in our troubleshooting efforts.

REVIEW QUESTIONS

1. You want to install Windows 2000 Professional on several computers with identical hardware configurations. You are thinking of using the SysPrep tool as a part of the disk duplication process. Which two components on the source and the target computers must be identical for this to work properly?

    A. Sound card
    B. Network adapter
    C. Hard disk controller driver
    D. Hardware Abstraction Layer
    E. Video adapter

2. To run the Setup Manager to automate the installation of Windows 2000 Professional, the following tasks must be completed:

    A. Copy the Windows 2000 deployment tools by extracting the files in the Wintools32.cab file on the Windows 2000 Professional CD-ROM.
    B. Copy the Windows 2000 deployment tools by extracting the files in Deploy.cab file on the Windows 2000 Professional CD-ROM.
    C. Run the autoset.exe application in the directory to which you extracted the file.
    D. Run the setupmgr.exe application in the directory to which you extracted the file.

3. Two images can be stored on a Windows 2000 server running RIS. What are they?

    A. PXE-compliant
    B. RIPrep
    C. CD-based
    D. Published images
    E. Third-party images

4. You are administering a network with 25 users, all of whom are upgrading their Windows NT 4.0 machines. You have procured the Windows 2000 Professional OS and have downloaded Service Pack 2. You are going to deploy Windows 2000 Professional on your client machines. How will you apply the service pack to all the Windows 2000 Professional deployment machines as a part of the upgrade of the OS?

    A. Type **update**

    B. Type **update -s:** *distribution folder*

    C. Type **update /syspart -s**

    D. Type **update /slip:** *distribution folder*

5. Oliver has set up a RIS server on his network to distribute images to 50 PXE-compliant computers in an Active Directory domain. To the user accounts he has set the proper user rights. All of the clients in the network are DHCP clients. Additionally, he has set up WINS for name resolution for non-2000 clients. Upon boot-up, none of the intended RIS clients are being offered RIS images. What can you do to help Oliver fix this situation?

    A. Authorize the RIS server in Active Directory.

    B. Install the DNS service; RIS requires DNS.

    C. Create RIS boot disks for the intended clients.

    D. Remove the WINS server from the network.

6. On a home computer with a cable Internet connection, you installed Windows 2000 Professional. Months later, you notice that a service pack is available, so you download and install it. A few months later, you add another service from the original Windows 2000 Professional installation CD-ROM. What should you now do?

    A. Do nothing. The service pack is not affected.

    B. Type **update /refreshservicepack** at the command prompt

    C. Run **setupmgr.exe -s**

    D. Reapply the service pack.

7. Which of the following automated installation options can make use of an answer file? (Choose all that apply.)

    A. Unattended installations

    B. Attended installations

    C. SysPrep tool disk images

    D. RIS image installations

8. What is the utility used to create a RIS boot disk?

    A. MAKEBOOT.EXE

    B. WINNT32 /RIS

    C. PXEBOOTR.EXE

    D. RBFG.EXE

9. You are setting up a Windows 2000 Professional OS for use at your office, Russell International. The install fails. Where will you start looking to determine the severity of the setup error?

   A. COMSETUP.LOG

   B. MMDET.LOG

   C. NETSETUP.LOG

   D. SETUPERR.LOG

10. As the admin for Griffin International, you are planning to deploy Windows 2000 Professional on several computers on your network. What are some ways you can quickly generate a report that will check that the computers you are considering for deployment are compatible with Windows 2000?

    A. Run COMPATCHK.EXE from the \Support folder of the installation CD-ROM.

    B. Download and run CHKUPGRD.EXE from the Windows Update Web site.

    C. Use the winnt32 /checkupgradeonly switch of the installation utility.

    D. Use the winnt32 /checkupgradenow switch of the installation utility.

11. In the question 10 scenario, you will be performing an upgrade of your client workstations rather than a clean install. Which of the following Operating Systems support an OS upgrade to Windows 2000 Professional?

    A. Windows 9x and Me

    B. Linux workstations

    C. NT 3.51 and NT 4 workstations

    D. NT 3.5 workstations

REVIEW ANSWERS

1. **C D** These two parts must be exactly alike for you to use SysPrep to duplicate an installation of Windows 2000 Professional from a source computer to a target computer. For example, the HAL cannot support a multiple processor system on one computer that generates the image and then be ported to a computer that is a uniprocessor. The installation will fail. **A** is wrong because the destination computers can have different peripheral devices. Plug and Play will detect them and set them up automatically. **B** and **E** are incorrect because of this as well.

2. **B** **D** To run the Setup Manager, you must first extract the tools from Deploy.cab, which is located in the \Support\Tools folder on the Windows 2000 Professional installation CD-ROM. Then, after the Setup Manager is extracted, start it by running setupmgr.exe. You will then be guided by a wizard through the process of generating an unattended setup file for a fully automated installation. **A** is incorrect because there is no such .cab file on the installation CD-ROM. **C** is incorrect because that is not the file used to start Setup Manager; in fact it also a make-believe file.

3. **B** **C** These two images can work with a RIS implementation. **A** is incorrect because, while PXE is a technology that is essential to (most) RIS installations, it describes the network card and not the image of the operating system. **D** is incorrect because Published is a term that applies to applications installed by Group Policy, not to RIS images. **E** doesn't apply because the RIS technology is Microsoft-specific.

4. **B** This is the command needed to enable service pack slipstreaming. The command will apply the service pack files to the distribution folder. Any clients that then perform an installation from this shared directory will have the service pack automatically installed as well. **A**, **C**, and **D** are all incorrect because of the syntax of the command. This is one of the areas for which you must know syntax exactly to answer the question correctly. Update by itself can be used to apply a service pack on a local machine that is already running Windows 2000 Professional.

5. **A** For the RIS server to offer installation images, it must first be authorized in Active Directory. **B**, while a true statement, is not necessary because you can assume from the question that the network has access to DNS. You would not be able to install Active Directory without DNS. **C** in incorrect because the computers are PXE-compliant, so a boot disk should not be necessary. **D** is incorrect because the mention of WINS is a smokescreen here, and will not affect the operation of RIS in any way. This is a common Microsoft exam tactic.

6. **D** When a new service is added to Windows 2000 Professional from the installation CD-ROM, you must reapply the previously installed service pack to ensure functionality. **A** is incorrect because of this reason. **B** is incorrect because while the update utility will be used to apply the service pack, this switch is not necessary. **C** is incorrect because this is not the correct utility to update service packs. Setup Manager is used to help generate automated installation scripts.

7. **A C D** All of these installation methods, with the exception of an attended installation, can use an answer file. **B** doesn't fit because by its nature, an installation that is attended will not need an answer file.

8. **D** RBFG.EXE is the utility to create a RIS boot disk. You can find it by connecting to the \\RIS_Server\Reminst\Admin\I386 directory. **A** is used to make boot disks, but the disks you will make with this tool are the Windows 2000 Setup disks. **B** is incorrect because there is no such switch for WINNT32, and it's not the correct utility anyway. **C** is, well, let me know if you ever find the PXEBOOR utility, bub.

9. **D** This is the log file that is generated when errors are encountered during the setup process. You can view this log by finding it in the %systemroot% directory and opening it with a text editor. The rest are legitimate log files, but they are used for other troubleshooting purposes. **A** is wrong because COMSETUP.LOG logs COM component problems. **B** is the log file that will help troubleshoot multimedia device detection. **C** is also wrong because it is used to troubleshoot computer name registration and workgroup or domain detection.

10. **B C** The CHKUPGRD.EXE program can be found on the Windows Update Web site and is called the Windows 2000 Readiness Analyzer when you are looking for it there. This program will run a minimal version of WINNT32.EXE to check the upgrade capability of the computer. The same thing applies to running winnt32 /checkupgradeonly. This switch will cause the winnt32 upgrade utility to generate a log file to report upgrade readiness. The file will be called UPGRADE.TXT on Windows 9*x* computers and WINNT32.LOG on NT 4 systems. **A** is incorrect because that utility does not exist, and same goes for answer **D**. The /checkupgradenow switch is close, but this is not horseshoes.

11. **A C** You will almost certainly be asked which operating systems can be upgraded to Windows 2000 Professional. **B** is incorrect because no upgrade path is defined for any UNIX systems. (I guess I will get e-mails from Linux gurus about whether installing Windows 2000 Professional on a Linux box constitutes an upgrade.) **D** is incorrect because you cannot upgrade directly from NT 3.5. You must first upgrade a NT 3.5 system to NT 3.51 or NT 4 before an upgrade is possible.

Implementing and Conducting Administration of Resources

	NEWBIE	SOME EXPERIENCE	EXPERT
ETA	4 hours	2 hours	1 hour

Now that you have installed Windows 2000 Professional on a system, you need to start making decisions about what is going to be accessed. Resource access defines what the operating system (OS) makes available to users. A user who is sitting down and opening a file on a local disk accesses resources locally. That same user can also access a resource that lives on a different computer. In either case of resource access, varying levels of security can be applied as access is made. As you'll see later in the chapter, the file system that holds the resource determines how it can be secured. If fact, much of what is discussed in this chapter will affect how you actually use the OS.

Resources are parts of your computer that are made available to users of the system, both local and remote. Most often, when we talk about *resources,* we are talking about files and folders stored on our fixed disks. These fixed disks have been prepared to hold the resources with *file systems.* Devices can be resources as well, like a printer or a CD-ROM device. Resource implementation tasks, then, include preparing the partitions with file systems, and creating folders, shares, and Internet-accessible resources. It also includes configuring security permissions to these resources. Administration tasks include modifying these permissions, and removing unnecessary partitions, folders, files, and shares. It also includes troubleshooting resource access problems for the users in your network.

A number of file systems are supported by Windows 2000. The two fixed-disk file types it supports are the file allocation table (FAT) and the NT File System (NTFS). The FAT file system support is kept for backward compatibility, floppy access, and dual-boot configuration. NTFS is a much more feature-rich file system, as you will be learning in this chapter and throughout your entire Windows 2000 education. Only computers running Windows NT or Windows 2000 support it. In Chapter 3, we'll talk much more extensively about the differences between the types of file systems used by Windows 2000 Professional.

Objective 2.01

Manage and Troubleshoot Access to Shared Folders

A *share* is a portion of your computer's resources that is made available to other computers on the network. The share is central to a network's functionality. After all, that's why we hook all of these computers up in the first place, so that files on one computer can be accessed, used, and modified by someone on another. With sharing, we make disk resources (folders and drives) network accessible. Without sharing, we have little more than *sneakernet* to get files back and forth between computers.

Local Lingo

Sneakernet The process of transporting files form one computer to another using floppy disks, by walking files from one computer to another. It's *net*working using your *sneakers*. Sneakernet. Get it? No one said the computer industry wasn't full of hilarity.

You can share resources in Windows 2000 Professional in two ways: through regular *network* sharing (we'll give this another name soon) or through a totally different beast called *Web* sharing. We'll talk more about Web sharing in Chapter 7; for this chapter, let's focus just on good ol' regular network sharing—that is, a couple of computers in a room or office building talking to each other and exchanging files.

The two versions of sharing resources are controlled by different pieces of server software. Sharing is made possible through the Server service, which is installed automatically on all Windows 2000 (as well as NT) computers by default. Furthermore, the Server service by default is configured to start automatically when the system boots up, and it runs in the background. This means that files that have already been shared will remain so even if no one is logged on at the computer. You can just turn on the computer and others will have access to shared folders.

The properties of the Server service can be examined by accessing the Services program in the Administrative Tools group. If you want to make changes to the way the Server service starts, from the Services utility, double-click the Server service icon to access the Properties dialog box, as shown in Figure 2-1.

From the General tab, you can configure startup behavior of the Server service (or any service, for that matter) to be either automatic or manual, and you can disable the service completely. You can also associate the startup of the service with a particular hardware profile from the Log On tab. This might be useful when a computer is not sharing any files at all, such as when a laptop is using a profile that is off the network. We will cover hardware profiles in Chapter 6.

If you look closely at the description of the Server service from the Services program, you might notice that the stated job of the Server service is to make a file or print resource available on Microsoft networks. (I'm paraphrasing just a bit.) But what does that mean? The Server software component actually makes shared resources available through a protocol called Server Message Blocks (SMBs), which is the "language" that Windows computers speak to one another when they are requesting and delivering shared files and printers. In other words, the client makes the request using the SMB protocol, and the request is answered because the server also "speaks" SMB.

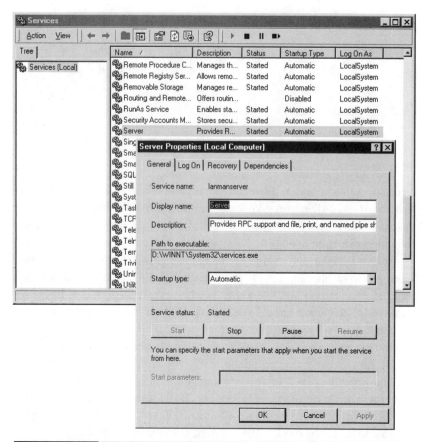

FIGURE 2-1 Configuring the Server service

Travel Advisory

To make your computer more secure, you can disable the Server service or not enable file and printer sharing on a Windows 9x computer. This is especially significant on a computer with "always on" Internet access, as with a cable or DSL connection.

So what is the client component that speaks SMB? The Workstation service. The Workstation service is the software that allows access to files that have been made available through the Server service. The Workstation service, like the Server service, installs and runs at startup time by default. These client-server communication topics will be revisited later in this book in Chapter 7 when we discuss interoperability of Windows 2000 Professional in a Novell environment.

Travel Advisory

I realize that I often make reference that "we'll talk about this in more detail later," or something like that. This is not because I am putting off discussing the subject matter; rather, I am trying to keep this chapter somewhat shorter than a Clancy novel. What should become apparent is that much of the information presented in this chapter is foundational to your understanding of Windows 2000. If you don't "get" sharing, or how shares are accessed, for example, you are going to have a hard time understanding other Windows 2000 topics.

In contrast to Server service sharing, the WWW (for World Wide Web) Publishing Service, which installs as a part of Internet Information Server (IIS), controls Web sharing. It is *not* installed by default on Windows 2000 Professional. The WWW Publishing Service's job is to make files available through a different protocol, in this case the Hypertext Transport Protocol (HTTP). But again, our focus for now is squarely on sharing via the Server service.

For the time being, let's concentrate on what this looks like from the client's point of view. From an end user standpoint, the big difference between SMB (regular) sharing and Web sharing is the program used when the user connects to a shared resource.

Local Lingo

SMB Server Message Blocks, an application-layer protocol used by Windows computers to share files and printers. SMB is not compatible with other vendor's client software, like the Novell client.

HTTP Hypertext Transfer Protocol, which also can be used for the purposes of sharing files and printers. HTTP is compatible with any computer that has a Web browser.

As you probably know, a client connects to a Web resource using a Web browser. Resources are located using the Uniform Resource Locator (URL) syntax, which looks something like this: http://computername/alias/file.

OK, enough of this Web talk for now. While a Web resource is usually accessed in only one way, users can access a "normally" shared resource in several ways. Here are three of the most common ways, which we will discuss later in the chapter in greater detail.

- By browsing the network using My Network Places
- By mapping a drive letter to a share and then accessing it through Windows Explorer
- By using the NET USE utility from the command line

But first things first. Let's figure out how to set up these shares before worrying about how to access them.

Create and Remove Shared Folders

In Windows 2000, you can make files and folders available to network users by using Windows Explorer, the Shared Folders utility, or from the command line by using the NET SHARE utility. To begin this process, first make sure that you are logged on as a member of the Administrators or the Power Users group. Only a member of at least one of these two groups can create shares (unless you delegate this ability to other users in Active Directory, but this is *way* beyond the scope of this book—so far, in fact, that you can forget I mentioned it—and don't think about pink elephants, either).

Exam Tip

For the Windows 2000 Professional exam, know that a user must be a member of the Administrators or Power Users group to share a resource.

From Windows Explorer, right-click on the folder you want to make available and choose Sharing. From the Sharing tab (shown in Figure 2-2) of the folder's Properties dialog box, name the share and click Apply. Notice the share name that is given to a shared folder when you click the Sharing button. The default name of the share will be the same name of the folder, but you don't have to use this name. Shares and folders can be given different names. One name, the folder name, is

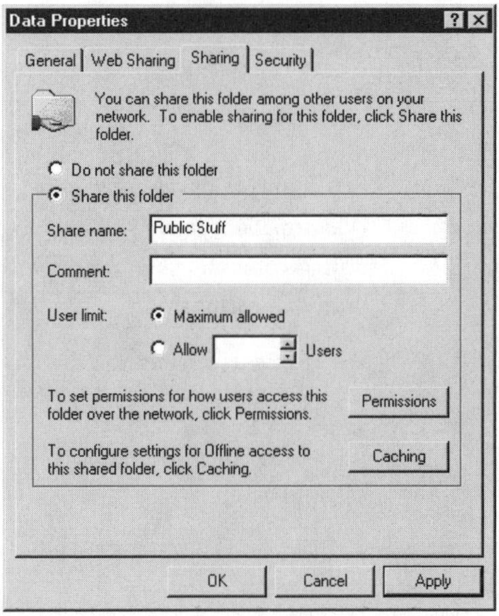

FIGURE 2-2   Setting up a share

used to access the folder locally, and the other name, the share name, is used to access the folder over the network. In other words, you could have a folder named "Pub1" on your system and share it by the name "Public Data."

You can configure many additional options from the Sharing tab of the Properties dialog box, as outlined in Table 2-1.

TABLE 2.1   Options in the Sharing Tab

Option	Does This
Do Not Share This Folder	Specifies that the folder is available locally, not over the network
Share This Folder	Specifies that the folder is available to network users as well as locally
Share Name	The descriptive name that network users will see when they access the share

(Continued)

TABLE 2.1 *CONTINUED*	
Option	**Does This**
Comment	Lets you optionally enter more descriptive information, possibly about the share's contents; users connecting over the network do not see this information
Permissions	Allows you to define how the share will be accessed
Caching	Specifies how folders are cached when the folder is offline

You can also set up sharing through the command prompt if you're into this kind of thing. Using the NET SHARE command, you can create, delete, or display shared resources. The syntax of the NET SHARE command is shown here:

```
NET SHARE sharename=drive:path
```

Where *sharename* is the network name of the shared resource (remember that it does not have to match the actual folder name of the resource), and *drive:path* is the way that the local machine addresses this resource (that is, what drive letter it's on, and what folders and subfolders it lives in).

Travel Advisory

As always, remember that you can use the net share /? command for a quick reference of the proper syntax.

A third way of setting up a share on Windows 2000 Professional computers is to use the Shared Folders utility, which is found in Computer Management. To launch Computer Management from the desktop, right-click My Computer and choose Manage. The Shared Folders node will appear in the left panel, between Performance Logs and Alerts and Device Manager, as shown in Figure 2-3.

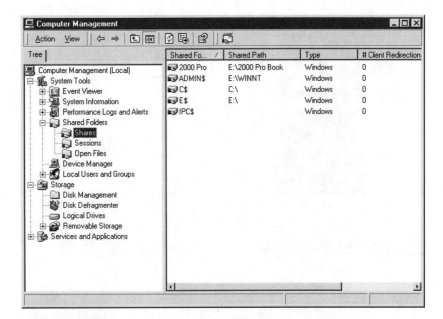

FIGURE 2-3   The shares listed in the Shared Folders utility

The Shared Folders utility exhibits all the shares that have been created on the computer and will also show you the sessions that are accessing the share, listed by user. In the Shared Folders utility, you can create new shares by completing the following steps:

1. Right-click the Shares folder and from the context menu choose New File Share. The Create Shared Folder Wizard starts, as shown in Figure 2-4, which will guide you the rest of the way.
2. From this dialog box, you will specify the path to the folder that you wish to be shared, or you can just browse to your hard drive and click on the folder you are after. Then fill in the name of the share (it doesn't have to be the same as the folder name), and click the Next button.
3. The next dialog box will allow you to assign initial permissions for the share. You can select from one of the predefined permissions or customize the share permissions that will be set. (More about share permissions in "Control Access to Shared Folders Using Permissions," a little later in this chapter.) When you are done, click the Finish button to set up the share.
4. The Create Shared Folder dialog box appears, verifying that the share had been successfully created, and asking you if you'd like to create another. To

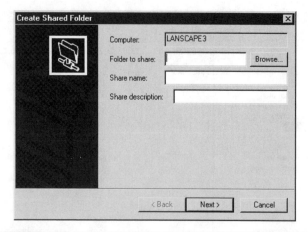

FIGURE 2-4   The Create Shared Folder Wizard

stop sharing a folder from the Shared Folders utility, simply right-click the share and select Stop Sharing from the context menu, as shown in Figure 2-5.

You may have noticed some shares listed in the Shared Folders utility whose share names end with a dollar sign ($). What is that all about? Who set those up?

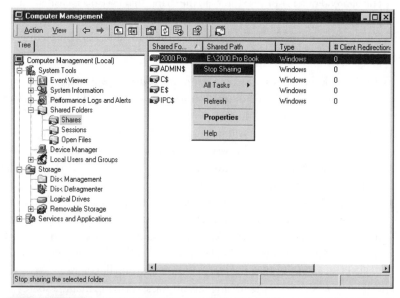

FIGURE 2-5   How to stop sharing a folder

Well, the answer is not who, but what. The Windows 2000 OS set up those shares, and they are your computer's *administrative shares.*

Windows 2000 automatically sets up these administrative shares to facilitate system administration form remote computers. It does, however, hide these shares from view as users are browsing the network.

The significance of the dollar sign after the share name means that the share will be hidden from view when using share access utilities like My Network Places. In fact, any share you create will be hidden from view if you append the share name with a dollar sign ($). This can be a good way to store software programs and other utilities that you may regularly use as a network administrator while keeping these files safe from the curious.

The following administrative shares are created on a Windows 2000 Professional computer by default:

- The *Driveletter$* share, where *driveletter* is the root of any logical drive. In Figure 2-5, you can see that the C:\ and E:\ drives have been shared.
- The ADMIN$ share points to the Windows 2000 installation folder, which is \WINNT if the defaults were kept at installation time.
- The IPC$ (Interprocess Communications) share allows remote adminis-tration of a computer and is used to view shared resources.
- The PRINT$ share may be present for remote printer administration.

If you go back through either Windows Explorer or the Shared Folders utility and try to administer the administrative shares, you may be in for a surprise. You cannot change any of the settings of the administrative shares, such as the per-missions. You might even notice that if you try to stop sharing an administrative share, it will be shared out again if the computer reboots. Does this mean that just anyone who has knowledge of these hidden shares can access your drive and wreak untold havoc? Not to worry. Only certain groups have access to the admin-istrative shares.

Travel Advisory

Only members of the Administrators and Backup Operators local groups can access the administrative shares (*driveletter$* shares) on Windows 2000 Professional and Windows 2000 Server member server computers. On Windows 2000 domain controllers, members of the Administrators, Backup Operators, and Server Operators groups can access these shares.

If you protect the user name and passwords of the users with access to the administrative shares, you are protecting these shares.

Connecting to Shared Resources

Once you've got a folder shared on the network, users can gain access to them in several ways. The list earlier in this chapter mentioned some of the common ways—one of which was by browsing through My Network Places.

My Network Places is probably the most intuitive tool for novice users to employ to gain shared folder access. By double-clicking on network objects, such as groups of computers and then on servers, users can be presented a listing of the shares that live on these servers. You can also use the My Network Places to map a network location through the use of the Add Network Place Wizard; this will create an easy to access method for you to connect to shared resources on the network.

1. To start the wizard, double-click the Add Network Place icon from the first My Network Places window. Figure 2-6 shows the wizard's Welcome screen.
2. You can either enter the name of the network place to which you want to connect or click Browse and search for it. You can use a URL path to a Web folder, a File Transfer Protocol (FTP) path to an FTP site, or a Universal Naming Convention (UNC) path name. Notice that when you browse for a shared folder and select it, the UNC pathname will be entered for your convenience.

We really can't go any further before making sure that you understand completely the UNC syntax for addressing network resources. A UNC path is a method

FIGURE 2-6   The Add Network Place Wizard opening screen

that you can use to connect to any resource on the network (that you have permission to access) by specifying a unique path, called the UNC path.

This syntax is vital to understand as we work with Windows 2000, because it is used so often to specify network resources. If you don't know what you're looking at when seeing a UNC path, not much else will make sense.

The UNC path syntax to access a network share is as follows:

*computername**sharename*

The *computername* is the name of the computer, or server, to which you would like to connect, while the *sharename* is the name of the share on that specific computer.

It is important that you not confuse this syntax with the MS-DOS path name, which will look like this: *C:\folder\subfolder1\subfolder2.* The UNC syntax is used to access the resource over the network, while the MS-DOS path is how the same resource is addressed locally. Notice that the UNC syntax makes no reference to a drive letter or to how deep in the folder hierarchy the resource may live. In Figure 2-7, you can see how resources on a computer look when accessed over the network versus locally.

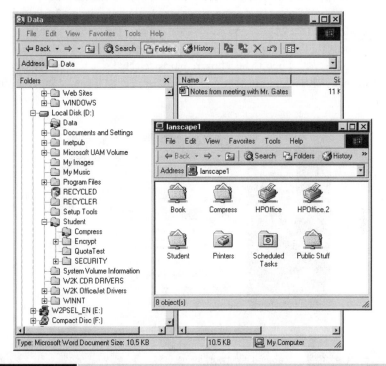

FIGURE 2-7   Viewing a resource locally versus over the network

In Figure 2-7, the window on the bottom (titled Data) shows the contents of my hard drive. On the right, inside the window titled lanscape1, is how my hard drive looks to someone accessing the computer using the syntax *computername* (you can use just the first half of the UNC syntax to see a list of all shares on a given server); notice that from the network side, you don't see all the folders, only those folders that have been shared.

You can also access network resources by mapping a network drive using Windows Explorer. After you have mapped a network drive, it will appear as another drive letter when the user accesses My Computer or Windows Explorer. You can map a network drive in several ways. Here's one way:

1. Either right-click My Computer or My Network Places and choose Map Network Drive.
2. The Map Network Drive dialog box appears, as shown on Figure 2-8. Choose the drive letter that will be associated with this network connection, and the path to the location. You can use any letter for the drive that is not already taken. You can specify the folder location by typing the UNC pathname of the folder, or click Browse to search for the folder location.

   Notice that the UNC pathname syntax is used even if you Browse out for the folder.
3. If you want this mapped network connection to be persistent, make sure the Reconnect At Logon checkbox remains selected. (It will be selected by default.) This will ensure that the mapped connection is part of a user profile,

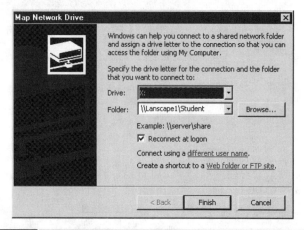

FIGURE 2-8 Mapping a network drive

which means that it will be a part of the drives seen in Windows Explorer each time the user logs on.

4. You can also specify a different user name that will be used to make this connection if you wish. To do this, click the hyperlink called "different user name" and then designate the account used for the connection.

Additionally, Mavis Beacon disciples can use the NET USE command to assign a user name, which is actually a fairly quick and painless way to map a network drive to a shared location. Similar to the NET SHARE command, the NET USE utility uses the following syntax:

```
NET USE x: \\computername\sharename
```

Where *x* is the drive letter that will be used for the mapped connection, and *computername\sharename* is the UNC address of the share. (I'm not one to say I told you so, but I told you so: you have to know the UNC path.)

Your users, however, will probably never have to know what the UNC syntax is, or what it means. That's fine, as they will most likely use graphical applications, like Explorer, to access shared resources. On the exam, you might even see questions from end users about the "H:\ drive going bad." That's understandable. I didn't know the difference between local and network drives until someone showed me. One of the benefits of a GUI-based OS like Windows is that any resources needed are just a few intuitive double-clicks away.

Control Access to Shared Folders Using Permissions

Sharing also provides a limited form of network security through the use of *share permissions,* which define what kind of access a user has when connecting to a share over the network.

It's important at this point to take a breath and realize that two kinds of permissions are available on Windows 2000 computers: share permissions and NTFS permissions. It's even more important that you not confuse the two. Share permissions define what happens only when a remote user is connecting to a resource. These permissions are meaningless if that same user were to sit down and log in *locally* at your computer. To control local access, you need NTFS permissions. NTFS permissions are discussed in the Objective 2.02 section, along with an explanation of what happens when share and NTFS permissions are combined.

The three levels of share permissions are described here:

Permission	Characteristics
Read	Allows a user to view files in a folder; lets users execute programs in the shared folder
Change	Allows users to change the data in a file; lets user delete a file within a share, so be judicious about who has change permission
Full Control	Allows full access to the shared folder, this including all permissions from Change; allows users to change permissions on the share

Further, these three permissions are restricted by two conditions, called allow and deny. Allow grants the specific permission to a shared resource, and it is the default selection for a permission setting. Deny will explicitly block the permission from being applied to a resource. The deny condition adds another layer of complexity to shared resources, and therefore should be used sparingly. For example, it is possible to deny read access to a resource while still allowing change access to be in effect. The result would be a folder in which a user could delete a file that she could otherwise not read.

Exam Tip

Remember that the deny permission overrides the allow permission. This concept will remain consistent throughout many other aspects of the operating system, so it's a good thing to have clear in your mind.

To configure share-level permissions to a network resource, you will edit the *access control list (ACL)* for that resource. The ACL is a list of user accounts and groups that are allowed to access a resource, and it lists what level of access is allowed. Each and every *object* in Windows 2000 Professional has an ACL associated with it that it checks every time an account needs access to the resource. Examples of objects include folders, files, network shares, and printers.

Travel Advisory

For practical purposes, when you don't want a user or group to access a resource, you simply do not include them in the list of users and groups in the Access Control List (ACL), which you are building. You don't need to add a group and then deny that group a given permission. Just don't add it in the first place.

To access the ACL, start from the Sharing tab of a folder's Properties dialog box. Click the Permissions button, as shown in Figure 2-9, to begin editing the ACL.

When you first share out a folder, you will notice that the ACL consists of only one entry that says the Everyone group is granted Full Control. If you want to edit the list of users and groups who can access the share and how they can access it, click the Add button and you can add a group or individual account. You can also remove groups by selecting them in the ACL and clicking, you guessed it, Remove.

After the user or group appears in the ACL, you can modify its level of access by either checking or unchecking the appropriate checkboxes in the Permissions property page, as shown in Figure 2-10.

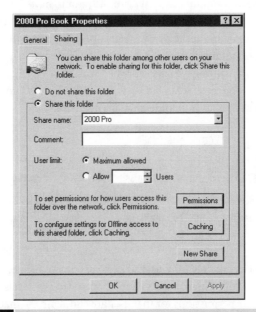

FIGURE 2-9 The Permissions button lets you lock down a share

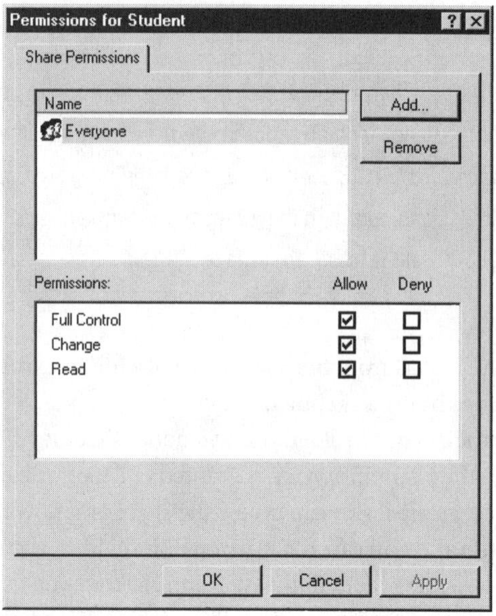

FIGURE 2-10   Setting share permissions

For example, if you want the local Administrator to have Full Control and the Everyone group to have the Read permission, you first uncheck the Full Control and Change permissions of the Everyone group, and then add the Administrator account and grant it Full Control by checking the Full Control box (Full Change and Read will automatically be checked when you select Full Control). The share will then let Everyone read files in the share, and the Administrator will be allowed Full Control to all files and subfolders within the share, as explained next.

Exam Tip

You should know that the default permission on a shared resource is the Everyone group has Full Control. As a best practice, you will typically remove this permission and then build the ACL to your own needs.

It is, of course, possible for a user to be a part of two or more groups within Windows 2000. And when those groups have different levels of access to a resource, the share permissions for that user are cumulative—that is, the permissions are added together.

To illustrate, suppose user Brian is a part of the Sales group, who has Read access to the \Commissions shared folder. That same user is in the Management (of course) group, who has the Full Control permission. What is Brian's permission when connecting to \Commissions? Full Control. Figure 2-11 shows how the combined permissions are evaluated.

Travel Advisory

Remember that if the Deny permission is in effect, either through group membership or by individual assignment, the Deny becomes effective for that particular permission. In the Brian example, if the Sales group were denied the Read permission, Brian would also be denied Read permission by virtue of his membership in the Sales group. In other words, the Deny permission overrides the Allow permission.

As mentioned, when a share is created, the special group Everyone is granted the Allow Full Control access permission to the share. This is a potential security hole, but it represents a design philosophy of Microsoft. Why share something if

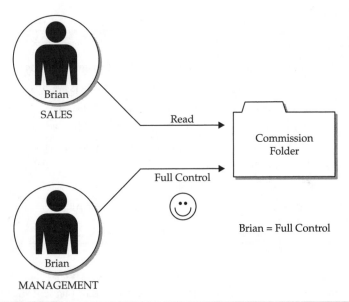

FIGURE 2-11   Share + share permissions

you don't want it accessible? It is up to you, the administrator, to tighten the security of resources on your computer, and you have some powerful options when you combine share permissions with NTFS permissions to do just that.

Travel Advisory

Be aware of the default behaviors of sharing (and those for just about anything else). Defaults might not be the type of behavior you want the operating system to display, and, in the case of sharing permissions, the wrong sharing choices may leave you open to security breaches.

One more point about sharing on a Windows 2000 Professional computer that must be mentioned: The number of concurrent connections is limited to a maximum of 10. In the case of Windows 2000 Server, the connections are unlimited by default. For this reason, dedicated file servers on larger networks usually use 2000 Server as their operating system. Windows 2000 Professional is more suited for smaller peer-to-peer networks.

Exam Tip

Remember this about shares:

- They are not effective locally, when a user is sitting down at a computer. They are effective only when other systems access folders over the network.
- They can be applied only to folders, not to individual files. (As a corollary, everything within a share is available, files and subfolders included.)
- Share permissions can be applied to any file system that is supported by Windows 2000 Professional.
- Share permissions, when combined, are cumulative. (The caveat here is that the Deny permission overrides the Allow permission.)

And as a coda about sharing, remember that sharing is not a function of the file system. It is a function of the Server service. You can implement sharing on both FAT and NTFS partitions. (You can also share out resources that the server retrieves using CDFS—the file system for CD-ROM drives.) Sharing is just a way to make something accessible on the network. As you'll see in the next objective, NTFS security is specific to a resource on an NTFS partition. Higher levels of security are one of the several features available on NTFS that aren't on any other file system. Something to keep in the back of your mind as we press on.

Manage and Troubleshoot Web Server Resources

Windows 2000 uses the services of Internet Information Services (IIS) and a subset of IIS called Peer Web Services (PWS), which is installed on Windows 2000 Professional computers. PWS is intended to act as a small-scale Web server for a small intranet or Internet site with limited traffic.

Web sharing will be dealt with in further detail in Chapter 7, when we talk about technologies that extend the network beyond our local office network. One could argue that since it is in essence a file sharing technology, it would be more appropriate to discuss here, but I think it's best to focus on smaller scale file and print sharing for now. We'll save the Web technologies for Chapter 7.

Monitor, Manage, and Troubleshoot Access to Files and Folders

O n a volume or partition formatted with NTFS, each file or folder has associated with it a set of NTFS *attributes*. Some of these attributes are the NTFS security permissions that are granted to users and groups when accessing the file or folder. Other attributes include the compression attribute, the encryption attribute, and the owner attribute, but those topics are not discussed here. The important thing to remember is that these attributes are available only on NTFS partitions, which is one of the many reasons that Microsoft strongly recommends that Windows 2000 be installed on an NTFS partition where possible.

The decision to format a drive is usually made at installation time, although you can convert a drive from the FAT file system to NTFS even after you've performed the Windows 2000 installation. (The conversion from FAT to NTFS will be fleshed out in Chapter 3.) To determine whether you're working with an NTFS partition, right-click the drive letter from Windows Explorer and choose Properties to look at the properties of the drive. The General tab will list what kind of file system the drive is using. Another quick way to know whether the drive is

NTFS is to look at the properties of any folder or file (This works on the drive letter itself, as it is really a folder in it own right.) If you see a Security tab listed, you're in business.

On the Security tab of a file or folder, you will configure the NTFS permissions, and most of the time you will be working with the standard permissions. But before we define these standard permissions, you should understand that the NTFS standard permissions are collections of *individual* NTFS security *attributes*. Click the Advanced button on the Security tab to see a complete listing of these individual security attributes, as shown in Figure 2-12.

Control Access to Files and Folders Using NTFS Permissions

One of the hallmarks of the NTFS permissions is that, unlike shared folder permissions, *they can be configured at the folder level and the individual file level.* Table 2-2 lists the standard folder permissions that can be assigned with the click of a mouse from the Security tab of the Properties dialog box for a folder. These standard folder permissions are collections of the security attributes mentioned previously.

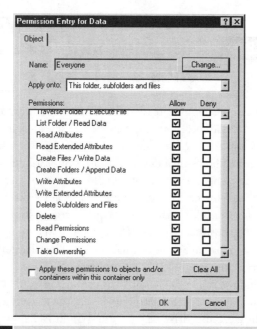

FIGURE 2-12 The individual NTFS security attributes

TABLE 2.2	Standard Folder Permissions
NTFS folder permission...	**Lets a User...**
Read	See files and subfolders and view folder ownership, permissions, and attributes
Write	Create new files and subfolders within the folder, change folder attributes, and view folder ownership and permissions
List Folder Contents	See names of the files and subfolders within a folder
Read and Execute	Move through folders to reach other files and folders, even if the users don't have permission for those folders; perform actions permitted by the Read permission and the List Folder Contents permission
Modify	Delete the folder, plus perform actions permitted by the Write, Read, and Execute permission
Full Control	Change permissions, take ownership, and delete subfolders and files, plus perform actions permitted by all other NTFS permissions

As with share permissions, each of the NTFS standard permissions (as well as individual attributes) has an Allow setting and a Deny setting. Also, as with shares, the Deny is trump over the Allow. To explicitly deny all access to a user or group to a particular resource, deny the Full Control permission. This turns off all other access to the resource.

So, from the Security tab, you will build the Access Control list specific for the NTFS permissions for a file or folder. The process will look almost exactly the same as when you built the ACL for shared resources using the Sharing tab.

Exam Tip

You should know that the default NTFS permission in the Everyone group is Full Control. As with shared folder permissions, a best practice when setting NTFS permissions is to remove the default permission and create your own ACL of users who may access the resource.

Here's how to begin to modify this default NTFS security behavior:

1. On the Security tab, click the Add button to open the Select Users, Computers, Or Groups dialog box shown in Figure 2-13. From this dialog box, you can select users and groups from the computer's local accounts database or from a domain listed in the Look In drop-down box at the top.

2. Select the user or group you want to add and then click the Add button. If you are selecting an account from a domain, you will notice that the list presented can grow quite large.

A shortcut in navigating the accounts list in Windows 2000 comes in handy. Instead of scrolling through the list, you can type the first letter or first few letters of an account or group you are trying to find. When you press ENTER

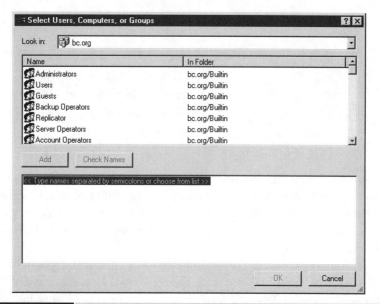

FIGURE 2-13   Adding a group or user to the ACL

on your keyboard, you will see a shortened list of all groups and accounts that start with the letters you just typed, making it much easier to find the intended account. If only one account or group starts with the letters you typed, it will automatically be added to the ACL without your having to click Add. To see how this works, type U and then press ENTER. (Make sure that your computer name is listed in the Look in drop-down box.) One of the accounts that should appear is the Users group, as well as any other groups and accounts that start with the letter U.

3. After you have made an addition to the ACL, configure access to the resource by highlighting a group or user account and selecting or deselecting the checkboxes that correspond to the level of access you wish to allow or deny.

Travel Advisory

It is possible to configure the ACL so that nobody has access to a resource. If you remove all groups and accounts from the ACL, nobody will be granted any kind of access whatsoever. That goes for you, too! (We'll discuss how to fix this if it occurs later when we talk about NTFS ownership.)

Although the file permissions are by default inherited from the parent folder in which the files live (more about this in "NTFS Permissions Inheritance"), NTFS permissions can also be used to secure individual files. Table 2-3 lists the standard NTFS file-level permissions that you can assign and the type of access that each permission implies.

TABLE 2.3   Standard NTFS File-Level Permissions

NTFS file permission...	Lets a User...
Read	Read the file and view file attributes, ownership, and permissions
Write	Overwrite the file, change file attributes, and view file ownership and permissions
	(Continued)

TABLE 2.3 *CONTINUED*

NTFS file permission...	Lets a User...
Read and Execute	Run applications and perform the actions permitted by the Read permission
Modify	Modify and delete the file, plus perform all actions permitted by the Write, Read, and Execute permissions
Full Control	Change permissions and take ownership, plus perform the actions permitted by all other NTFS permissions

As you can see, the only significant difference between folder and file permissions is that List Folder Contents is not one of the standard file permissions. What is really significant about discussing the two NTFS sets of permissions for folders and files is an understanding that *file permissions override folder permissions.*

It is possible, then, for a folder's NTFS permissions to be set to allow a user Read access, yet that same user would have Full control to a file within that folder. That's because the file's ACL would be king of the mountain when the account was used to access the file.

Furthermore, like its relative share permissions, NTFS permissions are *cumulative.* That is, a user's effective permission is a combination of the group permissions that an account has been assigned to, plus any individual permissions specifically assigned to that user.

To illustrate using the same example used in the discussion of shares, suppose that Brian is a part of the Sales group that has NTFS Read access to the \Bonuses folder. Brian is also part of the Management group, which has the NTFS Full Control permission. What is Brian's permission when connecting to \Bonuses? It's Full Control. This example is shown in Figure 2-14.

Optimize Access to Files and Folders

NTFS permissions differ from share permissions in two significant ways:

- *NTFS permissions are effective locally* when a user accesses a resource. Share permissions apply only when network connections are made to a resource.

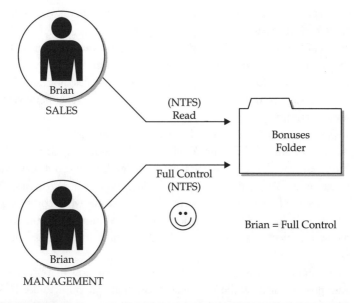

Brian

SALES

(NTFS)
Read

Bonuses
Folder

Full Control
(NTFS)

Brian = Full Control

Brian

MANAGEMENT

FIGURE 2-14   Applying NTFS + NTFS permissions

- *NTFS permissions can be applied to both folders and individual files.* Share permissions can be granted at the folder level only. The share permissions then apply to any files and subfolders within the share.

Local access means that the user is using the local machine. Local access to a file is made through the MS-DOS path name, and shared folder access is made using the UNC path. This fact also highlights one of the core differences between the Windows 2000 Professional and Windows 9*x* operating system families. Because Windows 9*x* is not capable of supporting NTFS locally, there is no way for a user of a shared machine to restrict local access to a file or folder. Anything on a partition that is formatted with the FAT (or FAT32) file system can be seen, changed, or deleted by *any* user who is able to log on to the machine. In the case of Windows 9*x*, no logon is even necessary. You can just press the Esc key while in any logon dialog box and then delete files to your heart's content. This is the main reason that Windows 2000 Professional is considered a *secure* platform and Windows 9*x* is not. The only way to make sure people don't have access to files on a Windows 9*x* machine is make sure they can only access them over the network; that way, you can at least apply share permissions.

As for the second point—NTFS permissions can be applied to both folders and individual files—does that mean that NTFS permissions are effective *only* locally? A good question, but the answer is no; they are effective *both* locally and when making connections over the network. This brings us to one of the most significant pieces of the resource permissions puzzle.

When share-level permissions and NTFS permissions are combined, the *most restrictive permission becomes the effective permission*. This is *crucial* information for you to know both for taking the exam, and for troubleshooting real-world access problems in a network. You will not have much success at either if you don't understand this point.

The permission settings behave in this way because each ACL is evaluated independently of one another. The Windows 2000 operating system is saying, in effect, "You may have *this* set of permissions at this level, but you only have *that* set of permissions at another level. So you only get *that* level of permission." This combination trait of the two sets of permissions, especially when combined with the ability to set individual file permissions on NTFS volumes, gives the administrator a powerful mechanism for controlling the granularity of access to network resources.

Let's illustrate again with the example from before: suppose that Brian is a part of the Sales group, which has the Read share access to the \Bonuses folder. He's also in the Management group, which has the NTFS Full Control permission. What is Brian's permission when connecting to \Bonuses? It's Read. This example is illustrated in Figure 2-15.

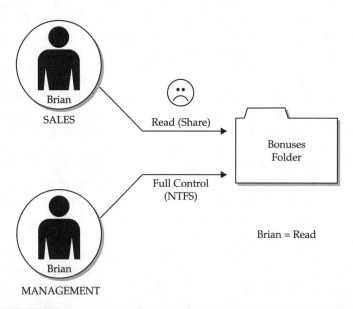

FIGURE 2-15 Combining Share + NTFS permissions

I can't stress enough how many times you are likely to be asked questions that test your understanding of how permissions interact, both on the 70-210 test and in others, especially the 70-215 (Server) test.

Exam Tip

Things you must remember about NTFS permissions (give me your test exam fee unless you know these by heart):

- NTFS permissions are effective locally, unlike share permissions.
- NTFS permissions can be applied to files as well as folders.
- File permissions override folder permissions.
- NTFS permissions are cumulative, with the exception of the Deny, which overrides Allow.
- When NTFS and Share permissions are combined, the effective permission is the most restrictive permission.

So, then, the advice given to new administrators: Share the disk resources you want users to access on an NTFS volume with the default network permissions (Everyone, Full Control) and then tighten down security via NTFS permissions. Don't bother setting share permissions because it adds another level of permissions to track and document, and they aren't effective locally anyway.

This strategy is recommended for a few reasons:

- It gives administrators maximum flexibility when designing and implementing file servers in a network.
- It ensures that files and folders will remain secure on computers that are shared by several users.
- It lets an administrator set security on files before they are even available on the network (assuming that you, the administrator, take the step of configuring NTFS permissions before sharing out the resource, which is a step you should take).

NTFS Permissions Inheritance

It's important in the MCSE track that you have a clear understanding of how NTFS permissions are inherited from parent folders. Not only will this understanding help you when answering questions regarding NTFS permissions, but it will set the foundation for understanding other types of permission inheritance, especially when dealing with Active Directory.

The default behavior of NTFS permissions is that the permissions you assign at the parent folder level are propagated to the subfolders and files that are contained in the parent. This default behavior is consistent throughout many other Windows 2000 technologies, so you will see this practice repeated time and again.

The good people at Microsoft have given us a visual cue, however, that permissions on a given folder or file have been inherited. When you look at the Security tab of the Properties dialog box, as shown in Figure 2-16, the boxes that have a gray shading indicate that the permissions checked have been inherited from the parent.

But what if you want this inheritance behavior to be prevented? What if you want to set NTFS permissions for individual files and folders, so that a user can be granted Full Control over a file that is stored in a folder that she has Read permission for? You can easily prevent this default permission inheritance from parent folder to subfolders and files that are contained within the parent. And when you configure this behavior, the folder for which you prevent permission inheritance becomes the new parent, and any new files or subfolders created in this new parent folder will inherit the new permissions just set.

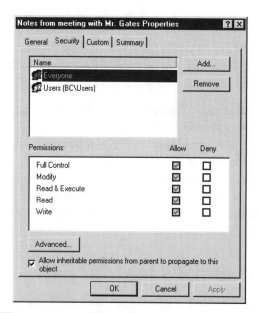

FIGURE 2-16   The gray-shading indicates inheritance

This inheritance blocking is done with a single click: just uncheck the box at the bottom of the Security tab that says Allow Inheritable Permissions From Parent To Propagate To This Object. You will be given two options when you perform this task: whether to copy previously inherited permissions or to remove existing permissions, as shown in Figure 2-17.

Copying existing permissions is preferred, because you can then edit the ACL that is already present. Most of the time, you will be making a few minor tweaks to the ACL. Choosing Remove will empty out the ACL and you will have to start from scratch.

Copying and Moving Considerations

When you copy or move files and folders, the NTFS permissions set on those objects might change. In fact, they often do. You must understand the specific rules that control how and when permissions change during copy and move operations. Like the discussion about NTFS permission inheritance, an understanding of concepts presented here will help you understand what happens to other NTFS attributes as *they* are copied or moved.

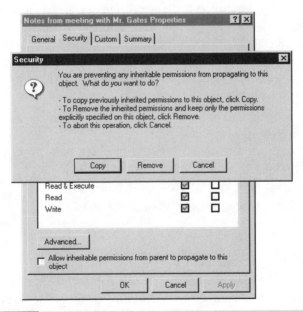

FIGURE 2-17   Options when preventing permission inheritance

Whenever you perform a *copy* from one folder to another, the permissions change. The file or folder copied inherits the permissions set for the destination folder. This behavior occurs regardless of whether your copy is from folder to folder on the same partition or the copy is from one partition to another.

Also, when a copy is performed, the user making the copy becomes the Owner of the copy and can modify the NTFS permissions on the copied resource. (More on this Ownership power is discussed later in "Special Access Permissions"—for now just think of this behavior as analogous to a Xerox machine. You take the copy with you, and do whatever you want with it and return the original to it owner.)

When a *move* is performed on a file or folder, the NTFS permissions may or may not change, depending on the destination directory of the move. It can get a little confusing, but here's how a move operation works:

- If you move a file or folder *within* the same NTFS partition—say from one folder to another on the C:\ drive—the file or folder *retains* its original permissions. The Owner attribute of the object also remains the same.

- If you move a file or folder *between* NTFS partitions—like when you drag and drop something from the C:\ drive to the D:\ drive—the file or folder *inherits* the permissions of the destination folder, and the Ownership also changes to the user performing the action. Windows treats a move between partitions, like from a folder on the C:\ drive to a folder on the D:\ drive, as a Copy and then a Delete. Thus, what is really happening is that the move operation between different partitions follows the rules of a Copy, which to the OS is what the file management operation actually is.

Travel Advisory

You must have at least the Modify permission for the source file or folder for a move, and you must have the Write permission for the destination folder to perform the move operation.

Finally, when you perform a move *or* copy of files and folders from an NTFS partition to a FAT partition, the files and folders *lose their NTFS permissions*. Why? FAT partitions don't support NTFS permissions. So take care when moving files and folders to FAT volumes, because carefully implemented NTFS permissions could be lost instantly.

Special Access Permissions

Fourteen special access permissions—14 security attributes—can be assigned to a NTFS folder or file. If you assign the standard NTFS permissions to a resource and then look at the Advanced properties from the Security tab, you will notice that some or all (in the case of Full Control) are checked, as shown in Figure 2-18.

Two special permissions are particularly useful when governing access to resources: the Change Permissions and Take Ownership permissions.

The *Change Permissions* attribute is useful for assigning to others the ability to control access to files and folders without giving them the Full Control permission. In this way, a user who has Change Permissions won't be able to delete or write to the file, but she can set user access, including setting her own account so that she has permission to delete the file. (This paradox is one reason that special permissions are used infrequently.)

Take Ownership is a somewhat more powerful permission because of the inherent ability that an Owner has over a file or folder. The next section covers this issue.

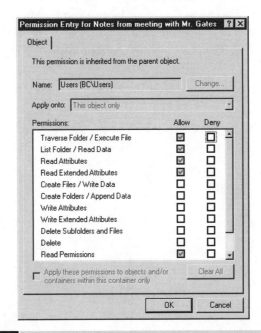

FIGURE 2-18   Setting special access permissions

Ownership

The Owner attribute is set for every file and folder on an NTFS partition. Each and every file placed on an NTFS partition is done so by its Owner, and this owner of a disk resource has the ability to edit the ACL permissions for that resource. That means that the owner of a file can lock everyone out, even the Administrator. The Owner attribute is another of the attributes tracked by Windows on an NTFS partition. It is not tracked on FAT volumes.

The Owner attribute is also used for several additional Windows functions, such as for tracking disk quota usage (which will be discussed in Chapter 3) and identifying system events.

Ownership of a resource can be taken, but never assigned. It's a one-way street, and this is a point that is important for you to understand. What can be assigned by the current Owner of a file or folder, an Administrator, or anyone with the Full Control permission, is the Take Ownership permission, which allows the assignees to take ownership of the resource. This ownership behavior assures accountability for files created on an NTFS partition.

As with a million shares of drkoop.com stock, there are some things you might not want to own. For example, I can't create a file called "The Editor of this book is an overpaid, talentless, slacker" and then give ownership to the layout person. I am the owner of that file until the layout person takes ownership from me (if he has the ability). Figure 2-19 illustrates the principle of NTFS Ownership.

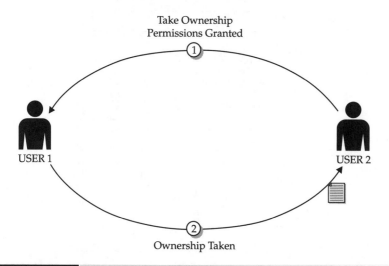

FIGURE 2-19   Ownership taken; only the ability to own is given

To view the current owner of a folder or file, open the Access Control Settings dialog box by clicking the Advanced button of the Security tab of an NTFS resource. As seen in Figure 2-20, the Owner tab of this dialog box will show the Owner of the resource as well as a list of the accounts and groups that have the ability to Take Ownership.

Additionally, the permission to Take Ownership is given to users or groups by editing the special permissions of the ACL, as shown earlier in Figure 2-18. The users given the NTFS permission Take Ownership will then be able to take ownership through the Owner tab.

This "one-way street" characteristic of Ownership is also important when considering disk quotas. This will be discussed more in Chapter 3, but for now, just imagine how effective quotas would be at limiting disk usage if every time a user was up against his or her quota limit, the user just gave away ownership of a couple megabytes' worth of files.

This bears repeating: *To become the owner of a resource, a user or group member with the Take Ownership permission must explicitly take ownership.* Ownership may never be given to another user. Remember that you can give someone the right to take ownership of a file, and then have that person perform the act of taking ownership, but you cannot give ownership to an individual without his or her knowledge.

FIGURE 2-20   Viewing and changing the current Owner of a file

Exam Tip

For the exam, know that only members of the Administrators group
have the right to take ownership of resources by default.

As I mentioned in the first paragraph of this section, the owner of a file can
lock everyone out, even the Administrator. What does an Administrator do when
a user has a file that's locked out to everyone, and the Administrator needs to see
what's in that file? What if that user has left the company? One of the powers of
the Administrator account and the Administrators local group is the ability to take
ownership of anything on a disk, regardless of the assigned permissions. So, then,
to resolve such a situation, the Administrator takes ownership from the user and
then, as the new owner, the Administrator can modify the ACL.

Travel Advisory

When an Administrator takes ownership of a resource in Windows 2000,
she may decide whether her account specifically will be the
owner of the resource or whether the entire Administrators
group is to be the owner.

Objective 2.03 # Connect to Local and Network Print Devices

When it comes to printing in the Windows 2000 environment, Microsoft uses
a bunch of terms most folks wouldn't find very obvious—it's kinda like a
whole new language. So, for the purposes of this lesson, we will be using all new
language. Consider this your language lesson. A quick question to get us started:
What is that thing on your desk that spits out a printed page? That's a printer, right?
Wrong. It is, at least for the purposes of this chapter and the exam, a *print device*.

Local Lingo

Print device   What used to be (before this section, anyway) called the printer.
The piece of equipment that prints your electronic files.

Printer   A piece of software that provides the necessary translation
so that an application can send information to a print device. The
printer is there to provide access to the print device on your desk.

Now that we have established that a printer is a piece of software and not a piece of hardware (again, don't walk around correcting your grandmother on this; the social consequences can be harsh), it really shouldn't be too much a leap of faith to imagine that this piece of software, the printer, is just another disk resource that can be shared on a network, just like other resources such as files and folders. And when this bundle of code is shared and available for other users to submit a print job to, that printer is known as a *shared printer.*

A computer providing this shared printer is a *print server.* Lots of Microsoft OSs can be set up as print servers. A Windows 9x box can be a print server, as well as a Windows 2000 Professional machine. Both of these OS flavors can quite capably handle the print server needs of most Microsoft-only networks. In addition, Windows 2000 Server OS print servers have the potential to become print servers for non-Microsoft client computers. (You should be aware of this now, but you won't need this information again until the Windows 2000 Server exam.)

Some print devices are connected directly to the network, just like any other computer. These types of print devices that are not directly connected to other computers are called *network print devices.* Figure 2-21 shows all the components of a Microsoft network printing environment.

Here we have the building blocks of network printing, which is probably a close second on the list of why networks were designed in the first place. With network

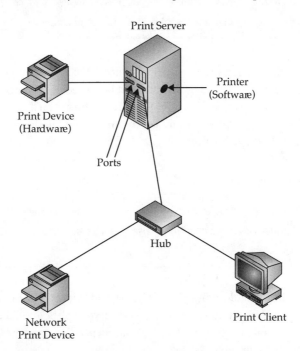

printing, we don't need printers...pardon me...print devices at every desk in an organization.

A printer needs a way to get its translated information to the print device. It accomplishes this through a specifically defined pathway, known as a *port*. These pathways of information can be one of several varieties, as you'll soon learn.

Connecting to Local and Network Printers

A printing device attached directly to the computer is known as a *local printer,* because it makes use of a local *port*. The local printer usually uses the LPT1 (parallel) port, but other ports qualify. The USB port also comes to mind as an example of a commonly used local printing port. This port selection simply defines which copper wires the 1's and 0's use to get from the printer to the print device. Most people who have home computers with a print device handy have set up a printer to use a local port.

Local Lingo

Port   An interface through which a device, in this case a print device, is connected to a computer. Ports can be thought of as the byway by which instructions are sent from a piece of software to a piece of hardware.

To access the physical print device in Windows 2000 Professional, you must first create a logical printer. To do so, you must be logged on as a member of the Administrators or Power Users group for that machine. You'll create a logical printer using the Add Printer Wizard, which can be found in the Printers folder either via Control Panel, My Computer, or the Start menu under Settings.

Exam Tip

For the Windows 2000 Professional exam, know that only members of the Administrators group and the Power Users group can install a local printer.

Double-click the Add Printer icon, and the Add Printer Wizard will launch. After clicking the Next button to get things started, you will be given the choice of adding either a local printer or a network printer, depending on where the printer is located, as shown in Figure 2-22.

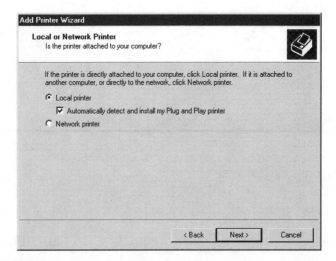

FIGURE 2-22   Choosing a local or network printer

The remainder of the questions in the Add Printer Wizard depend on whether you choose to install a local printer or network printer. If you are setting up a local printer, you will select a port that the print device is connected to and then find the print drivers to install.

The second way to get access to a print device is over a network connection. In the Local or Network Printer dialog box, if you choose to connect to a network printer, the wizard asks where the printer lives, as shown in Figure 2-23. The Locate Your Printer dialog box will let you connect to and install a shared printer by specifying a UNC path name (here's that UNC stuff again) or by browsing through a list of shared printers. Note that when you browse for a printer, the network printer will appear as just another share on the network: \\servername\printername, when the selection is made.

There is an even easier way to set up a network printer. A print client can connect and submit jobs to a printer that is shared using the exact same process that a client would use to connect to other shared resources. By simply browsing the network through My Network Places and double-clicking a shared printer, or by entering the UNC path to a printer in the Run dialog box from the Start menu, the client will automatically perform the installation without further user interaction. It's pretty cool.

Port Properties

Windows 2000 Professional supports local ports and TCP/IP logical ports. A TCP/IP port is used when a printer needs to send a print job to a network-interface print device, which is connected to the network with a network interface card (NIC).

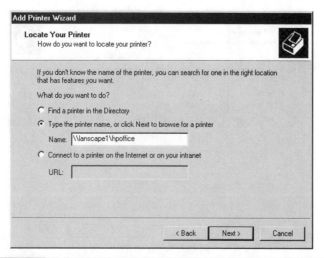

Connecting to a shared printer

You will configure your ports from the Ports tab of the printer's Properties dialog box.

1. To add a TCP/IP port, from the Ports tab, click the Add Port button. Then choose the Standard TCP/IP port from the next dialog box.
2. The Add Standard TCP/IP Port Wizard will launch, as shown in Figure 2-24. The TCP/IP Port Wizard will allow you to install a printer that sends its print jobs to a network printer, as opposed to a printer submitting jobs to your local printer port. This is common on networks today.

Adding a network print device

3. After you click Next, using the wizard is simple. You are asked for either the TCP/IP address of the print device or the device name.

4. In the next dialog boxes, you install and set up the port, so that the printer can now send its print jobs to an IP address rather than a local port.

Managing Printers

After you have set up a local printer on your computer, you will configure its settings through the Properties dialog box, which is accessed by right-clicking the printer from the Printers folder and choosing Properties.

From the Sharing tab, you can make available a local printer the same way you make folder resources available. When you share out an existing printer, you will specify the share name, which is the name that will be seen by network users when they browse the resources on your server. Additionally, you can configure driver support for Microsoft clients other than Windows 2000 if necessary. By default, the only driver that loads when setting up a shared printer on a Windows 2000 Professional box is the Intel print driver for Windows 2000. A Windows 2000 client connecting to this shared printer will then automatically download and install these drivers when the connection to the shared printer is made. To provide additional print driver support, click the Additional Drivers button at the bottom of the Sharing tab, which will bring up the Additional Drivers dialog box, as shown in Figure 2-25.

Print Pooling and Priorities

Printer pools and *print priorities* are typically used in high-volume printing environments, where many printers or print devices are needed to service the printing needs of network users. The two technologies are really two sides of the same coin, as you will see.

Print pooling is used to associate a *single printer* with *multiple print devices*. You would typically use a printer pool if many print devices of the same type are located on the network, so that they would all understand the instructions of one type of print driver. The print jobs submitted to a printer pool will be serviced by the first available print device, as illustrated in Figure 2-26. When you configure printer pools, however, you cannot specify what print device will be receiving the job. For that reason, it is wise to place the print devices in close physical proximity to one another, unless you are trying to incorporate your printing scheme with some kind of corporate exercise program.

To configure a printer pool, access the Ports tab from the Properties of a printer, as shown in Figure 2-27. At the bottom of this tab, check Enable Printer Pooling and then select all the ports you want the logical printer to send its 1's and

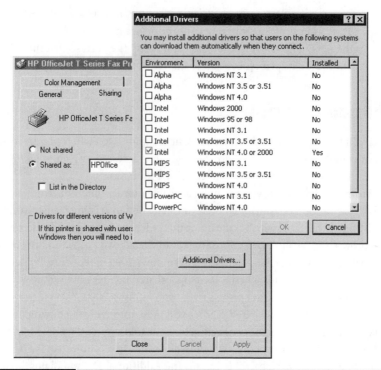

FIGURE 2-25 Configuring additional driver support

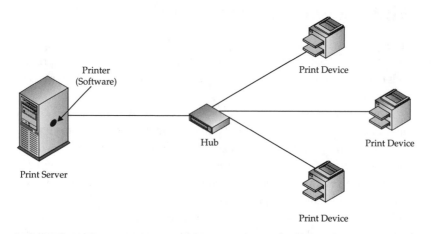

FIGURE 2-26 One printer, many print devices

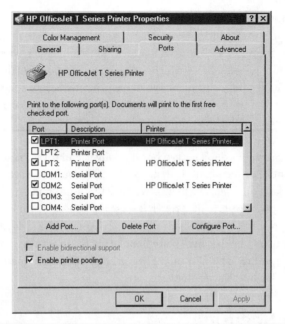

FIGURE 2-27   Enabling printer pooling

0's from. If you do not select the Enable Printer Pooling check box, you will only be able to configure one port per printer.

The flip side of printer pooling is setting printer priority. With printer priority, you will configure *multiple printers* to use a *single print device*. Catch that? Priority is the opposite of printer pooling, where one printer is using multiple print devices. When you set priority, you specify *how* print jobs are sent to the device. In this example, you have two logical printers that are pointed to the same physical port to submit their jobs, as illustrated in Figure 2-28.

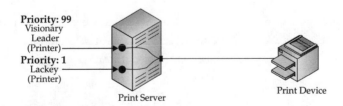

FIGURE 2-28   Many printers, one print device

You set the priority of a given printer from the Advanced tab of the Properties dialog box for a given printer. From this tab, you will be able to rank the priority of the printer from 1 to 99. The default priority for a printer is 1, which is the lowest ranking. Any printer that has a higher ranking gets first dibs on the print device that is associated with the printers. When the print manager on the system polls for print jobs, the printer with the higher priority will always print jobs in the queue before jobs in the lower priority printer.

Also notice from the Advanced tab that you can schedule the printer to be available at a certain time. This can be especially useful for users or groups that typically print large documents with no urgency. Say you have a network in which a user is working on drafts of a book—we'll call this user Brian—who often sends 40 to 50 page documents to the printer. If we set up a specific printer just for Brian and set this printer with a schedule of 11 P.M. to 5 A.M., the large documents won't be printed during the day, but they will be ready for Brian when he gets to the office in the morning. This frees up the normal network printer space from Brian's time-consuming 50-page printouts.

Printer Security

You will control which users have access to a Windows 2000 printer through the printer's Security tab, which is accessed through the Properties dialog box. You typically won't have to do much configuring of the Security permissions of printers, as the default security settings for printers is that the Everyone group has Print permission (unlike sharing and NTFS security, where the Everyone group gets Full Control).

Here are the three print permissions and what they mean:

Print Permission...	Lets a User...
Print	Connect to a printer and send print jobs to the printer
Manage Printers	Have administrative control over the printer; allows a user to pause and restart the printer, share and unshare the printer, and change printer properties
Manage Documents	Pause, restart, resume, and delete queued documents, but with no management of the properties of the printer

So what's the worst breach of print security that a normal user account could have? They could send a job to the printer. No big deal, at least to everyday network security. Users do have the ability to manage the documents they own—the documents they have sent to the printer.

Travel Advisory

For further information about network printing options and possible configurations, see the *Microsoft Windows 2000 Server Resource Kit,* Chapter 12, "Setting Up and Configuring Network Printers," from Microsoft Press.

Internet Printing

The WWW Publishing Service, a part of IIS, can make a printer available through a Web browser. This feature is new in Windows 2000 and is known as *Internet printing*. A new protocol, called Internet Print Protocol (IPP), allows users to print directly to a URL. When planning a print server deployment, remember that the Server service, which makes available shares through UNC pathnames, is installed automatically, whereas IIS services, which make printers available over HTTP, is not installed. You must install IIS and the WWW Publishing Service components on the computer to support Internet printing.

To install a printer that's been made available using IIS,

1. Start up your Web browser and type in the following syntax: *http://server-name/printers.*
2. Click the hyperlink of the printer you want to install, and under the Printer Actions menu, click the Connect hyperlink. If you have surfed the Web before, you can probably figure this out. You can also specify the URL when working through the Add Printer Wizard, as shown in Figure 2-29.

Finally, it is not uncommon in many networks to have a computer that is dedicated as a print server. This machine does not need to be one of your latest and greatest machines—in fact, it can be one of the oldest. Doesn't matter.

Travel Advisory

Take one of your older computers, possibly even one that has been pulled from production, and make it the dedicated print server. The speed of the processor is of little importance; the bottleneck in printing is *always* the speed of the print device.

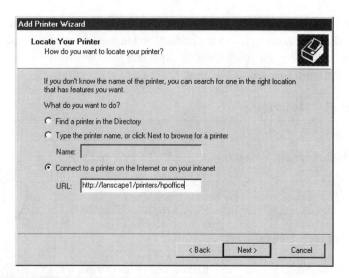

FIGURE 2-29   Connecting to a printer over the Web

Microsoft certification exams are famous for using disguises when testing your understanding of permissions. Some questions will look like they are asking you about moving and copying considerations, or about almost anything else, but they are really testing whether or not you grasp the security considerations discussed in this chapter. The trick is to read the question carefully to determine what is being asked, not to go for the head fake.

It cannot be overstated: *You almost certainly will not pass the exam without knowledge of the material covered in this chapter.* To the best of this author's recollection, a good 20 percent of the questions from both the Professional and Server tests covered these topics. You will give yourself a huge boost and a little margin for error with a thorough understanding of share and NTFS permissions.

I now step down from my soapbox.

✔ **Objective 2.01   Manage and Troubleshoot Access to Shared Folders.** In this objective, we looked at the significance of setting up network shares and then managing access with shared folder permissions. We also looked at considerations when share permissions are combined when users are part of groups that have different levels of share access to a resource.

✔ **Objective 2.02   Monitor, Manage, and Troubleshoot Access to Files and Folders.** This objective examined what security attributes are available in NTFS partitions. We distinguished between NTFS and share permissions and also looked at what happens when share and NTFS permissions are combined. We looked at NTFS permission inheritance and at some advanced NTFS attributes such as Ownership.

✔ **Objective 2.03   Connect to Local and Network Print Devices.** We discussed the characteristics of the Microsoft network print environment. Once we understand the terminology involved, we can set up local and network printers. We can then further manage our network printers so that they best meet our printing needs.

REVIEW QUESTIONS

1. You are the administrator of a laboratory in Los Alamos, California. You create and share a folder called \Thermonuclear Launch Codes on a computer running Windows 2000 Professional. You assign the Read share permission to user Matt and assign the Change share permission to the Research Scientists group. Matt is a member of the Research Scientist group. What will Matt's effective permission be to the folder when accessing it over the network?

   A. Read
   B. Change
   C. Full Control
   D. No Access

2. The government wants to move the folder in question 1 to a more powerful computer running Windows 2000 Professional. After the move is made, users call to complain they can no longer access the \Thermonuclear Launch Codes folder. What is the most likely cause of the problem?

   A. The disk signature on the target volume is corrupt.
   B. When you move a shared folder, Windows 2000 stops sharing the folder.
   C. Users must log off and log back on before being able to access a shared folder that was moved.
   D. To be able to move a shared folder, you must download the Microsoft Windows 2000 High Encryption Pack and apply it from the Windows Update Site.

3. Lindsey is a veterinarian at an animal clinic, and she has NTFS Read permission to the \Prescriptions folder. You are the Administrator at this clinic, and

you put a Clinical Trials.doc file in that folder and assigned Lindsey the Full Control permission to that file so that she can make regular updates to that file. You don't change anything on the \Prescriptions folder. What is Lindsey's effective permission when she accesses the Clinical Trials file?

   A. No Access

   B. Read

   C. Full Control

   D. None, but she will be able to change this because she has Full Control to the file

4. In the example in question 3, you decide to reorganize the directory structure of your NTFS partition to reflect your current business needs. You create a new folder called \Testing on the same partition and share out that folder, giving the group Everyone Read permission. You then move the Clinical Trials document over to this new folder. What now is Lindsey's permission to the file?

   A. Full Control. The NTFS permissions are unaffected by a move.

   B. No access. You need to create a new ACL for the file because of the deletion from the original location.

   C. Read. The share permission is now effective.

   D. This operation is not allowed because of the conflicting permissions.

5. You are the admin of a Windows 2000 peer-to-peer network for your small business. To help reduce TCO (and because you are a control freak), you don't want users to have the ability to share out folders. What groups can you safely put them in while meeting your goal?

   A. Administrators

   B. Backup Operators

   C. Power Users

   D. Server Operators

6. You set NTFS permissions on a folder named \Public on your Windows 2000 Professional computer. This folder contains several subfolders. Which folders inherit the permissions set on the \Public folder by default?

   A. \Public

   B. \Public and any first-tier folders

   C. \Public, first-tier subfolders and any second-tier subfolders

   D. All subfolders

7. You have given a user the NTFS Change permission to a file in the \Data folder. You then move the file to a folder on a FAT partition that the user has the Read permission to. What now will be the user's effective NTFS permissions after this move operation?

   A. Read
   B. Change
   C. Full Control
   D. All NTFS permissions will be lost.

8. You are creating a new printer in Windows 2000 Professional through the Add Printer Wizard. What settings are required during printer installation?

   A. Printer Name
   B. Share Name
   C. Port Location
   D. Location and Comment

9. You are the administrator of a Windows environment that includes a Windows 2000 Server domain and Windows 9x clients. The Windows 9x clients are not running the Windows 2000 Directory Service client or Microsoft Internet Print Services. Taking this into consideration, what methods can clients running Windows 9x use to connect to a network printer using the Add Printer Wizard?

   A. Enter a UNC name.
   B. Browse the network.
   C. Use a URL name.
   D. Search Active Directory directory services.

10. You are the admin of a Windows 2000 Professional computer called LEBOWSKI. An HP LaserJet 5 print device is connected to LPT 1 and shared out as LaserPrt. The accountant, who uses an MS-DOS client computer, calls to ask how she can connect to the network printer to print end-of-month reports. What is the syntax you should tell her to use?

    A. `Net use lpt1: \\lebowski\laserprt`
    B. `Net use lpt1: \\laserprt\lebowski`
    C. `Net print lpt1: \\lebowski\laserprt`
    D. `Net print lpt1: \\laserprt\lebowski`

11. On your Windows 2000 Professional computer, you want to connect to a network-interface print device using the Add Standard TCP/IP Printer Port Wizard. What can you specify to identify the port?

   A. A TCP/IP host name
   B. An IP address
   C. A Media Access Control (MAC) address
   D. A Windows Internet Naming Convention (WINS) computer name

REVIEW ANSWERS

1. **B** The effective permissions to a shared folder are the combination of the user and group permissions, with the least restrictive permission being the effective permission. The Deny permission will override the Allow permission, but that is not mentioned here. All other answers are incorrect because of this behavior of share permissions.

2. **B** Any time you move a shared folder, the Windows 2000 operating system stops sharing that folder. It must then be shared out from its new location. **A** is incorrect because a corrupt disk signature would most likely make the drive inaccessible in the first place, as it is an indicator of disk problems. It is written when the drive is viewed for the first time in Disk Administrator. **C** is incorrect because this will have no effect on whether or not the folder is shared after it has moved. **D** is incorrect for the same reason. The 128-bit High Encryption Pack can be applied to secure access, but it does not affect the actual sharing of the folder.

3. **C** Here you must remember that file permissions override folder permissions on NTFS volumes. Since she has Full Control to the file, this will be the effective permission. **A** and **B** are wrong because of this. **D** is partially true: she will be able to change the permissions because she has Full Control, but she won't have to change any configurations to make changes to the file.

4. **C** When Share and NTFS permissions are combined, the effective permission will be most restrictive of the combination of permissions. **A** is a true statement; the NTFS permissions will not be affected, but when combined with the share permissions, Full Control will not be the effective permission. **B** is incorrect because a new ACL creation is not necessary after a move; the ACL will travel with the moved item as long as it is within the same partition. **D** is just a false statement altogether.

5. **A** **C** Only these two groups can share out folders in a Windows 2000 workgroup. The Administrators local group has unrestricted access to the local machine. The Power Users local group doesn't have quite as many rights to the machine that an Administrator does, but close. One of these rights is the ability to share out resources. **B** is wrong because Backup Operators are pretty much limited to being able to backup and restore files. **D** is wrong because that group exists in Windows 2000 domains, not in workgroups.

6. **D** The default behavior for inheritance on NTFS volumes is that child objects inherit the permissions, or more technically the ACLs, of the parent. Any new folders and subfolders in the \Public folder get the permissions of \Public until these permissions are changed. **A**, **B**, and **C** are all incorrect because of this default inheritance behavior. You can block the inheritance by clearing the Allow Inheritable Permissions From Parent to Propagate To This Object checkbox.

7. **D** NTFS permissions will not be retained when you move a file or folder from an NTFS partition to a FAT partition. You should be especially careful of this when moving folders and files to a FAT partition. Any security you have on the resource could be lost. **A**, **B**, and **C** are all wrong because they assume a certain NTFS security, which will be non-existent.

8. **A** **C** You must give the printer a logical name that will be used by applications to address the printer as they submit jobs. The printer queue will also use this name. You must also specify a physical location for the print job to get to the print device. Specifying the port does this. **B** is incorrect because a printer need not be shared at setup time, if ever. **D** is also incorrect because this is optional information that makes it easier to search for a printer in Active Directory, but again it is not required.

9. **A** **B** When a client computer connects to a network printer, it is just connecting to another shared resource, and the addressing convention is the same as if the client had connected to a folder. If you know the print server name and the printer share name, you can speed up the printer installation process by not having to browse around the network. In fact, you don't even have to run the Add Printer Wizard to perform the install. Just choose Start | Run, and then enter the UNC path to the printer from the Run command line. Browsing the network is a perfectly acceptable way to connect, also. **C** is incorrect because while a down level client will be able to view the properties of a printer via a Uniform Resource Locator (URL), a printer cannot

be installed in this way. **D** is incorrect because your down level clients cannot search the Active Directory unless they have Active Directory Services client installed, and the question makes no mention of that.

10. **A** The NET USE command line syntax for connecting to a shared printer is net use lpt*x*: *servername**printsharename*, where *x* is the port number of the shared printer. **B** is wrong because the syntax of the utility has been reversed. **C** and **D** are wrong because print is not a valid parameter of the NET USE utility.

11. **A** **B** It helps in this question if you understand what a network-interface print device is. Because a network print device will have its own IP address, it stands to reason that it can be accessed by either a host name or an IP address. Both the name and IP address can be used to locate the port that will be used for the submission of print jobs. **C** is incorrect because a print device's MAC address is not used to establish a port connection when running the TCP/IP protocol. **D** is incorrect because the Windows 2000 port monitor uses either a host name or IP address to establish the port connection, not the NetBIOS name.

Managing Disk Drives and Volumes

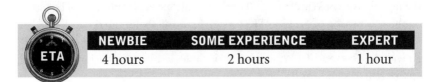

	NEWBIE	SOME EXPERIENCE	EXPERT
ETA	4 hours	2 hours	1 hour

In order for you to work with the operating system (OS), it must be able to retrieve information from the media used on your computer. Sounds simple enough, but the underlying task really isn't. To pull this off, the OS must be configured and able to work with various file systems. These file systems are worked with via the loading of various file system *drivers*, which are responsible for the retrieval of information from the file systems they are written to support. An example of this is the installation of CD-ROM file system drivers. CD-ROM media stores information on optical media (the CD) differently than a hard drive or floppy stores its information. In other words, CD-ROM File System (CDFS) drivers are needed to access the information stored on a CD, while NT file system (NTFS) drivers must be loaded to read data from an NTFS partition.

Fortunately, much of this driver configuration is done automatically by Windows 2000 at installation time, but this was not the case back in the DOS days. Because DOS was written before CDs became ubiquitous, this capability was not built into the MS-DOS operating system. Before CDs could be accessed, administrators had to make sure that DOS was told to load the Microsoft CD-ROM Extension (MSCDEX.EXE) as a part of autoexec.bat configuration. This driver enabled DOS to see the contents of a CD-ROM. The CDFS 32-bit driver replaced MSCDEX.EXE in the Windows 95 release and was incorporated into the OS, and since that version we don't need to give such drivers a whole lot of thought.

This chapter will take a look at the different file systems that are available on a Windows 2000 computer and also look at how physical media is prepared for formatting in these file systems. As always, much of our focus will be on some of the new abilities of Windows 2000 Professional. Special emphasis will be placed on the new version of NTFS, NTFS version 5, and all that it can do.

Finally, we will look at some backup considerations, and we'll get a little familiar with the new tool that Windows 2000 includes to configure backup jobs called, appropriately, Windows Backup.

Implement, Manage, and Troubleshoot Disk Devices

Objective 3.01

A computer's reason for existence is to work with data—to input, output, process, and *store* data. How an operating system works with storage devices is one of the first things you need to understand, because one of the items stored on such devices is the operating system itself. One of the reasons that DVD and CD-ROM devices are discussed first in this chapter is that, like any other program you purchase from the store, the Windows 2000 Professional operating system's installation files are distributed on a CD. If you want to install the OS, you have to know how to work with these devices.

DVD and CD-ROM Devices

Windows 2000 Professional uses two file systems to see and use optical (i.e. read by a beam of light) media. The CDFS is used for access to CD-ROM drives, and the Universal Disk Format (UDF) is used to access DVD drives. Both file systems are standards-based, which means that they comply with guidelines set forth by the International Standards Organization (ISO).

CDs and DVDs are both listed in the DVD/CD-ROM Drives area in Device Manager, which you use to manage the devices connected to you computer. Later in this chapter, we'll discuss the Device Manager in detail as you learn to set the properties of other devices.

To access Device Manager, right-click My Computer and choose Properties from the context menu, as shown in Figure 3-1. In the System Properties window, open the Hardware tab.

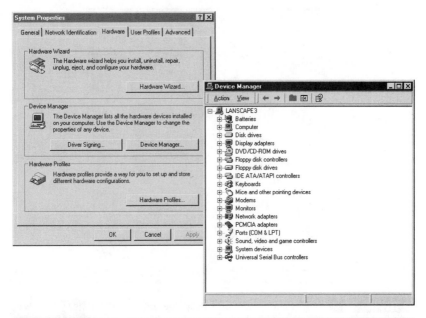

FIGURE 3-1   Viewing the Device Manager from the System Properties window

To start management of your DVD and CD-ROM devices, simply double-click the DVD/CD-ROM Drives node of Device Manager, and then double-click on the device you want to manage. You will then see three tabs in the Device Properties dialog box: General, Properties, and Driver.

The General tab (Figure 3-2) lists the device type, manufacturer, and location. It also shows the device status, indicating whether the device is working properly. If the device is not working properly, you can click the Troubleshooter button. Unfortunately, the Troubleshooter does little in the way of actual troubleshooting beyond asking you to make sure that a device is plugged in and has power. It is next to useless for experienced administrators.

The General tab of any device can also be used to configure the device's usage in a particular hardware profile. In the Device Usage area at the bottom of the window, you can set this behavior.

The Properties tab allows you to set device-specific options, such as volume and playback settings.

An optional tab, called Advanced Settings, is used to program a DVD device for the playback of any regionalized DVD media. From this tab, you can select a country and click OK. Usually, you can change the regional settings for the DVD device a limited number of times.

FIGURE 3-2   The General tab of the Properties window of a device

The Driver tab shows you information about the currently loaded driver, as well as buttons that let you see more driver details, uninstall the driver, or update the driver. If you click the Update Driver button, you will launch the Add/Remove Programs Wizard, which will prompt you for the location of the driver(s) you wish to update.

Removable Media Devices

Removable media are devices such as tape and Zip drives that are located outside the case that contains the workings of your computer. Zip drives were developed by the Iomega Corporation and first hit the market in the mid-1990s as a high-capacity replacement for floppy drives (a Zip disk can hold 100MB of data compared to the 1.44MB of storage available on a floppy disk). Removable storage media, such as Zip disks, can be read only using a corresponding reader device (a Zip drive) that's attached to the computer. Such devices have since been usurped by the commercial availability of CD-burner technologies, which let folks easily create 650-700MB CDs that are compatible with any computer with a CD-ROM drive—just about every PC in existence today. These removable types of storage can also be managed through the Device Manager.

Removable media devices are listed under the Disk Drives node, where you can double-click a device icon to manage the removable drive of your choice. Double-clicking will open the Properties window that contains General and Driver tabs that look pretty much the same as what you found when examining your CD-ROM and DVD devices. The Disk Properties tab contains options specific to the particular removable device you are managing. Whether or not other tabs appear in this Properties page will depend on the type of device installed, and of course Microsoft is not going to test your knowledge of a particular brand of removable media.

File System Considerations

Installation files are stored on a fixed disk in your computer's file system. The file system used to store files and retrieve all the files stored there, including the Windows 2000 Professional OS itself. In fact, one of the most important decisions associated with file management will be on what kind of file system you choose to hold the OS. The file system chosen at installation time will have a great influence on how you are able to use Windows 2000 and what kinds of features are available.

As mentioned in the previous chapter, Windows 2000 will support three types of file systems for partitions (or volumes) on a disk: FAT16, FAT32, and NTFS. Although a single disk can be divided into partitions and each of these partitions can be formatted with different file systems, a partition can use only one file system. Let's take a brief look at each of these file systems.

Local Lingo

Volume or partition   A logical area of a physical disk that is formatted with a file system so that data can be stored, secured, and retrieved. It is usually assigned a drive letter, such as C:\, but as we'll see it doesn't have to be. Throughout this book, these terms are used interchangeably in reference to a logical portion of disk space.

FAT16

FAT16 was first used with DOS way back when I was in parachute pants (that would be 1981). FAT16 divides the space on a fixed disk into 2^{16} storage locations, or *clusters*, and each of these locations is assigned a number. A cluster is the smallest unit of storage space on a FAT partition. A cluster can be used to store only a single file, or just a part of a single file, even if the file does not use up all the storage space. You can think of a cluster's use in the same way that you might use a personal storage space for the stuff that won't fit into your house: you rent out the entire space, even if you're going to store only a few things in just a fraction of the available space. Because hard disk space can be allocated to a file that doesn't use up all the space, it is usually best to keep cluster sizes as small as possible, especially when formatting larger volumes, as we'll see when we look at FAT32.

The location of files in these storage spaces is tracked by the use of a **file allocation table** (hence the acronym), which works in a way that is similar to the index of a book. It says, "File x is stored in the location starting with the number x and ends at location y." The read/write heads of the disk can quickly find and retrieve data from storage locations x through y.

The main advantage of FAT is that almost all operating systems support it. This makes FAT a good choice if the computer will be dual-booting with other operating systems. It is also a good choice for small partitions, which will operate with better performance when formatted with FAT16 instead of NTFS. This is because the overhead associated with the storage of files on FAT partitions is much smaller than with NTFS.

The FAT16 file system has two key drawbacks that make it an unlikely choice for most installations of Windows 2000 Professional: It was designed to be a single-user file system and does not support any kind of local security, and the maximum partition size is limited to 2GB.

FAT32

FAT32 is an updated version of FAT16 that uses smaller cluster sizes. Smaller cluster sizes result in a more efficient use of disk space, especially on larger drives. The average space saved when comparing data stored on a FAT32 partition versus a FAT16 partition is about 20 to 30 percent. One of the most appealing benefits of FAT32 over FAT16 is its ability to be used with today's much larger hard drive capacities. You probably won't need it anytime soon, but a FAT32 partition can be up to 2000GB in size!

The FAT32 file system was first introduced with the release of Windows 95 OEM Service Release 2 (OSR2), and it has been supported on all versions of Windows since, including Windows 2000. However, it is not compatible with earlier versions of Windows NT, which includes Windows NT 4.0.

NTFS

NTFS (general consensus is that it stands for New Technology File System, although you'd have better luck getting the formula for Coca-Cola than getting definitive word from Microsoft about that) was first used with the NT operating system.

NTFS provides the highest level of performance and features for Windows 2000 computers. NTFS version 5, which installs with Windows 2000, includes some significant enhancements. In fact, many of the technologies discussed in this book—such as compression, quotas, and encryption—are specific to NTFS, and more specifically to NTFS version 5.

NTFS supports partitions up to 2TB in size, and as with FAT32, cluster size is relatively small. This means that NTFS makes efficient use of disk space and is well suited for larger drives. One other significant advantage of NTFS is that it allows for local security of files and folders, which is especially important when two or more users are accessing the same computer. With NTFS, these users can be assigned different levels of permission to a resource, so that, for example, one user may have access to a particular file while the other user does not. This kind of security is not possible with either version of FAT.

You're not really taking full advantage of the Windows 2000 operating system capabilities unless you are using NTFS. NTFS includes technologies such as disk quotas, file encryption, local security, compression, and the hosting of a mounted drive, to name just a few. The longer you study the Windows 2000 operating systems, the more you will realize the benefits of NTFS. Even certain BackOffice Products, like Systems Management Server 2.0, simply won't install without an NTFS partition handy.

The main disadvantage of using NTFS is that only the NT and Windows 2000 OSs can recognize the NTFS file system. Windows 9x does not have the necessary file system drivers to access information on NTFS partitions, so if your computer dual-boots with Windows 9x, the NTFS partition will not even be seen on that installation.

Travel Advisory

You *can* still access information that is stored on an NTFS partition from a Windows 9x computer over the network. That's because the client request is serviced by the server, and the server calls the appropriate file system drivers necessary to retrieve the data before sending it back over the network. The client is not aware of what file system is being used to service the request.

Converting the File System

Windows 2000 provides a utility that allows you to convert both FAT16 and FAT32 volumes to NTFS volumes without affecting any of the data stored there. This is a big difference when compared to your other option for file system conversion: reformatting. Any time you format a drive, you will destroy any data on that drive and have to restore from backup. The FAT to NTFS conversion utility is called convert.exe, and it is run from the command prompt. Here is the syntax of the command (where *volume* is the drive letter that you want to convert):

```
convert volume /fs:ntfs
```

Of course, you can use the `convert /?` command to jog your memory about correct syntax when using this tool. For example, to convert the C:\ drive to NTFS, you would enter the command shown in Figure 3-3.

When the conversion process begins, it will attempt to lock the partition from use while the conversion is in process. If it cannot, like when trying to convert a partition with an open file, the conversion will begin the next time you boot the computer.

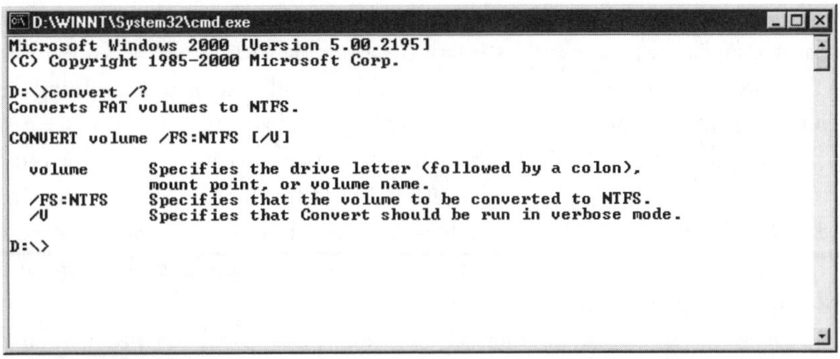

```
D:\WINNT\System32\cmd.exe                                    _ □ ×
Microsoft Windows 2000 [Version 5.00.2195]
(C) Copyright 1985-2000 Microsoft Corp.

D:\>convert /?
Converts FAT volumes to NTFS.

CONVERT volume /FS:NTFS [/V]

  volume      Specifies the drive letter (followed by a colon),
              mount point, or volume name.
  /FS:NTFS    Specifies that the volume to be converted to NTFS.
  /V          Specifies that Convert should be run in verbose mode.

D:\>
```

FIGURE 3-3 Converting a partition

Travel Advisory

The conversion of a FAT volume to an NTFS volume is a one-way process. You cannot convert NTFS to FAT without third-party utilities such as Partition Commander or Partition Magic. In Windows 2000, the only way to make an NTFS volume a FAT volume is to reformat, which would wipe out all the data on the volume. As is usually the case, a little planning in this area can go a long way.

The Microsoft Management Console

The Microsoft Management Console (MMC) is the framework around which all the tools used to manage Windows 2000 are built and provides a standard look and feel to all of the tools that is similar to the file management utility Windows Explorer.

By itself, the MMC has no functionality; it is just scaffolding around which the management tools are designed. The MMC is given management usefulness depending on which snap-in is loaded.

The MMC is not new to Windows 2000. The technology was first used to manage Microsoft BackOffice products such as Internet Information Server (IIS) 4.0, Systems Management Server (SMS) 2.0, and SQL Server 7. Anyone who studied or used those products is familiar with the MMC interface and with Microsoft's pledge that all future releases of Windows would be managed with MMC snap-ins. Those familiar with those products are also aware of how different (and easier to use) the MMC tools are than previous management utilities, such as NT 4's Server Manager and User Manager for Domains. Use of these tools required an extensive memorization of the available menus, whereas use of the MMC utilities can be done much more intuitively and visually by examining the contents of the console *tree* (the left pane) of a given snap-in.

The preconfigured MMC tools are meant to give you easy access to the most commonly performed management tasks without the hassle of adding snap-ins to an MMC each time you want to do something like add a user. Some of these preconfigured consoles give you access to one snap-in, and others, like Computer Management, give you access to several.

The MMC management interface offers many additional benefits, including

- It's highly customizable.
- MMC consoles can be saved and shared with other administrators, and snap-ins can be sent as e-mail attachments.
- Most snap-ins can be used for remote computer management.
- You can configure permissions so that MMC runs in author mode, which an administrator can manage, or in user mode, which limits what users can access.

On Windows 2000 computers, no default snap-ins are loaded when you launch the MMC. To open up a blank MMC, select Start | Run, and type **mmc** in the Run dialog box. When you first run the MMC, you will see a blank template, waiting for a snap-in as directed by you to begin providing functionality. Figure 3-4 shows an MMC waiting for instructions on what to manage.

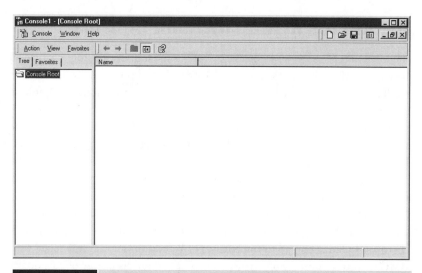

FIGURE 3-4   The MMC window before the addition of a snap-in

To add a snap-in to an MMC, you need to perform the following:

1. From the main console window, select Console | Add/Remove Snap-in to open the Add/Remove Snap-in dialog box.
2. Click the Add button to open the Add Standalone snap-in dialog box.
3. Select the snap-in you wish to add, and click the Add button.
4. You might be prompted here about which computer you wish to manage. In most cases, you will select the Local computer. When you are done click Finish.
5. Keep repeating steps 2, 3, and 4 to add snap-ins. In this way, you can create a single MMC that will gather all the tools you commonly use in a single location.
6. After you have added the snap-ins you want to create a console, you can save the console by selecting Console | Save As. Enter a name for your console. The custom consoles will be saved with a .msc extension by default.

The best place to save the console (in this author's opinion) is on your desktop, where it becomes a part of the user profile. In the case of an administrator, the custom MMC tool can be accessed anywhere with the implementation of a roaming profile (which is discussed in Chapter 4). From then on, you simply double-click one icon from the desktop to access all your day-to-day administrative tasks.

A collection of preconfigured MMCs is grouped in a folder called Administrative Tools on a Windows 2000 Professional machine. These administrative tools can be accessed from the Control Panel, as shown in Figure 3-5.

FIGURE 3-5   Accessing Administrative Tools

Unlike installations of Windows 2000 Server, there is no Start menu shortcut to the Administrative Tools when you first install Windows 2000 Professional. However, you can add this folder to the Start menu by dragging and dropping the Control Panel icon onto the Start menu. You will be prompted to create a shortcut if are trying to move the icon. Or (and this is probably the easiest way) you can access taskbar properties by right-clicking the taskbar and choosing Properties. Once in the properties of the taskbar, select the Advanced Page tab. You will see the option to Display Administrative Tools in the Start menu settings located at the bottom of the dialog box.

Configuring Disk Storage

The tool for managing and configuring the real estate on your network—that is, the disks and partitions—is a snap-in called Disk Management, which can be loaded in a custom MMC or run from a preconfigured MMC that includes the Disk Management snap-in.

Most people launch the Disk Management tool from the preconfigured Computer Management MMC snap-in. You can find this MMC in the Administrative Tools folder in the Control Panel, but a much faster way to launch this tool is simply to right-click My Computer from the desktop and choose Manage. From the Computer Management MMC, the Disk Management utility is easily accessible as one of the nodes on the console tree (under the Computer Management tools). You can also add the Disk Management snap-in by itself into a blank MMC. Figure 3-6 displays the Disk Management tool.

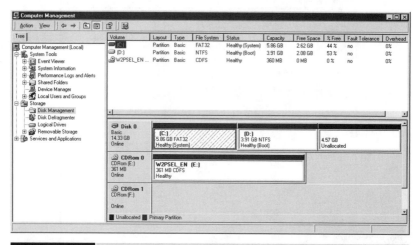

FIGURE 3-6   The Disk Management MMC (from Computer Management)

The Disk Management tool will also be discussed later in this chapter, in the section "Upgrading from Basic Storage to Dynamic Storage." Here, you'll learn how to use the tool to upgrade disk storage.

Monitor and Configure Hard Disk Drives

Windows 2000 supports two hard disk storage types: *basic* disks and *dynamic* disks. Basic disks use partition-based storage, which lets you divide a hard disk into up to four partitions, just as is the practice in NT 4.0, Windows 9*x*, and even DOS. Dynamic storage is a new system of storage in the Windows operating system world that divides hard disk space into volumes. Both storage types are concerned with separating the real estate on your hard drive into multiple, usable parts that will then be formatted with a file system. We'll tackle basic disks first, and then move on to a discussion of dynamic disks.

Basic Storage

Basic storage is a continuation of the disk storage that was used by earlier versions of Windows, and is therefore backward compatible with these and other operating systems. It works by setting up boundaries on the usable hard disk space called *partitions*. There are two types of partitions that can be configured on a basic disk: *primary* partitions and *extended* partitions. The first partition on a hard drive will be a primary partition, and all of the usable space in that primary partition will be assigned a drive letter. With basic storage, you can configure up to four primary partitions on a single disk. This limits you to using four drive letters to address the storage there. To get around this drive letter restriction, however, extended partitions can be used.

After the first primary partition has been configured, an extended partition may then be set up. Unlike primary partitions, the usable space in an extended partition can be further subdivided. Each subdivision of space in an extended partition is assigned a drive letter and called a *logical drive*. As a result of the subdivision possible in an extended partition, you can get around the four-drive-letter restriction that would be in effect by using primary partitions only.

When you use an extended partition, you reduce the number of primary partitions available by one, so that the new partitioning rule thus becomes: up to three primary partitions and one extended partition. It is not possible to have more that one extended partition on a single disk.

However, because you can divide extended partitions into multiple logical drives, one of the more common basic disk configurations is to have a single primary partition and a single extended partition. (Of course, the *most* common disk configuration for disks is that the entire drive is configured as a single primary partition that uses all of the available space.) This gives administrators almost all the partitioning flexibility they will ever need. Each logical drive on an extended partition can be formatted with different file systems if necessary, and each can serve as the boot partition for the operating system—that is, they can hold the operating system's installation directory. In this way, it is possible for a Windows 2000 computer to boot to a primary system partition that is formatted with FAT and then run off an extended boot partition that is formatted with NTFS.

The only restriction on extended partitions is that they can't be the *system* partition (the partition containing the hardware boot files), because extended partitions can't be marked as active. You will need to have your system partition on a primary partition for the computer to boot.

Travel Advisory

This is kind of backward, and is very confusing, but the *system* partition is used to hold necessary files to boot the computer. The operating system installation itself, the partition that holds the \WINNT directory, is actually called the *boot* partition. Got it? The system partition holds the boot files, the boot partition holds the operating system. Can these two partitions be one and the same? You bet. In fact, for most home computers, they are. (If your hard drive is just configured as one big C:\ drive, your system and boot partitions are the same drive.)

Basic disks are also an important consideration when you want to configure a computer for dual booting with non–Windows 2000 operating systems. That's because basic partitions are supported by operating systems other than Windows 2000 (like NT), which means that if you want to boot using an OS other than Windows 2000, you must configure the system partition on a basic disk.

Dynamic Storage

The new wrinkle in the area of disk storage is a Windows 2000 feature called dynamic disks, which divide the usable space on a hard disk into dynamic *volumes*. What is a volume, you ask? Like a partition, it divides up space on a disk. When you first install Windows 2000, the default type of disk will be a basic disk, and the space will be divided into partitions. When the disk is upgraded to a dynamic disk, those primary and extended partitions will become simple volumes (which are explained in the next section), but to an end user nothing will have changed. There won't be any more or less room on that volume than was on the partition, and it can still be addressed by the same drive letter. A volume looks and acts much the way that a partition does to everyday users, but to an administrator, there are some significant differences between the two.

One of these differences is that dynamic disks do not, and cannot, contain partitions or logical drives (subdivisions of extended partitions). This removes almost all restrictions placed by partition-based disk storage: for example, with dynamic disks you can have an unlimited number of volumes per disk.

This storage type is also important to understand if you want to implement advanced disk configurations. Dynamic storage supports three volume types: simple volumes, spanned volumes, and striped volumes. Most of these advanced configurations were available with Windows NT 4.0 on basic disks (although that's not technically correct; there was no distinction back then between the two types of disks) but are available now in Windows 2000 only on dynamic disks. Now let's take a look at each of these in more detail.

Exam Tip

Only Windows 2000 supports dynamic disks. You can't take a dynamic disk and plop it into an NT 4 machine.

Simple Volumes

A simple volume is simply (Pun? You decide.) storage space from a single dynamic drive. The cool part is that the space can come from either contiguous or non-contiguous space from that drive. These are analogous to a primary partition on a basic disk, and your end users will probably never know the difference. You would use a simple volume when you have enough space on a single disk to hold your entire volume.

Spanned Volumes

A spanned volume contains space that is located on from anywhere between 2 to 32 dynamic drives (one could say that the space *spans* many drives). Spanned volumes can be used to increase the size of a dynamic volume. When you create a spanned volume, the data is written sequentially across the drive set, filling up the available space on one physical drive before moving on to use the space on the next drive on the set. For example, you can configure a 1GB space from one drive, another 500MB from another drive, and 500MB more from a third drive for a total volume size of 2GB. All the space would be addressed by a single name, usually a drive letter like D:\, and again, end users would have no idea of which physical drive stores the data.

Administrators would usually set up a spanned volume when available space on a disk is getting low. When a volume is running out of disk space from one hard drive and you need to extend a volume's storage capacity by using space from another one, spanned volumes are the answer.

One of the drawbacks to spanned volumes is that it does not provide fault tolerance. In fact, because multiple drives are involved, it is a bit less fault tolerant than a simple volume. If one of the drives in the spanned set fails, you lose the entire volume and will have to restore the set from backup. You will also not see any increase in performance because the data is being written sequentially, accessing only one physical disk per I/O request.

Striped Volumes

A striped volume stores its data by writing data across between 2 and 32 dynamic drives in equal portions. The important thing to understand about striped volumes is that the areas of free space in a volume set must be of equal size, even though the disks that they exist on are not. This is because the operating system writes the data across all disks in the stripe set as it fills up. To help you visualize, think of a how a dealer deals out a hand of poker. Each player is going to get the same amount of cards, one card at a time. The dealer does not hand out two to one person, three to the next, and then skip the next. When the dealer is done dealing the "set," players have exactly five cards in front of them. The drivers controlling I/O operations on a striped volume act the same way. A single stripe in a stripe set can only be as big as the smallest area of free space on one of the disks on the set. Figure 3-7 illustrates a striped volume.

As with simple volumes and spanned volumes, the striped volume will be addressed as a single entity to end users, usually a drive letter. The drawback to

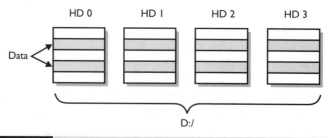

FIGURE 3-7 A striped volume

using striped sets is also the same: if you lose any of the disks in the set, the entire volume fails, and you must restore from backup.

So why would anyone use a striped set? Performance. Because the data is written across all the stripes in a set, you can take advantage of multiple I/O performance and increase the speed at which data reads and writes take place. You can also combine free space on multiple disks, but be careful when doing this because, for example, if you combined space from three disks, two with 1GB of free space, and one with 100MB of free space, you don't get 2100MB of storage, as you would with a spanned volume. You would instead have 300MB of space on your striped volume.

Mirrored Volumes and RAID 5 Volumes

Two other volume sets are available with Windows 2000, mirrored volumes and RAID 5 volumes (RAID stands for redundant array of independent disks). Both volume types are fault tolerant, but neither is available on Windows 2000 Professional computers. You shouldn't see any questions on the 70-210 exam on these fault tolerant volumes, but you will see questions on the 70-215 (Server) exam. We will discuss these volumes briefly, because it won't hurt for you to have some understanding of these volume types now.

Local Lingo

Fault tolerant   In the computer world, this refers to the ability of something to withstand the loss of data and keep performing. In the case of fault tolerant volume configurations, one of the disks could fail and need to be replaced, but an end user would never know the difference.

Mirrored volumes work by creating a duplicate copy of data across two physical drives. A standby copy of a hard drive is waiting in the event of a disk failure. When a disk failure occurs, the mirrored volume must be "broken" and then rebuilt, but access to the volume will continue uninterrupted (except in the event that a computer must be shut down to replace the failed drive).

RAID 5 volumes are striped sets that work across 3 to 32 physical dynamic disks that store the duplicate copies of data across the entire set in the form of *parity*. These RAID 5 sets, in fact, were known as *striping with parity* sets when configured in NT 4 Server computers. The parity information can be used to regenerate lost data in the event of the failure of a single disk in the RAID 5 array. Again, data access will remain uninterrupted even though a component has failed.

Upgrading from Basic Storage to Dynamic Storage

As you recall, a disk is configured as a basic disk when you install Windows 2000 Professional or perform an upgrade from a previous operating system. All partitioning information on the existing drive is carried over from the upgrade. To take advantage of the new features offered by dynamic disks, you must perform an upgrade of your disks.

Exam Tip

One important consideration to keep in mind as you study for the Windows 2000 Professional exam, as well as something you'll use in the real world, is that a physical disk can be either basic or dynamic, but not both. The process of configuring the disk as either basic or dynamic is done at the disk level, not at the partition level.

To perform a disk upgrade, you use the Disk Management MMC snap-in, which can be found under the Computer Management tools in the console. From the Disk Management utility, just right-click the drive you want to convert and choose Upgrade to Dynamic Disk, as shown in Figure 3-8.

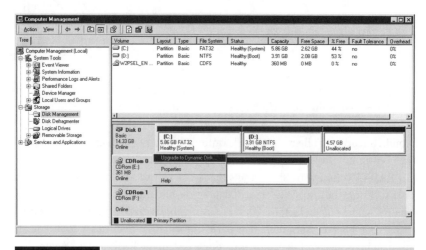

FIGURE 3-8   Converting to a dynamic disk

The Upgrade to Dynamic Disk dialog box appears, where you can select the disk you want to upgrade (I know that seems a little redundant) with a check box and then click the OK button. After your selection, the next box will ask you to click Upgrade to proceed, and then a confirmation dialog box appears warning you that there is no chicken exit for this procedure, as seen in Figure 3-9. Another confirmation dialog box warns you that any file systems mounted on the disk will be dismounted. You will need to click Yes to continue. The last warning you will receive is that a reboot will take place to complete the operation.

Even though other operating systems can't use the fault tolerant volumes created with Windows 2000 dynamic disks, the inverse is OK. Windows 2000 supports advanced configurations created on basic disks when created in NT 4.0. To illustrate, a volume set created in Windows NT can be read from and written to in Windows 2000.

Travel Advisory

Be sure to test any upgrades to dynamic storage before implementing in production. I won't name names here, but I've seen some very well-known computer maker's hard disks become very grumpy (i.e. "inoperable" or "hosed") when they were upgraded to dynamic storage. (This particular situation was resolved by installing the manufacturer-supplied hard disk I/O drivers, but it's not like you're going to get a call from Microsoft or the company who sells the computers telling you not to do this.) So test just to be sure.

As a last point about dynamic disks, note that to upgrade a disk from basic to dynamic storage, the target disk needs at least 1MB of free, nonpartitioned space for the operation to complete. This space is needed for Windows to re-create and

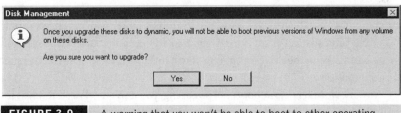

Disk Management

ⓘ   Once you upgrade these disks to dynamic, you will not be able to boot previous versions of Windows from any volume on these disks.

Are you sure you want to upgrade?

[Yes]   [No]

FIGURE 3-9   A warning that you won't be able to boot to other operating systems after the upgrade

store the volume information of the upgraded disk. This means that many computers with Windows 2000 Professional out of the box will not be candidates for an upgrade to dynamic disks immediately.

Travel Advisory
Most manufacturers configure the hard drive to partition all the available disk space into one primary partition—the C:\ drive. There won't be enough room on this disk for the upgrade to dynamic disks to go through. Usually, if you want to implement dynamic disks, it's better to start from scratch with a nonpartitioned hard drive.

Managing Storage

The Disk Management utility allows you to perform all your physical and logical disk space management. You will use Disk Management when you are adding new storage space to a computer, a fairly common administrative task as programs and files grow larger. How you will use Disk Management to help you add more space depends on whether or not the computer supports hot swapping.

Local Lingo
Hot swapping   The ability of a device to be added without shutting down the computer. Most hot-swappable hard drives come in special hardware arrays that are part of a high-end server package. In most cases, a computer running Windows 2000 Professional will not support the hot swapping of disk drives.

If your computer *does not* support hot swapping, you first need to shut down the computer. Add the new drive and restart the computer. The new drive should be detected automatically and listed in the Disk Management utility. You can now create partitions on the drive or upgrade it to a dynamic disk so that you can start creating volumes.

If your computer *does* support hot swapping, you don't need to shut down the computer. Add the disk to the array and then from the Action menu of Disk Management, choose the Rescan Disks command. The new drive should be detected and appear in the display.

After you add a new disk to the computer, you can divide that space into logical storage areas. Disk Management offers the ability to create, delete, and format partitions on basic drives, and it lets you create simple, spanned, or striped volumes on dynamic disks. The processes for creating new partitions and new volumes are similar. Both processes start with a right-click on an area of free space on a drive, which launches a wizard to help create the partition or volume on that drive. We'll illustrate with the creation of a volume.

1. Right-click an area of free space, and choose Create Volume. The Create Volume Wizard appears. Click Next to continue.
2. Select the type of volume to create, as shown in Figure 3-10. Note that only the volume types supported by your computer's hardware configuration are available. Choose the radio button of the volume you want to create, and click the Next button.
3. The Select Disks dialog box appears, where you will set the size of your new volume. The maximum volume size possible will be the amount of free space recognized. Choose the size of the volume and the disk you want it created on, and click Next.
4. The Assign Drive Letter or Path dialog box is next, where you will specify a drive letter or choose to mount the volume in an empty folder. Being able to assign an empty folder from another partition for this new drive will allow

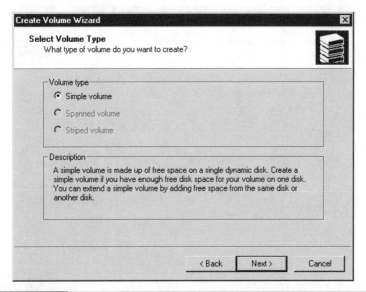

FIGURE 3-10   Select which type of volume you want to create

you to browse one folder hierarchy to get access to all your resources. For example, if you have drive C and you are in the process of building drive D, you could mount drive D to an empty folder in drive C. This would allow someone who is browsing the folder contents of drive C to double-click on the empty folder and be transparently redirected to drive D.

Travel Advisory

To mount a volume to an empty folder, the drive that will hold the empty folder must use **NTFS**.

---

5. Next, the Format Volume dialog box appears (Figure 3-11), and you will choose to format the volume with FAT16, FAT32, or NTFS. You can give the volume a label for informative purposes (your volume will still be accessed with the information you provided in the previous step), and perform a quick format. The quick format, however, does not scan the disk for potential bad sectors, so it is recommended that you use it only in test environments. After you've made your choice, click the Next button.

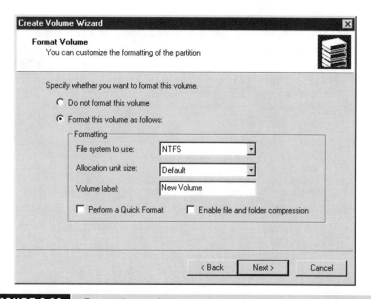

FIGURE 3-11 Formatting a volume

6. The Completing the Create Volume Wizard appears, which summarizes your selections. If you need to change any of them, click the Back button to return to the appropriate dialog box and make changes. If all is well, click the Finish button.

When you are creating a new partition on a basic disk, these steps will look pretty much the same. You right-click an area of free space and select a partition type to create, which will launch the Create Partition Wizard.

You will then be asked to select the partition type, specify the partition size, assign a drive letter or path, and then format the partition.

Additional Volume Management

One of the big advantages of third-party disk management utilities like Partition Magic or Partition Commander is the ability to add space to partitions without having to first delete and then re-create the partition, destroying the data contained therein. Windows 2000's dynamic storage now allows you to add space to partitions with the ability to *extend* a volume.

When you extend a volume, you are taking a single simple volume and adding more storage area to that volume from free space that exists on the same physical drive. Other than that, nothing else will change when accessing a volume that has been extended. The drive letter will remain unchanged; only the volume's capacity will have changed.

Travel Advisory

To extend a volume, the simple volume must be formatted as NTFS. You also cannot extend a system or boot partition, so this option will not be available on most C:\ drives.

Disk Quotas

Disk quotas are a powerful new feature available for managing storage on Windows 2000 NTFS volumes. Quotas let you determine who is hogging all of the disk space on a Windows 2000 Server or Windows 2000 Professional computer with all of their multi-gigabyte Napster downloads. However, you should recognize that even though it is available on any Windows 2000 computer with an NTFS volume, quota management is usually done only on file servers, where many network users may be storing files and your goal is to set limits on how much storage and individual can use. Disk quotas are not typically set on individual workstations.

Disk quotas also allow for a high degree of flexibility in their implementation. You can set disk quotas for all users, or you can limit disk usage on a per-user basis. You cannot, however, set quota limits on a per-group basis. I'll explain why in just a bit.

You enable quotas on a per-volume or per-partition basis. In other words, you configure quota tracking for the C:\ drive or the E:\ drive, but you will not set it up for hard disk 1. Furthermore, there's no way to set up quotas for a specific folder. The quota feature will be tracked for the contents of an entire volume.

So how are disk quotas monitored? They work by tracking file and folder ownership, which is why monitoring can occur only on a per-user basis, and not per group—groups do not own files or folders, individual user accounts do. Furthermore, quota limits are based on the uncompressed size of files or folders. A user up against his or her quota limit cannot compress files to free up space; the files will have to be deleted.

Travel Advisory

There is an exception to these quota rules, of course. The Administrators local group is the default owner of all files on a volume formatted with NTFS, and the Administrator account is exempt from all quota limits. This includes ownership of all files associated with a program installation. If the Administrator account were not exempt, it would severely limit what the Administrator could do.

You configure quota limits from the NTFS volume Properties dialog box of a given volume. You can configure the quota entries from Disk Administrator in either the top or bottom pane of the details pane by accessing a volume's Properties dialog box, but you can also access this dialog by right-clicking a drive letter in Windows Explorer.

After opening the Properties dialog box for a volume (again, I stress that you're working with a volume or partition, not a physical disk), click the Quota tab, shown in Figure 3-12. Quota tracking is disabled by default. You can turn it on by checking the Enable Quota Management box.

Once you have turned on quota tracking for a volume, it will be effective for all new users of that drive. Three general quota configuration options can be set from this tab, as described in the following table.

Option	What It Does
Deny Disk Space To Users Exceeding The Quota Limit	Users who try to save more information than their quota limit allows will receive an "out of disk space" message.
Select The Default Quota Limit For New Users On This Volume	Sets the quota for new users of the volume. You can limit disk space and use the drop-down boxes to set quotas and warning levels for disk usage.
Select The Quota Logging Options For This Volume	Specifies whether log events will be recorded when users exceed warning or quota limits. You may view these events in the system log.

After you enable quota entries, an interesting thing happens from the perspective of the end user. The size of the drive they are saving their work to becomes exactly the same as their quota entry. So, even though you might have set up a

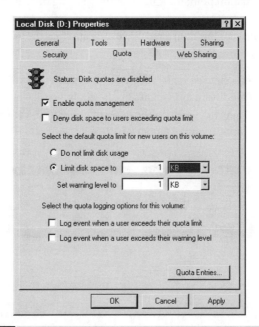

Enabling Windows 2000's quota feature

10GB volume for file storage, if you have set quota limits of 100MB, any user with that quota limit who logs on will see a volume of 100MB in size.

You will also note from an examination of the Quota tab that the utility can be used as a monitoring tool for disk space usage. In fact, the default choice by the operating system is that no disk space will be denied to new users until you set the configuration parameters.

You can monitor the disk space usage by each user by viewing the quota entries for the partition or drive. To view the quota entries, open the Properties window of the drive and open the Quota tab. At the bottom of the tab, you can click the Quota Entries button to view the list of users using hard drive space on that partition (shown in Figure 3-13). If you would like to change a user's quota limit, you can double-click the entry and modify the quota limit value.

This Quota Entries dialog box is also your management interface to monitor disk usage. Now that quota tracking has been enabled and you've told it how to behave, the results of that activity will be summarized here. The Status column next to the user's name will graphically display whether the user has exceeded a quota threshold.

- A green arrow means that the user's quota status is OK.
- An exclamation point indicates that the warning threshold has been tripped.
- An exclamation point in a red circle indicates that the user has exceeded allocated storage space.

You can also configure a higher degree of granularity for your quota settings from this tab. To modify an individual's quota, double-click a user name to bring up the individual quota entry dialog box shown in Figure 3-14. The options here mirror those that appear on the Quota tab. Remember that setting a quota entry

Status	Name	Logon Name	Amount Used	Quota Limit	Warning Level	Percent Used
OK		BUILTIN\Administrators	0 bytes	No Limit	No Limit	N/A
OK	Brian Culp	LANSCAPE1\bc	0 bytes	100 MB	90 MB	0
OK	J Lebowski	LANSCAPE1\The Dude	0 bytes	10 MB	9 MB	0

3 total item(s), 1 selected.

FIGURE 3-13   Examining individual quota entries

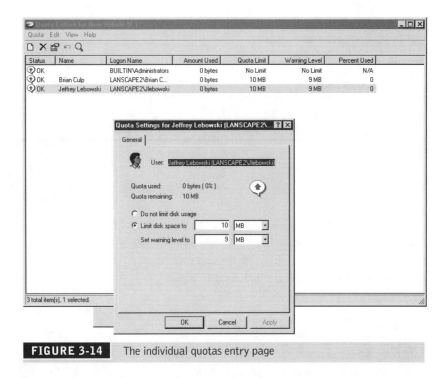

FIGURE 3-14 The individual quotas entry page

but not limiting disk space lets you see how much space a user is using, which is in many instances all the administrative leverage you will need.

Local Lingo

Granularity Techno-babble for being able to set a high degree of individual configurability—setting something one way for one user and another way for another user. If you hear this word used in a meeting in the same sentence as *drill down*, and/or have it suggested that you should address an issue *offline*, please excuse yourself and leave that meeting!

Finally, what should you do when a user's quota limits have been reached, and that user wants to save more stuff to your precious disk space? There are several ways to handle this situation. You can, as the Administrator, take ownership of the files. The files then would not be charged against the user's quota limit. Or you can tell that user to delete files that he or she no longer needs. As a last option, if the user does need all of the files, you could modify the quota entry settings for that user by increasing the quota value.

Travel Advisory

Remember that you are only human, and your first assumption of a quota limit may not have been realistic for all users. It is also important to know that you can change the quota value for a particular user after the initial setup of quotas.

As a final highlight regarding quotas, you should know that a user's quota entry cannot be deleted while he or she still owns any files or folders. To make a deletion of a quota entry, the files that the user owns must either be deleted or file ownership must be taken by another user.

Exam Tip

You are likely to see a troubleshooting question regarding what to do when a user is up against his or her quota limit.

To summarize our discussion on quotas, here are a few main points you should know about setting and configuring disk quotas as you sit down to take the Windows 2000 Professional exam:

- *Quotas are available only on NTFS partitions or volumes.* Quotas are one of those features of Windows 2000 that will not work on drives formatted with the FAT file system. You must be using NTFS on any drives that you wish to enable quotas on.
- *Disk usage is based on ownership.* An understanding of quotas requires that you be familiar with the concept of NTFS file and folder ownership. Recall that every file and folder on an NTFS volume has an owner, and quotas use this owner attribute to track disk usage. When a user creates or copies a file on an NTFS volume, Windows 2000 charges the disk space used against the users quota limit.
- *Disk quotas ignore compression.* Users are charged against their quota limit based on the uncompressed size of the files they own.

- *Free space for applications is based on quota limit.* When you enable quotas for a user, the free space that Windows 2000 reports to applications for the volume is the amount of space remaining for the user's quota limit.
- *Administrators are not charged against quota limits.* Since most of the files on an NTFS volume are owned by the Administrators local group by default (including the installation of the operating system, if applicable), it would be pointless to track usage by the Administrator. For this reason, you should perform all application installs when logged on as the Administrator.

File and Folder Compression

Each file and folder on an NTFS-formatted volume maintains a compression state (a compression attribute) that is either compressed or uncompressed. This feature of an NTFS volume enables you to compress files or folders, which, as the name implies, will ultimately let you store more data on an NTFS volume. The compression attribute on files and folders are furthermore managed independently, which means that a compressed folder can contain uncompressed files, and an uncompressed folder can hold a compressed file.

The setting to enable file and folder compression is set by clicking the Advanced button on the General tab of the Properties dialog box of each given file or folder. After choosing to look at the Advanced Properties, you can set the attribute with a simple click of the mouse, as shown in Figure 3-15.

FIGURE 3-15 Compressing a file or folder

A quick note here is necessary about the Compression attribute as it relates to the Encryption attribute, as you will configure them both from the same location. (We'll discuss encryption in Chapter 8.) These attributes are mutually exclusive: you can either enable compression or encryption, but not both at the same time.

The compression that NTFS applies is invisible to users and even applications accessing the compressed files. When a compressed file is requested by an application like Microsoft Word or even by an older DOS application, NTFS takes care of the decompression before presenting the file contents to a user.

Exam Tip

And what about the compression attribute on a FAT or FAT32 volume? You won't find a setting for compression on these FAT volumes because compression is available only on NTFS volumes. Don't let this trip you up on the exam!

Some file formats, such as JPG, MP3, and ZIP, exist in an already highly compressed state, and compressing them on an NTFS volume will have little impact on the space they use. Large ASCII text files (if you have any on your computer) and some executables are usually good candidates for compression.

Moving and Copying Considerations

As long as you weren't sleeping during Chapter 2's discussion of moving and copying considerations on NTFS attributes, you should have a pretty good handle on what happens when compresses files and folders are copied and moved between and within NTFS volumes.

Like security attributes, more often than not the compression attribute changes when files and folders are moved or copied.

- When you perform a copy from within the same NTFS volume, the copied files and folders inherit the compression attribute of the destination folder. Same goes for copies between different NTFS volumes.
- When you perform move operations within the same NTFS volume, the moved files and folders retain their original compression attribute.
- When you perform a move between different NTFS volumes, the moved files and folders inherit the compression attribute of the destination folder. Again, as with security attributes, this is because Windows 2000 treats the move between volumes as a copy operation and then deletes the original file or folder.

- And what about moves or copies to non-NTFS volumes, like to FAT drives or to a floppy disks? As you suspect, the compression attribute is not supported on these file systems, so the copied or moved file is uncompressed first before being copied or moved.

You can also easily determine which files and folders are compressed from Windows Explorer by setting the compressed files and folders to display in a different color. Simply select Tools | Folder Options from Windows Explorer. Then, from the View tab, select the Display Compressed Files And Folders With Alternate Color check box. From then on, compressed files and folders are displayed in blue.

Using the Windows 2000 Backup Utility

Windows 2000 also includes a backup utility called Windows Backup. The purpose of a backup is protect your data in the event of a system failure like the failure of a device or any other disaster such as the theft of a machine or a really angry user with a sledgehammer. But you know that already, don't you?

Windows Backup is run interactively through a graphical interface, which, if you've ever backed up *anything* in your life, you'll find intuitive to use. This interface can be configured either manually or via a series of wizards. The wizards can be used to back up, restore, and schedule backup jobs. Simply specify what you want to backup, with a few check boxes, select what kind of backup to perform, and where the backup job should be saved.

In Chapter 6, we'll discuss in more detail the mechanics of the Backup utility, including a discussion of the various types of data that can be backed up and the different kinds of backup operations that are possible.

What may be the most confusing thing about the Backup utility is where to find it. Most management tasks on a Windows 2000 computer are configured from a MMC snap-in. As mentioned earlier, many of these preconfigured MMC snap-ins are found under Start | Programs | Administrative Tools. To access the Backup utility, however, you will need to select Start | Programs | Accessories | System Tools | Backup. Figure 3-16 shows you where the configuration of backup jobs will start.

From this window, you can start the Backup Wizard, start the Restore Wizard, and create an emergency repair disk (ERD). The ERD will be discussed in Chapter 6 as well.

There's no law that says that you have to use the Windows Backup utility. Almost every tape drive vendor supplies its own software package for configuring

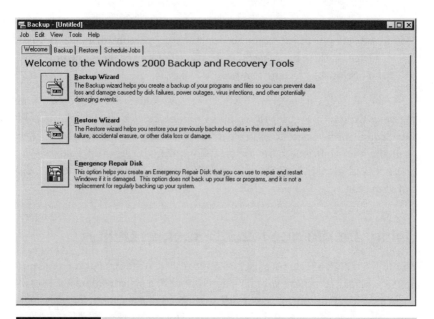

FIGURE 3-16   The Windows Backup utility

backups. In fact, the Windows Backup that is included with Windows 2000 was written by Veritas, Inc.

You can also schedule backup jobs from the Backup utility or manually configure backups to run by adding a task to the Windows 2000 Task Scheduler. I think you'll find the Backup utility the easier of the two to use for scheduling automated backups.

CHECKPOINT

✔ **Objective 3.01   Implement, Manage, and Troubleshoot Disk Devices.**
We discussed storage management considerations for DVD, CD-ROM, fixed disks, basic disks, and dynamic disks. We also looked at technologies for NTFS volumes that allow administrators to further control the network environment, including setting disk quotas for network users, setting compression on files and folders on a partition, and configuring backups on removable media.

REVIEW QUESTIONS

1. Artie Fufkin is planning an install of Windows 2000 Professional on your brand new computer running an Athlon 1.4GHz processor. He has two 20GB hard drives to work with. He doesn't want to use all the available space right away, but he wants to reserve the right to extend a volume to use the space on the second disk if necessary. What two considerations define the appropriate type of disk storage for this scenario?

   A. Basic disk
   B. Dynamic disk
   C. Simple volume
   D. Striped volume

2. You have been given a management directive to monitor disk usage by the users in your network. It seems that the file server's FAT32 G:\ drive is filling up fast with bad jokes, chain letters, and urban legends saved from forwarded e-mails. You try to enable disk quotas but are unsuccessful. What is the problem?

   A. Quota tracking doesn't set any limits on usage when you first enable it.
   B. Quotas only work on NTFS volumes.
   C. You have not specified the users to track in the disk quotas configuration dialog box.
   D. Quota tracking, by default, applies only to new users in Windows 2000.

3. Otis Hogswallop wants to change the file system on your G: drive from NTFS to FAT so that he can configure the system to dual-boot between Windows 2000 Professional and Windows 98. He also wants to preserve the existing data on that drive. How will Otis accomplish this?

   A. Type **convert drive_letter /fs: fat** from the command prompt.
   B. Type **convert drive_letter /fs: ntfs to /fs: fat** from the command prompt.
   C. Delete the partition and reformat with NTFS; the NTFS format leaves files unharmed.
   D. Back up all data, reformat the partition as FAT, and restore from backup.

4. Which of the following volume types are not supported on a Windows 2000 Professional computer?

   A. Striped volumes
   B. Mirrored volumes
   C. Spanned volumes
   D. RAID 5 volumes

5. Which of the following cannot be upgraded to dynamic disks?

   A. Disks from laptops

   B. Disks that don't have at least 1MB of unallocated free space

   C. Disks that are part of a striped set created in NT 4

   D. Disks that are part of a volume set created in NT 4

6. What are the available file systems that are supported for a Windows 2000 Professional installation? (Choose all that apply.)

   A. FAT16

   B. FAT32

   C. CDFS

   D. HPFS

   E. NTFS Version 5

7. You have compressed a 10MB file into 5MB. Now, you want to perform a copy of that file to a FAT32 partition. You are aware that the default behavior during a copy is that the file will inherit the destination directory's compression attribute. What procedure is necessary to ensure that the file maintains its compression state during the copy operation?

   A. You must perform the copy operation from the command line with the XCOPY command, using the /retain switch.

   B. You really can't change the default behavior; you must make sure to go back and set the compression attribute after the copy has taken place.

   C. Right-click and choose Cut, and then at the destination directory right-click again and choose Paste Special. Then specify that the compression attribute be retained.

   D. You can't maintain compression of a file on non-NTFS partitions.

8. You have a computer that supports hot-swapping capabilities. You add a disk to the array but do not see the disk when you go to configure it in Disk Management. What must you do to be able to see the new disk right away?

   A. Reboot the computer. Plug and Play will pick up the new disk and install appropriate drivers.

   B. In Disk Management, choose Action | Rescan Disk

   C. In Disk Management, choose Action | Import New Drive

   D. From the Control Panel, run the Add New Hardware Wizard.

9. You are the administrator of a network of Windows 2000 computers. You have a \Public storage folder shared out on an NTFS volume of a Windows 2000 Professional computer. You want to configure quota management on that folder so that the Sales group does not take up too much of the space. How should you configure quota management?

A. Set a quota limit for the Sales group on the NTFS volume.

B. Set quota limits for the \Public share for individual accounts of the Sales group.

C. Set quota limits for the Sales group on the \Public folder.

D. Set quota limits for the individual members of the Sales group on the NTFS volume.

10. Which of the following are true about Windows 2000 Professional dynamic disks?

A. Dynamic disks are supported only by Windows 2000.

B. You can add a dynamic disk to a NT4 computer.

C. Dynamic disks support division of disk space into partitions.

D. Dynamic disks support division of disk space into volumes.

REVIEW ANSWERS

1. **B** **C**   Free space from another disk can be added to a simple volume by extending the simple volume into a spanned volume. A spanned volume is composed of regions of free space on 2 to 32 dynamic disks. **A** is incorrect because none of the volume options are available on basic disks. Partitioning is the only method of dividing space on a basic disk, and a basic disk does not allow for extending the partition without third-party tools. **D** is not correct because a striped volume and a spanned volume are mutually exclusive. You will begin the process of creating spanned and striped volumes in the same way, but you will not be able to choose both when you select an area of unallocated space and run the Create Volume Wizard. Further, you will not be able to extend the striped volume once it is in place.

2. **B**   Quotas can be configured only on NTFS volumes. All of the other answers are true statements that apply to quotas, but none apply to this scenario.

3. **D**   You can't convert NTFS to FAT, and deleting the partition and reformatting with any file system would most certainly harm the data. The only way to accomplish this task is to restore from backup. **A** is incorrect because this is not an option of the convert command. **B** is incorrect for the same reason. **C** is incorrect because reformatting would blow away the data, not leave it unharmed.

4. **B** **D** Windows 2000 Professional does not support fault tolerant volumes. **B** is correct because a mirrored volume provides fault tolerance by making duplicate copies of data across two physical disks. **D** is also correct because RAID 5 provides fault tolerance by storing parity information, which can be used to regenerate data on a failed disk, across 3 to 32 drives in an array. Answers **A** and **C** are incorrect because neither striped nor spanned volumes provide fault tolerance for date. This is because only one copy of data is kept on the drives. Normal backup is the only way to guard data from disaster using these volume configurations.

5. **A** **B** Upgrading to dynamic disks is not supported on laptops or on disks with less than 1MB of free space. **C** and **D** are incorrect because it is possible, however, to upgrade any disks that are part of a striped set or volume set.

6. **A** **B** **E** Windows 2000 Professional can be installed on hard drives that have been formatted in any of the above file systems. **C** is incorrect because while Windows 2000 can read *from* CDFS media (CD-ROMs), you can't perform the installation on CDFS media. **D** is incorrect because HPFS is no longer supported by Windows 2000.

7. **D** Only NTFS drives support compression. This is the sort of head-fake that is likely on exams. Answer **A** sounds good, for example, but the command doesn't exist on XCOPY. None of the other possibilities exist, either. You can choose Paste Special from Microsoft Word, but not in file copy operations.

8. **B** All that is necessary if the computer supports hot-swapping is for you to select Action | Rescan Disk from the Disk Manager Utility. **A** is incorrect because a reboot, while it should work, is not the most efficient solution. **C** won't work because it's not a menu option. **D** is also unnecessary because answer **B** is all that is needed.

9. **D** Here you need to remember that quota limits are set for individual users and on entire volumes only. There is no way to set limits for groups of users, because quotas are based on ownership, and things are owned by individuals, not groups (with the exception of the Administrators group). Nor is there a way to set quota limits on folders; it's the whole volume or nothing. Therefore only choice **D** will let you accomplish your goal.

10. **A** **D** These statements are true. **B** is false because NT4 does not support dynamic disks, and **C** is false because partitioning is only supported on basic disks, not dynamic disks.

Configuring and Customizing the End User Experience

CHAPTER 4

	NEWBIE	SOME EXPERIENCE	EXPERT
ETA	3 hours	2 hours	1 hour

This chapter looks at the technologies that Windows 2000 provides to give both end users and administrators control over the operating system interface. These technologies allow a user to configure the desktop colors and mouse settings, and they extend to management capabilities such as deploying software to all users from a remote computer. We like to do things our own way. We also like to feel a sense of mastery over our machines; we like to get the computer system to do what we want, and we like it to look the way we want it to. User profiles are designed with this in mind. They are used to distinguish between different computing environments and are intended to personalize the Windows 2000 experience for each individual.

User profiles are great for configuring the overall look of the Windows 2000 Professional operating system, but there are many tools that will help make more meaningful changes to the user environment—like the Control Panel. The Control Panel allows users to configure a variety of settings that help define inter-action with the OS. Administrators can also lock down the user desktop through the employment of Group Policies. Group Policies are a powerful new tool set in Windows 2000 that works in many different ways to ease the burden of adminis-tration, thus reducing overall total cost of ownership for an operating system. One of the ways Group Policies can accomplish this, as we'll see later in the chapter, is to revoke from the user the ability to make certain changes.

This chapter will conclude with a discussion of fax support, and Accessibility Services. Accessibility Services are another important part of customizing the experience for users with special needs.

Configure and Manage User Profiles

Objective 4.01

Every user who has used Windows 2000 has worked with a user profile. That's because a user couldn't even get to the desktop without a profile. In other words, Windows 2000 will never present the desktop to a user without using a user profile, because part of a profile's job is to define how that desktop will look. User profiles make it possible to personalize the desktop environment based on the user's account name. In fact, profiles are so ingrained in the Windows experience that each and every time a new user account successfully logs on, a profile is created for that user account if one hasn't been configured by the administrator already.

What Is a Profile?

So what all is included in a user profile? A profile includes settings that are vital to the end user experience, such as the color and resolution of the desktop, any network connections or printers that have been mapped, and the location of the My Documents folder, to name a few. In brief, pretty much everything that will be a part of the user's interaction with the OS and any applications that are designed to work with user profiles will be found in a user's profile. Profiles can be assigned to a single user or to an entire group of users. If a profile is assigned to an entire group of users, each of the users in the group will receive a consistent desktop every time he or she logs on.

Two types of profiles are available: *local and roaming*. By default, user profiles are local, meaning that they are stored and accessed locally at the computer the user logs on from. However, users access their roaming profiles on a network server, which means that they will receive the same desktop environment from any computer on the network.

Also by default, users can make changes to their profiles. For example, they can change the screen saver and appearance of the icons as they please. An administrator can decide to make each of the two types of profiles *mandatory*, which restricts user modifications to the desktop somewhat, as we'll see in just a minute.

Local Profiles

As mentioned, when a user first logs on to a computer, a profile is created for that user *locally*, right there on the hard disk of the machine (unless that user has been previously configured to use a roaming profile). This includes the Administrator account the first time it's used to log on to the computer. The local profile for all users is generated by making a copy of two profile folders created when Windows 2000 is installed. The two profile folders involved in this process are the All Users profile folder and the Default User profile folder. A quick glance at the contents of these two folders gives you an idea of the kinds of settings that define a profile. You can see these two profile folders under the Documents and Settings folder on the *%systemroot%* drive, as shown in Figure 4-1. As you can see in the figure, the settings of the All Users folder will define what shortcuts are found on the Start menu for all users of this computer.

Here's how it all shakes out:

1. When a user logs on for the first time, the system checks to see whether a local user profile exists, which appears as a folder with the user's account name located under Documents and Settings. This Documents and Settings folder is created on the boot partition when you install the Windows 2000 Professional operating system.

2. If a folder for that user is not present at logon time, a profile folder that matches the account name is automatically created by copying the contents of the Default User folder to a new folder that will bear the name of the user account who is logging on.

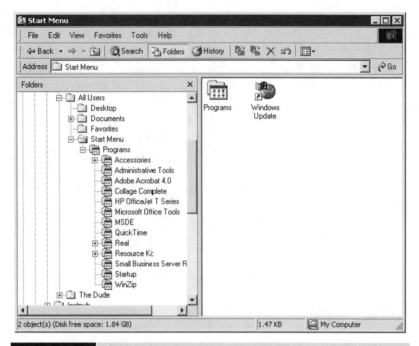

FIGURE 4-1   The settings of the All Users profile folder

3. The user's profile and the All Users profile from this point on remain in distinct folders, but their contents are merged when a user's desktop environment is generated. For example, after I created a user called The Dude, a folder is created for that user when he logs on, as shown in Figure 4-2.

You can even manage the contents of desktops for new users by adding and deleting from the contents of the All Users folder and the Default Users folder, although I recommend messing around only with the Default User folder, whose contents affect only those users who have no user profile created.

Travel Advisory

Be careful about what you change in the All Users folder, because changes made here will affect all users of the computer. This includes you, the administrator.

Windows 2000 keeps track of all the profiles that have been created on the local machine in the System Properties dialog box. To launch this Control Panel

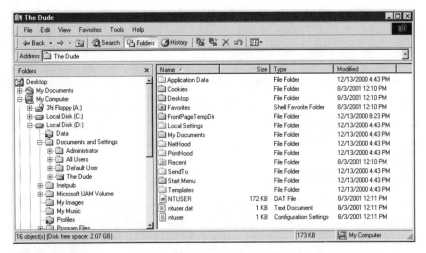

FIGURE 4-2 The Dude's user profile folder is created when logging on the first time

program, you can right-click My Computer and choose Properties. The list of profiles contained on a particular system is kept on the User Profiles tab, and if you want to configure roaming profiles that's where you go. Figure 4-3 displays the profiles that exist on my system.

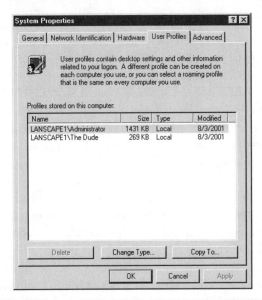

FIGURE 4-3 The User Profiles tab

The drawback of the local user profile is that it is available only at the computer where the profile was created. This becomes unwieldy in an environment where users are constantly moving among computers, because a new profile gets created for the user at every computer he or she uses. In this scenario, a user would have a hard time maintaining a consistent desktop environment and may spend otherwise productive time rearranging the look and feel of each desktop. To avoid this situation, and for users to maintain a consistent desktop environment, you should use a roaming profile.

Roaming Profiles

You can copy any of the local user profiles to a network server so that other users in the network can also enjoy the profile you have set up for them. This feature is called a *roaming profile*. Roaming profiles allow a user to move from one computer to another in a network and get the same desktop no matter what computer they are logging on to the network from. When a user is using a roaming profile, the contents of the profile are retrieved from a network share at logon time and downloaded to the local computer to create the user's desktop.

> **Travel Advisory**
>
> When you are setting up the share to store user profiles, be sure that users have the ability to read and write to this share; if they can't read from the share they can't get their profile, and if they make changes to their desktop they can't be saved without having the write permission.

You can create a roaming profile in a couple of ways. If you want to enable a user's desktop to be consistent from anywhere on the network, you can specify that the account use a network share to store its profile. The procedure for this will be discussed in a minute. If, on the other hand, you want to use roaming profiles as a management device so that many users will receive the same environment, you can copy an existing local profile to a network share and then point all your users to that share with the properties of their account (you will also usually make this profile mandatory).

It's usually wise to create a user profile that will be used as a template for the roaming profile. After you have the desktop settings as you want, you use the System applet in Control Panel to copy the profile to the network location.

1. In the User Profiles tab of the System Properties window, select the profile you wish to make available as a Roaming Profile and click the Copy To button.
2. In the Copy To dialog that opens, click the Browse button.
3. Select a shared directory where you want to place the profile, as shown in Figure 4-4. Click OK.

Travel Advisory

Always use the System applet to do the copying of the user profile. You cannot just drag and drop profile folders from Windows Explorer. (Well, you *can*, but the profiles won't work. Part of the profile settings are registry-specific, and the System program provides a graphical interface to the registry, whereas Windows Explorer does not. See "The Registry" later in this chapter.)

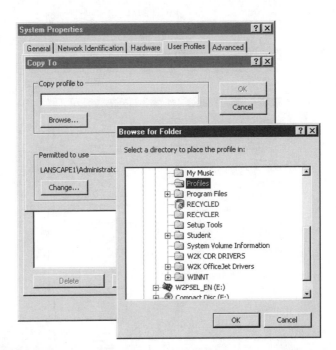

FIGURE 4-4   Copying a profile

After the profile you want to use has been copied to the network share, it is ready for use as a roaming profile. A user needs to be pointed to that profile folder at logon time.

To configure this second part of the Roaming profile process, you'll work from the Properties page of a user account.

1. On a Windows 2000 Professional computer in a workgroup, open Computer Management by right-clicking My Computer and choosing Manage.
2. Access the Properties dialog box for the user account by double-clicking the user account in the Users folder of the Users and Groups node.
3. From the Profile tab (shown in Figure 4-5), enter the share location in the Profile Path text box using the UNC path to that location.

Travel Advisory

You will almost never configure a roaming profile for a user in a workgroup environment. If you have to create multiple accounts for users to access multiple computers anyway, what's the point of using the roaming profile? Why store your profile on a different computer when you'll be using a completely different account? There isn't really a good reason. It is too much administrative overhead for little to no benefit.

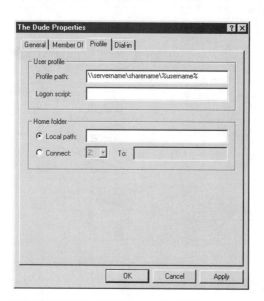

FIGURE 4-5   Specifying a profile path

You should view the discussion of roaming profiles in workgroup environments as one for illustrative purposes only. In a Windows 2000 Active Directory Domain environment, the tool to configure user accounts is called Active Directory Users and Computers. The rest of the discussion assumes that the roaming profile has been configured in a domain.

Also, it is good practice to use the *%username%* variable when configuring roaming profiles for individual accounts. The *%username%* variable takes the user's account name and creates a private folder for that user's profile using that name. For example, you can create a share called \profiles on a server called \\server1. The Profile Path box would be filled in with \\server1\profiles\%*username*%. The folder for that user will be created as a subfolder of the \profiles folder, and only the user would have the Full Control permission to the folder.

Now the magic happens. When that user logs on to the domain from any computer using the domain account, the user's profile will be accessed from the server holding the profile, and a local copy of the roaming user profile is copied to the user's computer. Any changes that are made to the desktop environment during the session are saved back to the server when the user logs off. The next time the user logs on, the desktop settings will appear just as they were at the user's last session.

Mandatory Profiles

If the user has been set up to use a *mandatory* profile, the changes made during the last session will *not* be saved as the user logs off. Mandatory profiles are an ideal solution when many users share the same profile, such as might be found in a computer kiosk or in a highly secure environment where you do not want users making changes to the desktop.

Saving changes made to desktop settings at logoff time, or not saving them (there's a Hamlet reference here somewhere) is the difference between a normal user profile—either local or roaming—and a mandatory profile. Users of a mandatory profile will still be able to manipulate desktops to their heart's content during their session, but the changes that are made during that session are not saved to the network version of the profile. As a result, the next time the user logs on, the original desktop will appear.

But we still haven't discussed how to make a profile mandatory. You can make a profile of either type mandatory in one of two ways: by renaming the NTUSER.DAT file NTUSER.MAN, or by renaming the profile folder by adding a *.man* extension to it. For example, you can configure a mandatory profile for a user named The Dude by renaming the \The Dude folder to \The Dude.man, or by looking in the \The Dude folder for the NTUSER.DAT file and renaming it to NTUSER.MAN. It's up to you.

If you haven't modified the default settings for the display of hidden files, you won't see the NTUSER.DAT file in Windows Explorer. Well, that's not really accurate. You will see the file; it just won't have the .DAT extension that you are looking for. It can be rather confusing, so it will be discussed in the next paragraph. You must enable the display of hidden files before you can find NTUSER.DAT. To do this, open the Folder Options dialog box, which is accessed by choosing Tools | Folder Options from Windows Explorer (or by selecting the Folder Options icon in Control Panel).

You still aren't done. When you first look in a folder where you want to set a mandatory profile, the NTUSER.DAT file that you see is not what it seems. It is really a text file called NTUSER.DAT.LOG, and renaming it will do nothing toward configuring a mandatory profile. To see all the file extensions correctly, you might want to uncheck the Hide File Extensions For Known File Types box in Folder Options. You'll then see the NTUSER.DAT file that you will rename to make your user profile mandatory.

If you mistakenly rename the .LOG file, you'll end up creating a new file called NTUSER.MAN.TXT. Windows will then create a new NTUSER.DAT.LOG file next time the user logs on, resulting in multiple NTUSER files in the same folder.

If, on the other hand, you append the profile folder with a .man extension as your method of configuring mandatory profiles, be cautioned that if the server holding the profile is not available, the user will not be able to log on. Conversely, if you rename the NTUSER.DAT file and the profile server is unavailable, the user will log on using a locally cached version of the profile.

Configure Support for Multiple Locations

As the focus of this chapter has to do with the end user experience, you will notice that a great deal of time is focused on the appearance of the desktop. That's because, to a great extent, the desktop *defines* the end user experience; it is the user's portal to accessing their system, and the less time users have to worry about the desktop, the more productive they can be.

We typically don't give the language settings much thought on a day-to-day basis, but the language that the desktop uses is one of the key factors in defining the end user experience. Believe me, you would give it a lot of thought if you came in and your desktop was in Greek one day (unless you were Greek). So, to allow the Windows 2000 Professional OS to be understood by almost anyone on the globe, it has the capability to use and understand almost any language on the planet. It actually comes in three different multilingual versions: the English version, the Translated version, and the MultiLanguage version. Each version offers varying degrees of language support:

- The English version allows a user to view, edit, and print information in more than 60 languages.
- The Translated version provides the same support as the English version, and it also includes a language-specific interface for menus, help files, dialog boxes, and file system components.
- The MultiLanguage version provides the same support as the Translated version, and it allows the (presumably bilingual) user to switch the user interface language.

While it will take you years of study to learn new languages, it takes a Windows 2000 computer a matter of seconds. You will perform your configuration of multiple languages in the Regional Options program accessed from the Control Panel. In the Regional Options window, click the appropriate check box in front of each language that you need your computer to support, as shown in Figure 4-6. You can configure several settings from this dialog box. On the General tab, you can configure the current locale setting. The Input Locale tab will allow you to add more locales to your system, and even modify input locales to change

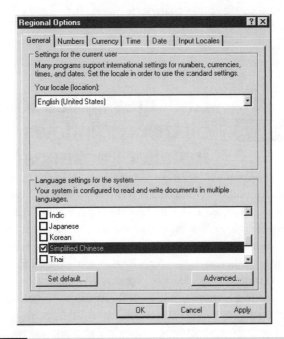

FIGURE 4-6   Setting the Regional Options

keyboard layouts. And you can set system language settings that will support viewing and editing documents in other languages. Any check box enabled here will require the corresponding language groups to be installed from the Windows 2000 Professional Setup CD.

Which version you choose will, of course, be dependent on the multilingual needs of your organization. The MultiLanguage version, for example, is ideal when full multilingual support is necessary to ensure the smooth execution of the business model.

Finally, when you have the MultiLanguage version of Windows 2000 Professional installed, you will see a Menus and Dialogs drop-down list on the General tab in the Regional Options dialog box. You can select any installed language from this drop-down list. This new language can apply to a particular user logging on or to all users accessing that computer.

Travel Advisory

Selecting a different language in the Menus and Dialogs drop-down list affects only menu items, help files, and such that are bundled with the operating system. The language for files not bundled with the operating system, including some of the desktop icons, will not be affected by the change in language.

Objective 4.03 Manage Applications by Using Windows Installer Packages

The proper use of the Windows Installer can help you take great strides in lowering the much talked about Total Cost of Ownership (TCO) of your network. Its purpose is to reduce the cost of software deployment by reducing the number of visits made to desk side. An understanding of the Windows Installer calls into play several areas of Windows 2000 expertise, and most of these areas deal with new technologies. This means that you are likely to be peppered with questions about this feature on the both the Windows 2000 Professional and Server exams. It's a good idea to become familiar with this service, even if there are other ways of getting software to your clients in a real-world network.

The Windows Installer is an operating service that helps manage or repair software installations. The Windows Installer can be set to manage the features and components of an application that is to be deployed—for example, you can configure some components not to install or to run right from the CD-ROM if needed without being installed with the rest of the application, conserving hard disk space.

However, two limitations govern the use of the Windows Installer: First, for applications to take advantage of the service, the installation routine must be packaged in an .msi file. The second is that it relies on the application of Group Policies, which are available only to Windows 2000 computers.

Local Lingo

.msi file   A Microsoft Installer file. This setup file is created by software vendors like Microsoft as an alternative to the setup routine that has been used for years to install application packages, the setup.exe file. The .msi file used by the Windows Installer Service is a little database that defines all of the installation options available. One of the first places it showed up was in the Office 2000 suite of applications, which were installed using an .msi file. If you have ever done a custom setup of Office 2000, you have been exposed to the installation options that are available through an .msi file.

The Windows Installer becomes a more powerful operating system feature when combined with Windows 2000 Servers running Active Directory. Active Directory is the database of users and computers that resides on the Windows 2000 Servers that are domain controllers.

The first step in the Windows Installer process is copying the .msi file to a network share. Then you have to create a Group Policy Object that will be used to facilitate the package's installation. This is where the Windows 2000 domain controller usually comes in. Finally, you need to add the package to the Group Policy object and filter that object to apply to the domain users or computers that you target for application distribution. Sound easy? It is, after you have done it a few times. There is really no shortcut that will get you familiar with the Group Policy objects other than practice, though. You will have to get your hands dirty with this one. We will be fleshing out the concepts and technologies of Group Policies throughout this book, and indeed throughout the entire MCSE track. Only a limited knowledge of Group Policies is needed at this time.

> **Local Lingo**
>
> **Feature**   A feature is part of an application, like the conversion features of Word. Installation of an application includes everything needed for proper operation, such as the addition of Registry entries, the configuration of shortcuts, addition of program groups, and installation of necessary EXE and DLL files. The instructions in the .msi file tell the installation routine which of these files to install.

Installation Options: Publishing vs. Assigning

Windows Installer packages can be installed on target computers via one of two mechanisms: as published applications or as assigned applications.

Publishing Applications

When you publish an application, users will be able to choose whether or not they will install the application. A published application will appear in the Add/Remove Programs applet in the Control Panel and will typically be installed from there—simply a matter of choosing the application and clicking Add. A rule of publishing packages is that packages cannot be published to computers, only to users.

Assigning Applications

When an application is assigned to users or computers, the package is automatically installed. This is accomplished when the user launches the program through the Start menu, or when the user opens a file that was created in that application. For example, opening a .doc file would cause the installation of Word. When an application is assigned to a computer, it is installed the next time *any* user logs on, before the desktop is presented.

> **Local Lingo**
>
> **Document invocation**   The process of installing an application at the time that an application file is accessed.

Objective 4.04

Configure and Troubleshoot Desktop Settings

In Windows 2000 Professional, the desktop is presented after a user has success-fully entered a user name and password. It is generated by using the contents of a user profile. After the desktop has been presented, the user will be offered many options for configuring the desktop to suit individual preferences. Configuring desktop settings allows a user to customize most user interface elements such as the Start menu, taskbar, toolbars, and the desktop background; these settings can be saved for the next time a user accesses the computer in a profile, as discussed previously in this chapter.

Two common methods exist for configuring the desktop settings: through the various user interface components supporting the desktop or through Group Policy. These two methods accomplish the same things, but they differ in their approach to desktop administration. Generally speaking, the user interface components let end users manage their desktops, while Group Policies are applied so that administrators can do the desktop management. We will start with a discussion of these user interface components first, and then we'll turn the discussion to Group Policy.

Exam Tip

Group Policy is a new feature of Windows 2000 that's available in Active Directory domains. This technology serves as a cornerstone to managing Windows 2000 domains. You can expect to see this topic covered in great detail throughout your study of Windows 2000. Even though you won't be expected to know a whole lot about Group Policy for *this* exam, the sooner you have an understanding of Group Policy, the sooner you will understand Windows 2000.

Customizing the Taskbar and Start Menu

The taskbar and Start menu are important launching points for modifying system settings and running applications, and modifying the contents of these areas has a great impact on overall user friendliness. The easiest way to customize the taskbar and Start menu is by right-clicking any blank area of the taskbar and choosing Properties from the context menu. The Taskbar And Start Menu Properties dialog box has two tabs: General and Advanced.

On the General tab of the Taskbar And Start Menu Properties dialog box, you will be able to specify whether or not the taskbar is always visible, and whether or not to use personalized menus, the scourge of Office 2000 users everywhere. (In informal surveys, it has run a close second to Clip-It as things least liked with the program.) Table 4-1 describes the options configurable from the General tab.

TABLE 4.1	General Tab Options
When you select...	**It does this...**
Always On Top	Specifies that the taskbar is always visible; enabled by default.
Auto Hide	Hides the taskbar when working in programs unless your mouse travels to the bottom of the screen; disabled by default.
Show Small Icons In Start Menu	Reduces the size of the Start menu icons; useful if you have created many shortcuts on the Start menu and if you don't need bifocals.
Show Clock	Displays the clock in the right corner of the taskbar (unless you've moved the taskbar somewhere else). This area is known as the System Tray; you can adjust the date and time by double-clicking the clock; enabled by default.
Use Personalized Menus	Hides applications that have not been used recently. You can display menu options that have been hidden by clicking the chevron (double-arrow) at the bottom of a menu; enabled by default.

The Advanced tab of the Taskbar And Start Menu Properties dialog box allows you to customize your Start menu further. It lets you add or remove shortcuts from the Start menu, re-sort the menu's contents, as well as select from other menu settings. From here, for example, you can enable the display of the Administrative Tools group from the Start menu, something that most administrators like to have enabled. Figure 4-7 shows the Advanced tab of this dialog box, where you can set many of the Start menu options.

You've probably played around with some of these features by now on either Windows 9x or NT-based computers, and while a few different bells and whistles can be configured here, this isn't considered meat and potatoes Windows 2000 administration. You will become comfortable with the options to manage the desktop environment mostly by trying out a few of the features. It's all part of taking the operating system out for a test drive.

The Control Panel

Another utility used to configure a wide range of computer options is the Control Panel (shown in Figure 4-8). You can access the Control Panel in three ways: by selecting Start | Settings | Control Panel, by opening Windows Explorer and

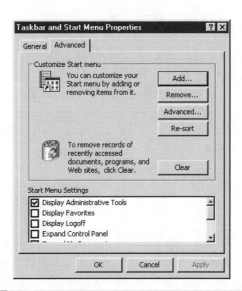

FIGURE 4-7   Configuring the Start menu

FIGURE 4-8 The Control Panel window

choosing Control Panel from the left side of the window, or by opening My Computer and double-clicking the Control Panel icon.

Table 4-2 describes all the Control Panel icons and what configuration settings they manage. It will serve as a valuable reference as you are working with Windows 2000 Professional. Most of these programs will be discussed in detail throughout this book.

TABLE 4.2 Control Panel Icons

When you select...	You can do this...
Accessibility Options	Configure options to make Windows 2000 more accessible to users with limited vision, hearing, or mobility.

(Continued)

TABLE 4.2	*CONTINUED*
When you select...	**You can do this...**
Add/Remove Hardware	Install, remove, or troubleshoot hardware, especially hardware that is not plug and play compliant.
Add/Remove Programs	Change or remove programs that are curently installed on your computer; accessed when adding Windows 2000 components.
Administrative Tools	Access the preconfigured MMC snap-ins that are most useful for managing day-to-day administrative operations—Event Viewer, Performance, Local Security Policy, and Computer Management.
Date/Time	Set the time and date, as well as the time zone for your computer; handy when you're traveling.
Display	Configure the computer's background, screen resolution, color scheme, and multiple monitor support with appropriate hardware.
Folder Options	Set folder options such as the look of folder contents, general folder properties, file associations, and support for offline files.
Fonts	Manage the fonts installed on your computer.
Game Controllers	Add, remove, and configure game controllers, including joysticks and game pads.
Internet Options	Set Internet connection settings, including security, content settings, and Internet programs.
Keyboard	Configure keyboard settings, including speed and input locales. Configure mouse settings, including button configuration, pointer appearance, and motion settings.

(Continued)

TABLE 4.2 *CONTINUED*	
When you select...	**You can do this...**
Network and Dial-up Connections	Set network connectivity, including which protocols to use, and includes a Wizard to create new network connections. Administrators will be use this dialog box often.
Phone and Modem Options	Set telephone dialing options, such as what area code you are dialing from, which modem to use, and the properties of that modem.
Power Options	Configure power schemes, enable hibernation, and set UPS options.
Regional Options	Set regional settings like what currency is used in money calculations, and set input locales.
Scanners and Cameras	Add a scanner or digital camera device to the computer, and configure and troubleshoot its operation.
Scheduled Tasks	Configure tasks to be run according to customized schedules.
Sounds and Multimedia	Set up audio options such as what sounds occur at specified events; set the output and input devices.
System	Change a computer's identity, configure virtual memory settings, and manage user profiles.
Users and Passwords	Create and manage users and passwords. Can also use Local Users and Groups, found in Computer Management. This icon will not be found on Windows 2000 Server computers.

Several Control Panel programs can be accessed from places other than the desktop. Most of these access methods will be mentioned when the applicable settings are discussed in this book, and some of them have already been addressed, but I'll give you a couple of for examples here:

- To access the Internet options, right-click the Internet Explorer icon and choose Properties.
- To access the Date/Time options, double-click the clock in the System Tray.
- To access the System options, right-click My Computer and choose Properties.
- To access the Network and Dial-up Connections options, right-click My Network Places and choose Properties.

You also need to be aware that the job of the Control Panel is to provide a safe and user-friendly way to edit the *Registry.*

The Registry

The Registry is a database of settings the operating system uses as a central repository of configuration information. The Registry information is the DNA of the system; it tells the computer how to look and act. For example, when you change the color scheme on your Windows 2000 Professional system to Rainy Day, the changes to the window bars, screen, and other interface elements, are recorded in the Registry.

You can edit the Registry directly with the Registry Editor, which can be launched using either of two commands: `regedit.exe` or `regedt32.exe`. These are actually two versions of the Registry Editor. Regedit.exe is the Windows 9*x* version, and it includes better search capabilities than its cousin and is visually arranged like Windows Explorer, which makes it easy to navigate. Regedt32.exe lacks some of the search features of regedit.exe, but it has better security. For example, you can use the regedt32.exe tool in read-only mode, ensuring that damage is not accidentally done to the Registry. The Windows NT Registry Editor, regedt32.exe, is shown in Figure 4-9.

The Registry is organized into a hierarchical tree format of keys and subkeys that represent logical areas of computer configuration. By default, you will see five keys when you open the Registry Editor. Each will be opened in its own window with the regedt32 tool, as shown in Figure 4-9. The registry keys and their configuration information are listed in Table 4-3.

If you have to edit the Registry, you will usually be working with HKEY_ LOCAL_MACHINE, which contains all the settings that tell hardware and services how to behave. For example, a Registry setting here tells the network card what Internet Protocol (IP) address to use at startup time and what services are bound to it.

Many of the keys and entries in the Registry are cryptic. The first couple of times you have to edit the Registry, you will likely be performing the changes from

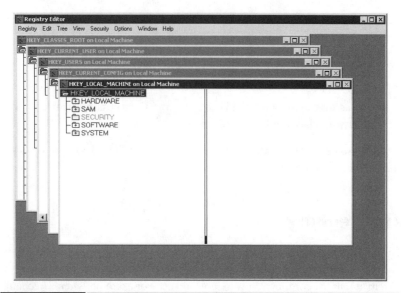

FIGURE 4-9 The regedt32 utility

TABLE 4.3	The Registry Configuration Keys
Registry Key	**Configuration Information**
HKEY_CLASSES_ROOT	Information associated with Windows Explorer to properly associate file types with applications. For example, this area of the Registry will store a setting that tells the system .doc files are to be opened with Microsoft Word.
HKEY_CURRENT_USER	Information about the user currently logged on to the computer.
HKEY_LOCAL_MACHINE	Hardware and software configuration information: how hardware is used, startup parameters, bindings, drivers used, and so on.
HKEY_USERS	Configuration information that is not specific to any one user of the machine.
HKEY_CURRENT_CONFIG	Hardware profile information that is used during system startup.

some kind of reference material. It is not necessary to have a mastery of the Registry to pass the Windows 2000 Professional exam.

You should know that making the wrong change to the Registry can have disastrous results, such as rendering the computer inoperable. It is recommended that you make backups of your Registry before making changes. This can be done from either Registry Editor utility. In the Registry menu of either tool, choose either the Save Key option from the regedt32 editor, or the Export Registry File option from regedit.

> **Travel Advisory**
>
> Treat editing the Registry like brain surgery on your computer. It is meant for configuration changes that can't be made through the Control Panel. You won't need to make many of these changes in day-to-day administration.

Group Policies

Up to now, we've been dealing with the configuration settings that are applied by an individual user at his or her computer, or changes made by an administrator of that machine for all users. But what if the administrator wants to take more control of the user environment, dictating the look and feel of the desktop experience? What if, for example, the administrator of a computer or even a network wants to remove access to the Control Panel altogether for ordinary users? Group Policy is the answer.

Group Policies are a powerful new technology built into Windows 2000 that lets an administrator manage the Windows 2000 computing experience. It is the lever with which Information Technology department policies and rules will be translated into overall computing practice.

The topic of Group Policies is a large one, as I hinted at earlier in this chapter, and you will be spending a great amount of time getting familiar with Group Policies as you continue to study Windows 2000. In fact, the Active Directory core exam that you will likely be ramping up for soon covers little else besides Group Policy. Fortunately, Microsoft has recognized the expanse of this topic and you will see only a small portion of Group Policy covered here and in the Windows 2000 Professional exam. To try and cover all the Group Policy material for this exam would be like trying to take a sip of water from a fire hose.

You should recognize for now that Group Policy Objects (GPOs) can be applied to many objects in a Windows 2000 computing enterprise. They can be applied to *local* machines, to *domains*, to *sites*, and to *organizational units* (OUs). Three of these objects, however, are specific to Windows 2000 Active Directory domains, and are not applicable in the discussion of the 70-210 test, which assumes that you are installing Windows 2000 Professional in a Workgroup environment. In this case, only the Local Group Policy settings apply to the user environment.

Local Policies

When you start up Windows 2000 Professional, you may have noticed the dialog box telling you that Windows 2000 was "Applying Security Settings" as you were waiting for the logon dialog box to be displayed. Why do you see this message and just what is being applied?

The desktop settings of a computer not on a Windows 2000 domain running Active Directory are enforced with a default Local Security Policy that is created at installation time. In this way, the Local Security Policy behaves like a user profile: you are getting one before you are presented the desktop. The user profile specifies what the desktop will *look* like, and the Local Security Policy specifies what you can *do* on that desktop. These default Local Security Policy settings can be viewed and managed using the Local Computer Policy node of the Group Policy snap-in, as shown in Figure 4-10.

You can begin working with the Local Security Policy of a system in two ways: You can add the Group Policy snap-in to a custom MMC, and you can launch the Local Security Settings preconfigured snap-in.

Using the MMC option when adding the Group Policy snap-in, make sure that the Group Policy will apply to the Local Machine. The Local Security Settings preconfigured snap-in is found in under the Administrative Tools folder in the Contol Panel. Note that the Local Security Settings tool is actually a subset of the

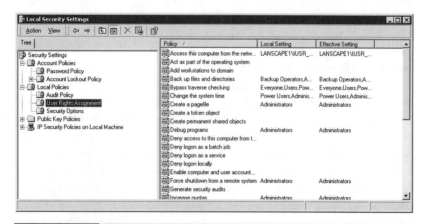

FIGURE 4-10   The Local Security settings

Group Policy settings. The security settings can be found in the Group Policy snap-in by expanding Local Computer Policy, Computer Configuration, and then Windows Settings, which will then show you the Security Settings node.

With the Local Security Settings, you can configure the user rights on a given computer, such as who can shut down the system or who can increase quotas. You can also set passwords and account policies from their respective nodes. For example, you can specify that passwords for users on this machine must be at least six characters in length. To configure a policy, just double-click a setting to open its Properties dialog box, as shown in Figure 4-11.

You can further configure almost all aspects of the user environment through the settings of the Local GPO. To do this, make sure that the interface you are using is the Group Policy snap-in, which gives you a huge range of management options, including the administrative templates, which are used mostly to manage the desktop environment. They contain many of the settings that we associate with a user profile. The Local Security Settings are specific to, well, security options.

Let's return to our earlier scenario where an administrator might not want users to access the Control Panel. This can be enabled in Group Policy (and this can be a bit hard to follow) by *enabling* the policy that *disables* the display of the Control Panel. This setting can be found under the User Configuration node of Group Policy by expanding Administrative Templates and then clicking on the Control Panel node, as shown in Figure 4-12. The setting can then be enabled by double-clicking the policy option and choosing to enable the policy.

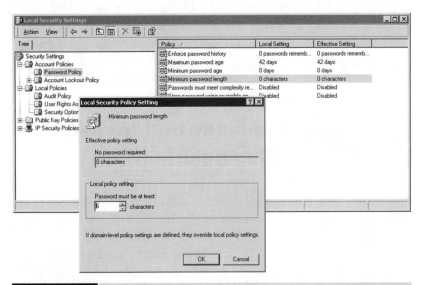

FIGURE 4-11 Configuring a policy

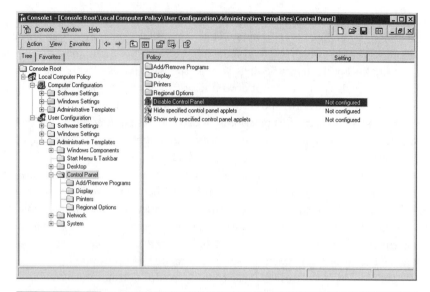

 **FIGURE 4-12** Turning off the Control Panel with Group Policy

Exam Tip

These are just a few examples of the settings possible with Group Policy. You won't be expected to memorize any part of the Group Policy snap-in; just know what it is used for. We will be returning to the Group Policy editor from time to time throughout this book to configure different management tasks where appropriate.

Objective 4.05 # Configure and Troubleshoot Fax Support

Windows 2000 Professional includes the software needed to send and receive faxes through a fax-capable modem. If Windows 2000 detects the presence of a fax device, it installs the Fax Service and the Windows NT fax driver. The Fax Service will then appear in the Services window, and the Windows NT fax driver will appear in the Printers folder as a printer named Fax. After the Fax Service has been installed, you need to start it through the Services node of Computer

Management, which is launched by right-clicking My Computer and choosing Manage. Click Services and Applications and then click Services. Then find the Fax Service and start it, as shown in Figure 4-13.

After your fax device has been set up and configured, documents to be faxed from an application are treated in the same way that they are printed, except the destination printer for faxed documents becomes Fax.

Faxes can also be received through the fax device. The Windows 2000 Fax Monitor listens for incoming faxes and receives the fax as a TIF graphical image. When the image file is received, it can be saved to a folder, sent via e-mail, or sent along to a print device. Any of these three options are available, but routing the TIF file to the Received Faxes folder is the default setting.

Local Lingo

TIF (or TIFF) An acronym for *tagged image file format,* one of the most widely supported file formats for storing bit-mapped images on personal computers. TIF graphics can be any resolution, and they can be black and white, gray-scaled, or color. Files in TIF format often end with a *.tif* extension.

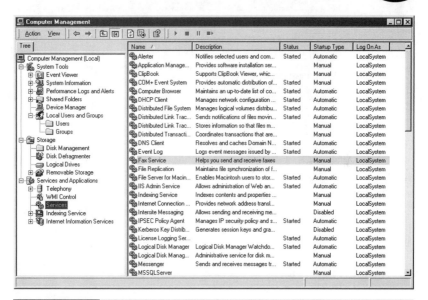

FIGURE 4-13 Starting the Fax Service

The image files can either be read by the Imaging for Windows Preview utility or by any installed application capable of viewing TIF files.

Travel Advisory

To route faxes to a network printer or to an e-mail profile, the Fax Service must be configured with a logon account with the necessary rights to read the users e-mail profile, to access a network printer, or both. You need to be aware of this when considering the default behavior: the Fax Service is configured to use the Local System account, which does not support network printing or local e-mail profile access.

You can further manage and customize fax support from two places: from the Fax applet in the Control Panel and from icons in the Fax program group by choosing Start | Programs | Accessories | Communications. For example, extensive user information can be added to outgoing faxes by double-clicking the Fax icon on the Control Panel to open the Fax Properties window shown in Figure 4-14.

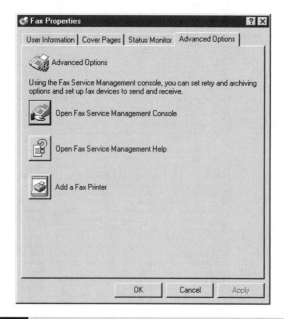

FIGURE 4-14 Fax Properties window

The Fax Properties window contains four tabs:

- **User Information**   Lets you fill in information you want to appear on the cover page.
- **Cover Pages**   Let you set additional cover page options, like specifying a preconfigured page.
- **Status Monitor**   Configures the behavior when faxes are sent or received.
- **Advanced Options**   Contains options for managing the Fax Service, looking up fax help, and adding fax printers.

So far, we've been working with the Fax Service properties in general. For more specific options, click the Open Fax Service Management Console button to further configure the individual fax devices attached to your computer. The Fax Management MMC snap-in will appear with two nodes: Devices and Logging. When you select the Devices node, you can configure individual fax device properties by right-clicking the device and choosing Properties to open the window shown in Figure 4-15.

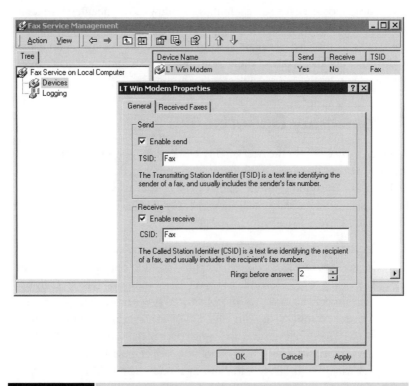

FIGURE 4-15   The individual fax device Properties window

In this window, you can configure the properties of the specific fax device, including how to handle incoming faxes, as mentioned. From the General tab you can enable the sending and/or receiving of faxes. The Received Faxes tab presents up to three options about how to handle incoming faxes, depending on how your computer is configured. These options include saving the fax to a local folder, directly outputting the fax to a print device, and e-mailing it to a mailbox. Saving to a local folder is the default choice.

Configure and Troubleshoot Accessibility Services

Objective 4.06

The keyboard is not the ideal input device for everybody. And not everyone can hear the beep and bell sounds made by Windows 2000. To accommodate preferences and alternative accessibilities, Windows 2000 includes Accessibility Services that makes it easier for people with disabilities to interact with the OS. These tools are installed by default at setup time. The Accessibility Options applet in the Control Panel is one of these tools, and you can find the others from the Start menu under the Accessibility program group.

Accessibility Options

You can use five tabs in the Accessibility Options program in Control Panel to manage many of these accessibility features: Keyboard, Sound, Display, Mouse, and General. The options on these tabs can be used to assist people with various hearing, sight, and mobility challenges. The special behavior options that can be set from these five tabs are summarized here:

- **Keyboard**   Allows you to specify the use of StickyKeys, FilterKeys, and ToggleKeys. *StickyKeys* will let a user press a multiple-key combination without having to hold down all the keys at the same time. This is especially useful for users who can't press more that one key at a time, yet need to access a keystroke command like Ctrl-Alt-Delete. *FilterKeys* ignores repeated keystrokes. *ToggleKeys* makes a noise when Caps Lock, Num Lock, or Scroll Lock keys are pressed. The Settings buttons for each of these further modify the behavior of each. Figure 4-16 shows these options from the Keyboard tab.
- **Sound**   Lets you specify whether to use the SoundSentry and ShowSounds. *SoundSentry* generates a visual warning whenever the computer makes a sound. *ShowSounds* displays captions for speech and sounds on a computer.

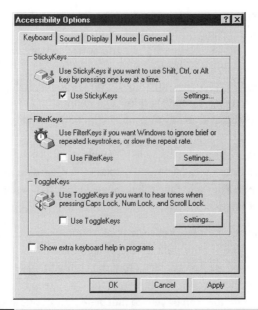

FIGURE 4-16   Configuring keyboard accessibility

- **Display**   Allows you to use the high-contrast settings that use fonts and colors designed for easy reading. Click the Settings button to set the specifics of the high-contrast setting.
- **Mouse**   Lets you use the MouseKeys option, which has the ability to control the pointer with keystrokes on the numeric keypad instead of a pointing device. The Settings button allows you to configure speed and acceleration settings.
- **General**   Used to control how the computer will react to idle time and to control how notifications are delivered when an accessibility feature is enabled or disabled. From here you can also configure whether or not the accessibility features will apply only to the logged on user or to all users of the system. You can also specify a SerialKey device, an alternative keyboard and mouse hardware used as the input device that connects to a computer's serial port.

Other Accessibility Utilities

Other important accessibility features can be configured via the Start menu. (Again, the path is Start | Programs | Accessories | Accessibility.) Three important accessibility utilities for people with limited sight, hearing, and mobility are readily available: the Magnifier, the Narrator, and the On-Screen Keyboard. Here is a summation of these three utilities.

- **The Narrator**   A text-to-speech converter that reads the text displayed on the desktop, including contents of an active window and any text you select or type. The Narrator is not guaranteed to work with all applications; however, it usually does.
- **The Magnifier**   Makes anything appearing on the desktop more readable by creating a separate window that follows the movements of the mouse to display a greatly magnified view of the desktop, a high-contrast view of the desktop, or both.
- **The On-Screen Keyboard**   Helps people who have difficulty using a keyboard to enter text strings. It displays a keyboard on the desktop to enable users with mobility impairments to type data using a pointing device or joystick.

You can manage the startup of these applications by selecting the application individually or by starting the Utility Manager application, which is found in Start | Programs | Accessories | Accessibility. From the Utility Manager application, you can select to start the Narrator, Magnifier, or the On-Screen Keyboard utility.

Each of these utilities can be started independently of one another, and independently of the Utility Manager, by clicking their corresponding icon in the Accessibility program group. However, most users with visual or mobility impairments will need greater capabilities than these three utilities can offer. The Microsoft Accessibility Web site at **http://www.microsoft.com/enable** contains a comprehensive list of hardware and software designed to assist computer users with visual, auditory, or mobility impairments.

CHECKPOINT

✔ **Objective 4.01**   **Configure and Manage User Profiles.** We discussed the purpose and process of user profile creation. We looked at the differences between a local profile and a roaming profile. We also discussed how to make user profiles mandatory.

✔ **Objective 4.02**   **Configure Support for Multiple Locations.** In this section we discussed the options available to configure Windows 2000 Professional to operate in multilingual environments.

✔ **Objective 4.03   Manage Applications by Using Windows Installer Packages.** We discussed the technologies behind automatic software distributions and its role in lowering the TCO of Windows 2000. We also looked at the different installation options available for applications distributed with Windows Installer Packages.

✔ **Objective 4.04   Configure and Troubleshoot Desktop Settings.** We focused largely in this section on the options available in the Control Panel, including an understanding of how the Control Panel is really a graphical interface to the Registry. We examined a couple of tools that can make direct edits to the Registry. Also, we started to get familiar with Group Policies and how they can be used to manage the desktop environment.

✔ **Objective 4.05   Configure and Troubleshoot Fax Support.** We looked at how to set up a fax print device in Windows 2000. We also looked at some of the considerations for directing the output of a received fax.

✔ **Objective 4.06   Configure and Troubleshoot Accessibility Services.** In the chapter's final section, we looked at the Windows 2000 Accessibility services, including situations when certain Accessibility options would be most appropriate. Finally, we investigated how many of these Accessibility services could be configured at one time by using the Accessibility Wizard.

REVIEW QUESTIONS

1. Nigel Tufnel is an administrator of a Windows 2000 network and is interested in configuring an environment in which users can log on to any computer and have their desktop settings follow them. What does he need to do?

   A. Configure all Windows 2000 Professional computers to join an Active Directory domain, and then create a profile pointing to the Active Directory.

   B. Configure all Windows 2000 Professional computers to join the domain, and then configure a roaming profile for each user.

   C. Configure all Windows 2000 Professional computers to join a workgroup, and then set their domain user accounts to point to a shared location.

   D. Nigel can't do this without third-party tools.

2. You are administering a small network and want to keep profile administration to a minimum. Each user has his or her own desk and uses the same computer every day. You also want to let users configure their desktops as they wish, figuring that happy workers make productive workers, even if you really don't want to see pictures of their parakeets every time you walk by their desks. What kind of user profile should you use?

   A. Local
   B. Mandatory
   C. Roaming
   D. Active Directory-Integrated

3. You receive a call from a user who is trying to configure the fax settings from Control Panel, and he reports that he does not have an Advanced Options tab as he does on his home system. He tells you that the driver must be corrupt. What should you do to fix this situation?

   A. Tell the user to update the driver using the Device Manager Update Device Driver Wizard.
   B. The user is using the wrong utility to do this. The fax settings are specific to the application he is faxing from.
   C. Have the user check the resource settings for any possible conflicts in Device Manager.
   D. Nothing. It is working as designed.

4. Lloyd Dobler is the administrator of a large network and is using Windows Installer to deploy a software application on computers running Windows 2000 Professional. He does not want to advertise the application on the users' desktop or on the Start menu. How should Lloyd deploy the network's software package?

   A. Assign applications to users.
   B. Assign applications to computers.
   C. Publish applications to users.
   D. Publish applications to computers.

5. You want to use Windows Installer to deploy an application to computers running Windows 2000 Professional. You want to configure the install to take place only when the users first try to use the application to cut down on network bandwidth usage during the install procedure. You would also like to configure the installer so that only authorized users can perform the install. What steps do you need to take?

    A. Assign the application to computers.

    B. Assign the application to users.

    C. Set the Deny check box on the Apply Group Policy permission for the Authenticated Users group. Create a new group containing the authorized users and grant the group Allow permission for Apply Group Policy.

    D. Clear the Allow check box on the Assign Group Policy permission for the Authenticated Users group. Create a new group containing the authorized users and grant the group Allow permission for Apply Group Policy.

6. What utility is used to configure a roaming profile for a user?

    A. User Profile Editor

    B. Control Panel | System Program | User Profiles tab

    C. Local Users and Groups

    D. User Manager

7. You are working on a computer that is a part of a Windows 2000 Professional workgroup. You log on with a user account that is a member of the local Administrators group, but you do not see the Administrative tools when you are trying to start the Event Viewer from the Start menu. What can you do to correct this situation?

    A. Log on as the Administrator account, not the user account.

    B. Right-click the Start menu, and add the Administrative tools through the General tab of the Start Menu Properties dialog box.

    C. Right-click the Start menu, and add the Administrative tools through the Advanced tab of the Start Menu Properties dialog box.

    D. Right-click the Start Menu, and add the Administrative tools through the Management tab of the Start Menu Properties dialog box.

8. One of your company's offices is located in China, and letters need to be viewed and edited as a part of regular correspondence to manufacturers there. You have the bilingual staff needed to accomplish this, and the computers they are using currently are Windows 2000 Professional localized English versions. How will you configure their Windows 2000 Professional computers to allow for the creation and editing of documents in the Chinese language?

    A. In Control Panel, use the Regional Options icon.

    B. In Control Panel, use the Additional Languages icon.

    C. Upgrade the OS to the MultiLanguage version.

    D. In Control Panel, configure the Locale settings for two locales.

9. One morning, you configure the use of StickyKeys on a Windows 2000 Professional computer for a user who needs this option to press multiple key combinations. He gives it a try, and everything is working properly when you leave. That afternoon, the user calls to report that the StickyKeys were not working when he came back from lunch. What do you think is most likely the problem?

A. The user has logged on using a different user account.

B. The user's Accessibility Options were deleted during a Group Policy refresh.

C. The Accessibility Options drivers have been corrupted.

D. The Accessibility Options have been configured to reset automatically if the computer is idle for a period of time.

REVIEW ANSWERS

1. **B**   After joining computers to a domain, you can configure roaming profiles for the accounts by modifying the properties of the domain accounts. The path specified must be a network share that the user has read and change permission to. Profiles work best in domains. It's possible to configure roaming profiles in workgroups, but it's not really worth the administrative overhead and security holes involved.

2. **A**   A local profile would be sufficient in this small network because the profiles are created automatically when users log on for the first time, and they are able to make changes to the desktop environment that will be saved for the next time they log on. **B** is incorrect because a mandatory profile would not let users make changes to the desktop. **C** is not a necessary step because a local profile would require less administrative overhead, and the users are not switching computers often, if at all. **D** is incorrect because Active Directory-Integrated is a description of DNS zones, not user profiles.

3. **D**   For the Advanced Options tab to be displayed, the user must be logged on as an Administrator or have Administrator privileges assigned. Since the question assumes a regular user, the fax settings are working as designed. When the regular user is using his home system, he is using an account with Administrator privileges. **A** will not work because there is no mention of the fax device not working, just that the Advanced Options tab is not available. **C** is wrong for the same reason. Resource conflicts would cause problems with the operation of the device. **B** is incorrect because there is an Advanced Options tab in Windows 2000 where you can configure fax settings.

4. **C** Publishing an application to users makes the Windows Installer package available for installation. To install a published application, the application can be clicked in the Add/Remove Programs applet in the Control Panel, or the application installation can be invoked by opening a file associated with the application. Published programs appear in the Add/Remove Programs dialog box. Publishing an application to users does not create a shortcut to the application on the users' desktops when targeted users log on. **A** and **B** are incorrect because an applications assignment would either install the application automatically (computer assignment) or place a shortcut in the users' Start menu. **D** is incorrect because applications cannot be published to computers.

5. **B** **D** Assigning an application to a user advertises the application to all targeted users at their next logon. The assigned application is installed the first time the user attempts to launch the program via the Start menu or by activating the Installer through document invocation.

6. **C** The Local Users and Groups utility is used to point the users profile to a network share, making it a roaming profile. **A** is incorrect because there is no such tool. **B** is also not right because while a list of profiles is displayed here, it is used to copy profiles, not to specify what type of profile is used. **D** is the local user management tool in NT 4 and does not apply to Windows 2000 Professional.

7. **C** From the Advanced tab of the Start Menu Properties dialog box, you can configure such settings as the display of Administrative tools, Logoff, and Favorites. **A** is incorrect because the user is already part of the local Administrators group, so that won't help matters. **B** and **D** are wrong because you won't find the configuration help you need from those tabs. (The Management tab, in fact, does not exist.)

8. **A** Localized versions of Windows 2000 Professional support localized user interfaces for the language selected. In addition, they have the ability to view, edit, and print documents in more than 60 different languages. You will enable multilingual editing and viewing through the Regional Options icon in the Control Panel. **B** is incorrect because no such icon exists in Control Panel. **C** is incorrect because it is not a necessary step in this case. **D** is unnecessary because the locale settings would configure such things as time, currency, and the input language used.

9. **D** In the Accessibility Options icon in Control Panel, you can set how long the accessibility features will be active if the computer is idle. You should first check the General tab of this dialog box to see if settings have been disabled after an idle period, such as a lunch break. **A** is wrong because the Accessibility settings will be computer-wide. **B** is incorrect because a Group Policy refresh is unlikely to reset the Accessibility settings. **C** is incorrect because the Accessibility Options do not rely on drivers. Corrupt drivers imply a problem with devices, not the operating system itself.

Implementing, Managing, and Troubleshooting Hardware Devices and Drivers

	NEWBIE	SOME EXPERIENCE	EXPERT
ETA	5 hours	3 hours	1 hour

Implementing a device means that you install and configure the device to a functional state within the operating system. Consider a display adapter device: It's this inanimate object made of silicon and aluminum wire that takes pulses of electricity and sends them to a monitor, which in turn shoots electrons through a gun at one end of a tube so that the electrons, in a very precise pattern, light up an array of red, green, and blue phosphorus dots at the other end of the tube. The dots glow because they've been hit with an electron for all of about 1/60 of a second or so. Each phosphorous dot that's hit glows in harmony with its neighbors to paint a picture on your monitor. That picture will be repainted again about 30 times a second, sometimes much more often, each picture slightly different from the last picture that is being drawn during a game of Half-Life that you are playing at 3:00 A.M.!

Fortunately, you don't have to think about all this complexity. As far as administrators are concerned, implementing is a two-step dance. First, the device is *physically* connected to the computer's bus. It has to have a way to transport data to the processor. Then the device needs to be *logically* connected to the operating system, so that the OS and the device can successfully communicate, and so that the operating system doesn't reply "Huh?" when the device has something to say. We logically connect devices to the OS through the installation of drivers.

Troubleshooting is the process of isolating the source of a system error and taking corrective measures as needed. Almost all computer books include sections on troubleshooting. Almost none of them will help you troubleshoot a fraction as well as old-fashioned field experience. And as the aim of this book is to get you prepared for an exam, I can only give you a few heads up in this area and cannot begin to cover all the problems and challenges you are likely to encounter in the real world. Here goes.

Implement, Manage, and Troubleshoot Display Devices

A video adapter is an output device—usually a card that's attached to the motherboard, although some computers come with integrated video adapters that send information, and lots of it, to your monitor. You will set up your video adapter the same way you set up other hardware devices on your computer, either through the magic of Plug and Play or by using the Add/Remove Hardware Wizard in the Control Panel.

If the video adapter is a Plug and Play device, you simply need to shut down your computer and install the card. When you reboot, Windows 2000 Professional will automatically detect and install drivers for this new card.

If the card is not Plug and Play, you will need the help of the Add/Remove Hardware applet in the Control Panel. The Add/Remove Hardware program helps in the addition of non–Plug and Play devices on Windows 2000 computers. The Add/Remove Hardware program will ask you what device is being installed, and where to find the drivers for the new device. Like many administrative tasks, the process is completed by providing answers to a wizard.

Travel Advisory

These steps look pretty much the same when using the Add/Remove Hardware applet to install any type of device. We will not go through the wizard every time a new device is mentioned in this chapter, because the skills here will port well to other device installs.

Following are the steps you will take when configuring a video adapter that is not Plug and Play:

1. To begin installing a video adapter that was not detected by Windows 2000, open the Control Panel and double-click the Add/Remove Hardware applet. This will launch the Add/Remove Hardware Wizard Welcome screen, shown in Figure 5-1.

FIGURE 5-1   The Welcome screen of the Add/Remove Hardware Wizard

2. Click Next, and the Choose a Hardware Task dialog box appears. You can either install or uninstall, depending on the radio button you choose. In our case, we are adding a video adapter, so keep the default choice and click Next. Windows 2000 will then look for Plug and Play devices. (If you're saying to yourself, "Why? I thought I was running the Add/Remove Hardware Wizard because there was no Plug and Play capability in the first place! What's wrong with these people?", remember that certain computers have hot-swap capability, and devices can be added while the machine is on. In that case, Windows wouldn't know to do a bus rescan to determine what devices were there. That's why.)

3. After the scan is complete, the Choose a Hardware Device dialog box appears, showing you a list of all the devices that are currently installed for troubleshooting. Since the last dialog box grouped Adding and Troubleshooting a device together, the Wizard assumes that you might want to troubleshoot a device first. We want to install a new device, so choose the first option, Add A New Device, and click Next.

4. The Find New Hardware dialog box appears, as shown in Figure 5-2. Windows 2000 Professional will ask you if it should try to find devices that are not Plug and Play compatible. In real-world use, this scan is unlikely to turn up anything new. If the scan at startup time fails to detect a device, it probably won't be detected. Since you know what device you are trying to set up anyway, I recommend you click No, I Want To Select The Hardware From A List radio button and select Next.

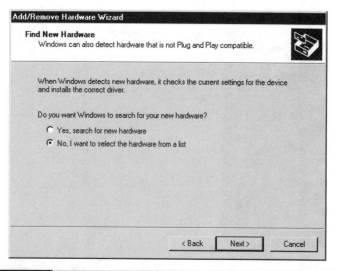

FIGURE 5-2   Tell Windows 2000 not to scan for new hardware

5. The Hardware Type dialog box appears next, as shown in Figure 5-3. This dialog box asks you that first vital piece of information: what to install. Make your selection and click Next. Windows 2000 will then retrieve a list of devices for which it has drivers. We will be selecting the display adapter type from the list.

6. The next dialog box you see will depend on what device you just told the Wizard you wanted to install. The Select a Device Driver dialog box presents you with a list of devices for which Windows 2000 already has a driver. Most of the time, these devices will be detected, so the choice for many installations with the Add/Remove Hardware Wizard is the Have Disk button. Figure 5-4 shows you this dialog box.

7. Now you are supplying the second vital piece of information to the Wizard: where to find the drivers. In fact, the drivers *are* the devices to Windows 2000, so when you locate and specify the drivers used, you are setting up the device.

8. After you have pointed Windows 2000 to the appropriate device drivers, the Start Hardware Installation dialog box appears, as shown in Figure 5-5. If the driver is the one you intended, click Next to begin the installation.

9. After the drivers have been installed, the Completing the Add/Remove Hardware Wizard dialog box will summarize what has just been done. Click the Finish button to exit the Add/Remove Hardware Wizard.

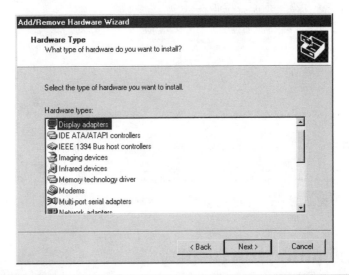

FIGURE 5-3 Tell Windows 2000 what kind of device you are installing

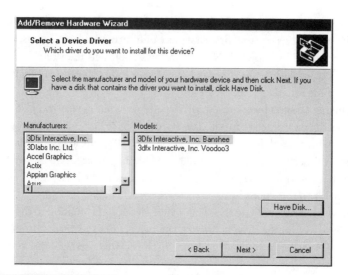

FIGURE 5-4 Make the driver selection

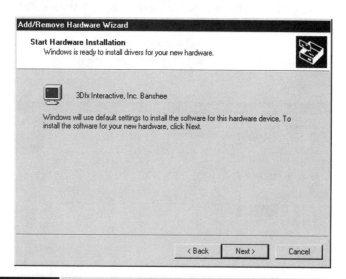

FIGURE 5-5 The installation begins after verification here

Configuring the Display

After you've installed the video card, you will configure the options of the adapter through the Display Properties dialog box. To get there, you can right-click on any free space on the desktop and choose Properties. Keep in mind that you are looking at the Display program in the Control Panel (as we discussed earlier) when you do so. From this dialog box, the options for configuring the video adapter will be on the Settings tab shown in Figure 5-6.

You will be able to set the following options directly on this tab:

- **Colors**   Lets you set the color depth for your adapter. The choices available on this drop-down list will be determined by the capabilities of the adapter. Most video cards today can display 16 million colors without breaking a sweat.

- **Screen Area**   Configures the resolution of the video adapter. Be aware that not all monitors support all screen resolutions, so just because you are able to configure a given screen area here doesn't mean that you should. This will be discussed further in the "Troubleshooting the Display" section later.

When you change either of these settings, you will be shown an informational dialog box (Figure 5-7), which informs you that the settings are about to be changed temporarily. If you configure a setting that is not supported by the monitor, the monitor will return to its original settings in 15 seconds. You can accept the new settings by clicking the OK button.

To configure advanced settings for the video adapter, click the Advanced button on the Settings tab, and up pops the Monitor And Video Adapter Properties dialog box, as shown in Figure 5-8, with the General tab selected by default.

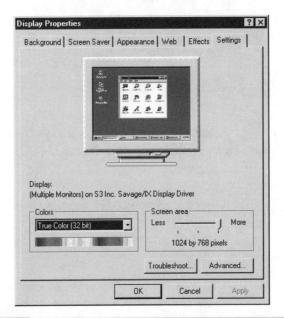

FIGURE 5-6   The Settings tab of the Display Properties dialog box

FIGURE 5-7 The 15-second informational dialog box

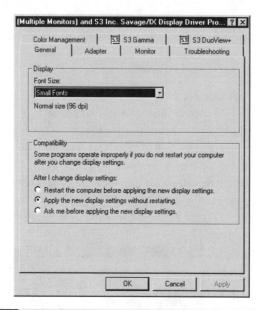

FIGURE 5-8 Setting the advanced properties of your display

The five tabs in the Advanced Properties dialog box let you further configure how the screen looks on your computer, as Table 5-1 describes.

TABLE 5.1 The Tabs of the Advanced Properties Dialog Box

This tab...	Lets you configure...
General	Font size for the display and what action Windows will take when you change the settings.

(Continued)

TABLE 5.1	*CONTINUED*
This tab...	**Lets you configure...**
Adapter	Properties of your video adapter; the Properties button here will provide you with the Device Manager interface to the device.
Monitor	Properties of your monitor, including the refresh frequency; as a safeguard to the blank monitor situation described earlier, you can hide all unsupported refresh rates with the check box. Figure 5-9 shows this tab for reference.
Troubleshooting	How Windows 2000 uses your graphics hardware.
Color Management	The color profiles used on the computer.

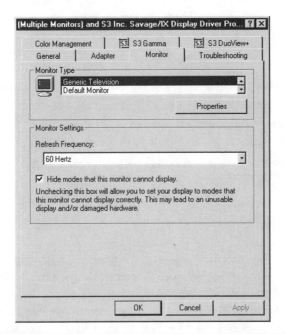

FIGURE 5-9   The Monitor tab

Travel Advisory

Some video adapter manufacturers will write device drivers that will add a few more tabs—or even a *lot* more—on the Advanced Monitor Properties dialog box. So if you see more tabs than are mentioned here, you have one of these adapters.

Supporting Multiple Monitors

For many Windows veterans, the display properties will look familiar. Although Windows 2000 sports a few display items not shown in previous Windows versions, nothing should be confusing here—many have been toying with these same display properties since the first Bush administration.

However, new to the NT family of operating systems is *multiple monitor support*. When Windows 2000 multiple monitor support is installed, you can extend the working desktop over the span of 2 to 10 monitors.

To support this feature, however, a motherboard must contain a Peripheral Components Interconnect (PCI) or Accelerated Graphics Port (AGP) video adapter for each monitor that will show the desktop. Most computers that run Windows 2000 Professional (like the one you are likely using) will have only three to five free PCI slots, and motherboards with multiple AGP slots are rare indeed.

Travel Assistance

PCI and AGP are technologies that define how expansion cards attach and send information to motherboards. The AGP bus was developed specifically for video cards and is a faster expansion bus compared to PCI. If you have a choice, go for the AGP card. For further information about AGP, PCI, and buses in general, please refer to the Webopedia at **http://www.webopedia.com.**

You should be aware of a few gotchas when configuring multiple monitors on systems that have an integrated video adapter. As always, it is crucial to recognize default behavior: by default, Windows 2000 recognizes the first detected video adapter as the primary display adapter. The *primary display adapter* is the display adapter that is responsible for showing the Windows 2000 log on screen. It is also the default screen space responsible displaying an application when the application is started up. You may then extend the application to the other displays. When you are using only one monitor, it is the primary display adapter.

However, if your system has a video card and an integrated adapter *before* the setup of the operating system, Windows 2000 will disable the integrated adapter; it changes your primary adapter, still assuming that you are going to use only one of those adapters (you haven't told it to use two adapters yet).

And when you add a second adapter *after* Windows 2000 is installed, the newly installed video adapter becomes the primary and the integrated adapter becomes the secondary.

Exam Tip

If your computer has an on-board video adapter and you plan to implement multiple monitors, you should *always* install Windows 2000 Professional on that system before you install the second video adapter.

Windows 2000 multiple monitor support lets you configure different settings, such as resolution and color depth, for the different monitors. You will configure multiple monitor support from the same place you are already used to configuring the properties of the display: the Settings tab of the Display Properties dialog box. This time, however, you should see a box on the Settings tab for every video adapter you have installed. To extend your desktop, click the number of the monitor that will be your additional display and choose the checkbox that says Extend My Windows Desktop Onto This Monitor.

Troubleshooting the Display

An unreadable display or no video output is commonly caused by a video adapter and monitor mismatch. This commonly occurs when a new video card is placed in a system that has an older monitor. The new video card, which has about three times as much memory as your first computer, might easily handle a 1280 x 1024 resolution at 80 Hz, but your monitor has nowhere near the capabilities to paint a picture that detailed that fast. It's like dropping a NASCAR engine into an AMC Gremlin. That car isn't going to perform quite like you planned.

I have seen just this scenario many times, and the result is that a monitor won't display anything. Sometimes the monitor will help with a message like

"Outside Scan Range," but other times, nothing works. (It will usually be reported as "My monitor is broken," or "The computer has crashed.") To troubleshoot this situation, you will need to restart the computer in Safe Mode or try booting to the Last Known Good Configuration, although chances are that the former solution will be necessary to resolve the problem. Safe Mode starts Windows 2000 with a minimal set of drivers, including a VGA video adapter with a limited number of colors and low resolution and refresh rates. Using these Safe Mode settings, Windows 2000 should display a picture on *any* color monitor. From within Safe Mode, you can reset the display settings so that the monitor can paint a picture on the screen once again.

Sometimes, non–Plug and Play capable devices will require that you configure available resources and dedicate them to the video adapter. This will be a rare instance on a Windows 2000 box but one you should be aware of nonetheless. System resources needed to support video adapters include I/O and memory addresses, direct memory access (DMA) channels, and interrupt request (IRQ) lines.

Travel Assistance

For more information on the resources that are assigned to devices, please see *Mike Meyers' A+ Certification Passport* (Osborne/McGraw-Hill).

Implement, Manage, and Troubleshoot Mobile Computer Hardware

Mobile computing often involves using battery power as an energy source, and Windows 2000 represents a quantum leap forward from NT 4 in the power-saving features it supports. These features are particularly useful on laptop computers, where the operating system and hardware can work in harmony to play a significant role in reducing consumption of battery life. The reduced power consumption technology in use on laptops is commonly used to reduce power usage of desktop computers as well.

Windows 2000 Professional supports two power-management specifications: Advanced Power Management (APM) and Advanced Configuration and Power Interface (ACPI). ACPI-compliant computers can take full advantage of reduced power consumption by controlling power requirements for Plug and

Play hardware devices. ACPI is a more advanced form of power management that needs the support of both the operating system and the computer hardware. In an ACPI machine, the operating system manages all of the power requirements for your computer subsystems and peripherals. ACPI lets the operating system direct power to devices as they need it, preventing unnecessary power demands on your system.

You will notice if a computer is ACPI compliant by looking in the Device Manager under the Computer node. Look under the System Devices to see if any ACPI devices are listed. If your computer supports APM, you should see an APM tab in the Power Options applet in the Control Panel.

As mentioned, with ACPI systems, the operating system is tasked with the management of power consumption. This is accomplished mostly by having things turned off when they are not in use. The monitor and hard disks are two components that when shut down conserve the most power.

You will enable and configure APM and ACPI power options from the Power Options program in the Control Panel, as shown in Figure 5-10. The Power Options dialog box has five tabs: Power Schemes, Advanced, Hibernate, APM, and UPS. Furthermore, the program will let you configure only the features that match your system's hardware capabilities.

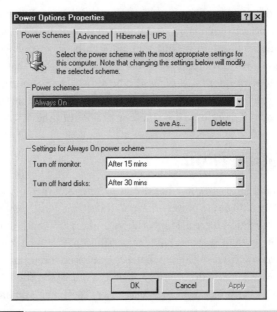

FIGURE 5-10   Setting power options

Travel Advisory

The Power Options dialog box automatically detects what is available on your computer and shows you only the options that you can control. If APM is not available on your system, for example, you will not see an APM tab. Likewise, you may not see a UPS tab if you don't have a UPS device installed on your machine.

From this dialog box, you can configure the following power conservation behavior:

- Create a new power scheme or edit one that already exists.
- Enable or disable Hibernation mode.
- Configure power alarms and Standby mode.
- Specify a UPS device and how it will behave.
- Configure APM on non-ACPI computers that support APM.

Standby Mode

Putting a computer in Standby mode causes the hard drive and monitor to be shut down, and the power remains on just enough to supply the RAM with power to hold its contents. You usually get out of Standby with a key sequence or by pressing the CPU's power button, and one of the main advantages is that restoration of your working environment is very rapid. The drawback to Standby is that (battery) power is still used, albeit at a significantly reduced rate, but this can still cause a battery to empty if Standby is used for long periods of time.

Hibernation Mode

When a computer hibernates, it writes all of the contents of memory to a file on the hard disk and then turns the power off. Upon restart, the computer grabs the contents of the hibernation file, called hiberfil.sys, and copies it back into memory. It takes a little longer than Standby, but you can still come right back to your working space just as you left it, even though the computer has been shut off and is not consuming power. Hibernation will be available as one of the Shut Down options after you enable it in the Control Panel. Again, every computer is different, but most computers can be restored from Hibernation by hitting the power switch.

Travel Advisory

Lots of third-party tools manage power consumption, and almost every laptop manufacturer supplies its own. These third-party utilities can sometimes conflict with Windows 2000's power management. Some laptops will not even let you in the Power Options dialog box, directing you instead to their own power-management software. If you are upgrading a computer that has one of these tools running, you might want to disable it so that Windows 2000 power support is installed, even if it is not used.

Uninterruptible Power Supply (UPS)

A UPS protects your computer from a sudden loss of electrical power, and subsequent sudden loss of your screenplay (to which you've just added a showstopper scene), by supplying backup battery power. This battery power is intended to run long enough to let you perform a safe shutdown that will save all of your current work, thus ensuring your Oscar nomination. The UPS is a safeguard; you are not meant to run your system on UPS power all the time.

Most UPS's will be connected to a computer's serial port, although you should follow manufacturer's instructions for installation, of course. After it is physically installed, the UPS status appears on the UPS tab of the Power Options dialog box. From the UPS tab, you can configure how the computer will behave in the event of a power loss. For example, with some UPSs, you can have the system page you if the power goes off.

As with backup devices, many UPS manufacturers will ship their own proprietary configurations, which in many cases are more robust than what is offered with the Windows 2000 Control Panel, so you may be using a totally different interface to your UPS in the a production environment.

Exam Tip

As a final note on this topic, remember that the contents of the Power Options can vary from computer to computer. If you know the purpose and configuration options of the tabs discussed here, you should be able to answer any questions that will be thrown at you on the 70-210 exam.

Configuring Card Services

If you've used a laptop computer, you've likely worked with Personal Computer Memory Card Industry Association (PCMCIA) card devices. These cards allows for laptops to change their configurations easily, depending on what type of card is used. The nice thing about PCMCIA cards is that they support hot swapping, which lets you exchange your cards while the computer is running. There are three types of PCMCIA card standards, and Microsoft expects you to know the differences between each:

- **Type I** Cards can be up to 3.3 millimeters (mm) thick. Type I cards are used typically to add memory to a laptop.
- **Type II** Cards can be up to 5 mm thick. These are the most common type of card used and are typically used to add a network card or modem to a computer
- **Type III** Cards can be up to 10.5 mm thick. Type III cards are usually used to connect a portable hard drive.

PCMCIA card devices fully support Plug and Play, and as such will work just like any other Plug and Play device. The difference here is that you will not need to shut down the computer to add the device.

Objective 5.03

Implement, Manage, and Troubleshoot Input and Output Devices

Windows 2000 supports a wide variety of input/output (I/O) devices, each requiring driver installation, configuration, and (occasional, hopefully) troubleshooting to achieve proper operation. We've already taken a look at some of the most common of these I/O devices in the display adapter and disk devices. Again, the job of these I/O devices is simply to transport data in the form of electrical pulses from one place to another—or more specifically from one device to the CPU, and then from the CPU to a device.

To implement and manage hardware devices successfully, you must be familiar with the use and purpose of one very important tool: the Device Manager. Fortunately, many people are already familiar with this tool as it is pretty much the same as is has been for several years, starting with Windows 95. If you are familiar with the Device Manager and take the scenic tour of the Windows 2000 version, there shouldn't be too much in this objective that will trip you up.

The job of Device Manager is to gather information about all the devices that have been recognized by Windows 2000. It also provides an interface from which you can manage and configure these devices. We have already seen examples of Device Manager at work, and we will see more from Device Manager in Chapter 6 when we configure hardware profiles.

For each device discovered by Device Manager, the following information can be gathered:

- Whether or not the device is working properly
- The settings for the device
- The resources used by the device

The Device Manager also lets you update drivers and print out a report about all the device information on your computer. You can launch this utility in one of a couple of ways:

- From the System applet in the Control Panel, choose the Hardware tab and then click on the Device Manager button.
- You can also run Device Manager from the Computer Management snap-in, under the System Tools node.

And while Microsoft thinks enough of the aforementioned I/O devices to devote an exam objective to each, the rest of the devices that may be connected to a particular computer are lumped into one objective. The following hardware I/O devices are also important in the day-to-day operation of any modern machine:

- Multimedia hardware
- Modems
- Wireless devices, especially Infrared Data Association (IrDA) devices
- Universal serial bus (USB) devices
- Smart cards

Let's take a closer look at installing and configuring each of these devices.

USB Devices

The USB is an external bus that allows for the connection of USB devices through a USB port. Support of USB is necessary at both the BIOS and the operating system level, and some previous versions of Windows did not support the USB bus. Windows 2000 Professional does support this bus, though, and if USB is also enabled in the BIOS, you will see Universal Serial Bus Controllers listed in Device Manager. You can then configure the USB device by double-clicking the controller to bring up the dialog box shown in Figure 5-11.

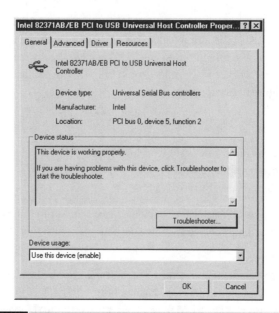

FIGURE 5-11 Set the USB controller properties with this dialog box

One of the advantages of the USB is that most USB devices are hot swappable. Another advantage of the USB is its scalability. A single USB controller can support up to 127 devices simultaneously, usually with one or more USB hubs. That means that a wide variety of printers, scanners, mice, modems, and other devices can use the same USB roadway to transfer their 1's and 0's to the motherboard, and they can be plugged in and removed as easily as an Atari joystick. The bus is also capable of data transfer rates of 12Mbps, which may not sound terribly fast today but is still faster than many network cards in use running at 10Mbps.

Four tabs appear in the USB controller Properties dialog box that let you set the optional behavior about your controller, as described in the following list:

- **General** Lists the device type and the device status, and allows you to disable the device with the drop-down box. You can also run a troubleshooter if the device is not working properly by clicking the Troubleshooter button.

- **Advanced** Lets you play traffic cop on the USB roadway. You can configure how much bandwidth each device connected to the USB controller can use.

- **Driver** Shows the driver properties and lets you remove or update the currently installed drivers.

- **Resources** Shows all of the resources used by the USB controller.

Imaging Devices

Scanners and digital cameras fall under the category of imaging devices, and are managed with a Control Panel applet named, appropriately enough, Scanners and Cameras. Figure 5-12 shows you the Properties dialog box of the Scanners and Cameras applet.

Scanners and digital cameras both do essentially the same thing: they take an image of something and store it as digital data that can be understood by the computer. Scanners have the ability to scan text as well but are really just working with a picture of the text.

The Scanners and Cameras Properties window only has one dialog box that lists the imaging devices currently installed on your computer. You can click the Add button to add a device, the Remove button to remove one, and the Troubleshoot button to begin using the Troubleshooting Wizard. Clicking the Properties button with the desired device selected displays a device-specific dialog box, where you can configure further options, as shown in Figure 5-13.

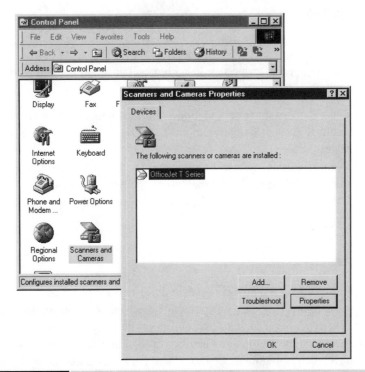

FIGURE 5-12   Manage your imaging devices here

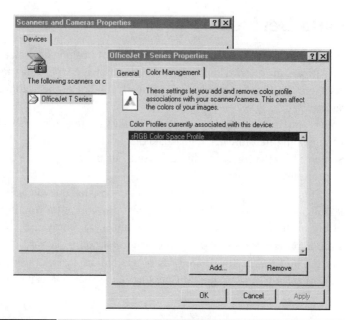

FIGURE 5-13 Configuring additional imaging options

The device-specific Properties dialog box will normally contain three tabs with the following information:

- **General**   Lists the make and model of the imaging device, as well as its status. You can click a button that will test the device as you can see from Figure 5-13.
- **Events**   Allows you to associate an event with an application, like automatically linking a scanned image to an application for editing.
- **Color Management**   Lets you set a color profile with a given scanner or camera.

Modems

Installation of modems is no different than the installation of any other device. If it supports Plug and Play, the modem should be recognized automatically and the appropriate driver installed. If it does not support Plug and Play, the device must be set up through the Add/Remove Hardware program in the Control Panel.

You will then configure modems through the Phone and Modem Options applet in the Control Panel. When you double-click this icon, you will see the

Phone And Modem Options Properties dialog box, as shown in Figure 5-14. To begin management of a modem, select the Modems tab and double-click the modem you wish to manage. In the figure, the Modems tab is already selected.

You are also able to manage modems by using the Device Manager and double-clicking the modem object there. Once you have selected the modem to manage, you will see the modem's own Properties dialog box, as shown in Figure 5-15. Modem options will vary according to manufacturer, but there are generally seven tabs in this dialog box that are used to modify modem behavior. These tabs are described in the following section.

- **General**   Like other General tabs, displays the make and model of the modem and lets you run a troubleshooter. Also lets you disable the device.
- **Modem**   Lets you control the speaker volume, the maximum port speed, and whether or not to Wait for a dial tone before dialing.
- **Diagnostics**   Can be used to perform additional troubleshooting. You can run a test from here that will check the operating system's ability to communicate with the modem.
- **Advanced**   Allows you to specify additional initialization commands. You can also configure communications port behavior that will be used for transmit and receive buffers, and manage the default call preferences.

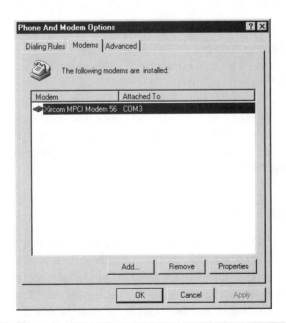

FIGURE 5-14   The Phone and Modem Options Properties dialog box

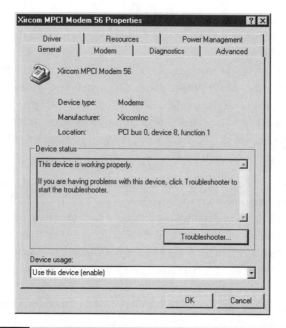

FIGURE 5-15   Use this dialog box to configure your modem

- **Driver**   Displays information about the currently loaded driver and allows you to update or remove the installed driver.
- **Resources**   Lists the resources used by the modem, including the memory and interrupt request (IRQ) settings. Useful if conflicts need to be resolved with non–Plug and Play devices on your computer.
- **Power Management**   Lets you set device power consumption options, such as letting the modem bring the computer out of standby mode (so that the system could still receive an incoming fax while in standby, for example).

Wireless Devices

Most internal IrDA devices should be discovered and installed by Windows 2000 Setup automatically, or once you start Windows 2000 Professional after installing one of these devices. If the IrDA device is not found by either of these methods, you can always do the installation using that old saw, the Add/Remove Hardware Program, as you will likely do when connecting a wireless device to a serial port. To configure your wireless device, you will use the Wireless Link program in the Control Panel. Then, from the Hardware tab, select the device you want to configure and click Properties.

> ### Exam Tip
> IrDA is a new feature in Windows 2000, so you can expect a question that mentions configuring an IrDA device.

Multimedia Devices

Typical multimedia devices include CD-ROM, DVD, digital camera, Musical Instrument Digital Interface (MIDI), and scanner hardware.

You are probably familiar with DVD already, and we have already discussed how to configure these devices back in Chapter 3 when we talked about disk management. You should know that the main difference between a DVD and a CD-ROM is the amount of data it can hold. DVDs are capable of storing anywhere from 8 to 40 times as much data as a standard 650MB CD-ROM. The big problem right now is that there really isn't much everyday use for this kind of static storage other than movies, and who really wants to cuddle up with a date and a bowl of popcorn to watch a show on your ViewSonic? Me neither.

Also, as we mentioned in previous chapters, Windows 2000 Professional supports DVD through the automatic installation of the Universal Disk Format (UDF) file system.

> ### Travel Advisory
> UDF in Windows 2000 does not support write operations for DVD formats that support recording. Third-party software is necessary to record DVD media in Windows 2000.

Any installed devices should appear in Device Manager. As mentioned, you can perform many administrative tasks from here, and Administrative privileges are required to do most of them. One example of this is updating device drivers, which you won't be able to do while logged on as a regular user. If an installed device does not appear in Device Manager, this might be because it is missing a driver or has been disabled or otherwise improperly configured in the BIOS.

Just as in Windows 9x, you can use the Add/Remove Hardware Wizard to add any drivers for devices that Windows 2000 Professional doesn't automatically detect. Unlike Windows 9x, Plug and Play usually works as advertised. The requisites are that when the hardware is detected, the drivers must exist in the drivers.cab file in the Windows installation (there are thousands of drivers in this file), or the driver must be readily available on disk, usually a CD-ROM. You will also be able to use the Add/Remove Hardware interface to remove, unplug, or troubleshoot hardware.

Exam Tip

You will use the Scanners and Cameras program in the Control Panel to install a digital imaging device that was not detected by Plug and Play.

Drivers for Personal Computer/Smart Card–compliant Plug and Play smart cards and readers are included with the operating system. To use smart cards, the network must support a Public Key Infrastructure (PKI) and an Enterprise Certification Authority (CA). Of course, every computer that will use a smart card will require a smart card reader.

Travel Advisory

Windows 2000 does not support non–Personal Computer/Smart Card–compliant or non–Plug and Play–compliant smart card readers.

If a device is controlled by the BIOS and is not functioning properly, you will likely need to update the BIOS. You will be notified of devices that are not working through Device Manager's warning and failure icons. The most common cause of this will be a resource conflict like an IRQ line. However, resource conflicts are rare with Plug and Play devices due to the nature of Plug and Play, which eliminates resource conflicts by dynamically assigning resources to devices upon startup. To see which resources are in use by which device, use the Resource by Type and Resources by Connection views.

Objective 5.04   Update Drivers

A *device driver* is software that acts as intermediary between the Windows 2000 operating system and a specific piece of hardware. New drivers are being developed and tested all the time that add new functionality, fix bugs, or just get something to work faster. Managing device drivers involves updating these drivers when necessary and deciding how to handle drivers that have not been tested for reliability.

A number of procedures exist for updating installed drivers. Most manufacturers are in constant development with drivers and will typically post new drivers to their Web sites for download. Further, many manufacturers include a setup routine when they distribute device drivers, and installation is simply a matter of double-clicking the setup executable. Another of the more simple ways is to use the Windows Update tool, which will update many core operating system drivers, as has been discussed in Chapter 1.

This tool also works in reverse. If a driver needs to be removed, you can connect to the Windows Update site and follow the instructions to restore the previous configuration, or you can run the Update Wizard and Uninstall tool. This is a system tool available with the System Information snap-in.

The Upgrade Device Driver Wizard

You can update most other drivers by accessing the properties of the device in Device Manager:

1. Click the Driver tab, and click Update Driver. This click will launch the Upgrade Device Driver Wizard, whose Welcome screen is shown in Figure 5-16.
2. Click Next, and you will see the Install Hardware Device Drivers dialog box. These dialog boxes, and almost all of the steps of the Upgrade Device Driver Wizard, look much like the Add New Hardware Wizard. You tell the Wizard

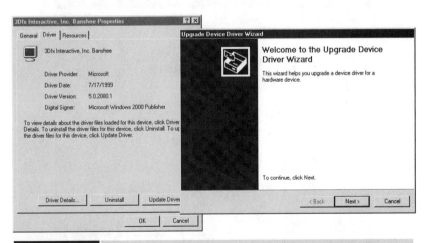

FIGURE 5-16   The Upgrade Device Driver Wizard Welcome page

where to find the new files by making your selection, as shown in Figure 5-17, and then click Next.

3. The next dialog box asks you where to find the updated drivers, as shown in Figure 5-18. You can have the Wizard look on a floppy or CD-ROM, search the network, or use the Microsoft Update utility. Make your selection based on where the files are and click Next.

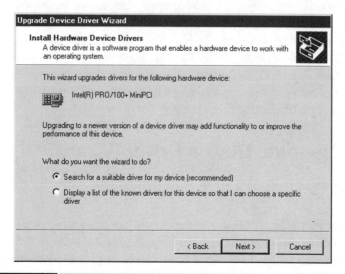

FIGURE 5-17   The Install Hardware Device Drivers dialog box

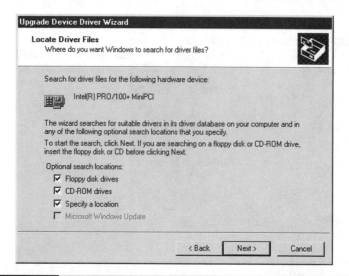

FIGURE 5-18   Search for the updated driver

4. The Driver Files Search dialog box appears, letting you confirm the location and filename of the driver to be installed. Click Next if the appropriate driver is selected and the driver installation process will begin. When finished, the Completing the Upgrade Device Driver Wizard dialog box appears.

Exam Tip

Administrator privileges are necessary to install device drivers manually, but Plug and Play devices that are detected and automatically installed do not require that the user be logged on as an Admin.

Driver Signing

In the past, Microsoft has blamed operating system issues on poorly written drivers that cause conflicts, usually in the area of memory conflicts. These conflicts will prevent a device from working properly and can even cause the operating system to crash. (I'm sure that the writers of the bad drivers have their own view of what's poorly written, but that's another debate.)

One of Microsoft's answers to drivers that cause havoc on a system has been the Hardware Compatibility List (HCL), a list of hardware devices that have earned the Microsoft stamp of approval after being tested by the folks in Redmond. Installing devices that appear on the HCL was first discussed in Chapter 1.

One of the other mechanisms that's newly available is *driver signing*, a signature that's associated with a driver installation file that certifies that it has been tested and is safe for installation.

You will be able to specify how Windows 2000 Professional will respond to unsigned drivers through the Driver Signing Options dialog box, found on the Hardware tab of the System Properties dialog box. When you click the Driver Signing button, you can set three levels of behavior before the driver is installed: Ignore, Warn, and Block, as seen in Figure 5-19. The default is set to Warn you when drivers are unsigned, giving you the option of whether on not to perform the install.

Exam Tip

Driver signing is another new feature of Windows 2000 Professional, which means a likely exam question candidate on the 70-210.

FIGURE 5-19 Driver signing options—notice the default

Objective 5.05

Monitor and Configure Multiple Processing Units

The Windows 2000 operating system kernel is scalable, in that it is able to use multiple processors to execute processes and threads. Windows 2000 Professional includes support for one or two processors. Even though supported in Windows 2000 Professional, you will typically use multiprocessor machines with installations of Server, and more specifically on application servers like Web servers, because of the processor-intensive nature of applications that can be running on a server. Typical Professional front-end applications, like Microsoft Access or Internet Explorer, are not considered processor-intensive when compared to back-end applications like SQL Server or Internet Information Server (IIS). One example of an exception to this would be in the case of a graphics-rendering program.

Local Lingo

Scalable A catch-all term that simply means adding more without changing how the thing works. Lots of things are described as scalable, like Active Directory or TCP/IP, which is scalable because it works just as well for a 2-workstation network as it does for 2 million-workstation network. In this case, the addition of more than one processor makes the Windows kernel *scalable*.

Support for multiple processors is provided by the hardware abstraction layer (HAL), a hardware-specific operating system component. Different computers will use different HALs. The function of the HAL is to isolate the rest of the Windows 2000 operating system from the underlying hardware. If you want to implement a system with multiple processors, you typically need to upgrade the HAL. To do this, you must go to the computer device Properties dialog box in Device Manager. You will then upgrade the HAL with the Upgrade Device Driver Wizard. Upgrading to an incompatible HAL is likely to cause a critical system failure.

Travel Advisory

This procedure upgrades only the driver on your computer. If your system has only one processor, upgrading the HAL isn't going to suddenly make it a multiple processor computer. In fact, if you have a HAL that supports two processors on a computer that only has one processor, the computer will likely be able to process instructions about as well as a doorstop. (Or be about as useful as the pets.com mascot—check out pets.com and try to order dog food if you didn't catch that one.)

Uniprocessor computers contain the simple Programmable Interrupt Controller (PIC) hardware, referred to as Standard PC in Device Manager. The HAL for a computer containing ACPI and PIC hardware is not upgradeable to the HAL for a PIC computer that is not ACPI compliant.

Performance Console

Once you install your second processor, you will use the Performance Console to monitor your new symmetric multiprocessing (SMP) system. Performance monitoring starts by establishing a baseline of satisfactory performance and then continuing to monitor the system to identify bottlenecks that impact performance. Following are the primary processor-specific objects to monitor:

- Processor counters that monitor each processor individually
- System counters that monitor all processors as a single unit
- Process counters that monitor each application running on the processors

The Performance Console will be explored in much greater detail in Chapter 6. Stay tuned.

> **Local Lingo**
>
> **Symmetric multiprocessing (SMP)** A description of the methodology involved when multiple processors execute the instructions of an application. With SMP, all processors share the same memory space and work on the same copy of an application. SMP's cousin is *Asymmetric multiprocessing (ASMP)*, in which each processor can operate on independent tasks. For example, one processor could be dedicated to operating system instructions and the other processor could handle applications. Windows 2000 supports SMP, not ASMP.

Task Manager

Another important tool for multiprocessor systems is the Task Manager, which will be used to verify that the second processor has been recognized by the operating system. Probably more importantly, you can also configure the use of multiple processors through the Task Manager. On the Processes tab, you will associate each processor with the processes that are running on the computer. This configuration of processes to run across multiple processors is called processor *affinity*, and you won't be able to configure this for just any old application. To take advantage of two or more processors, a process has to be *multithreaded*.

To set processor affinity, right-click the process you want to associate with a specific processor and select the Processor Affinity option. Then, from the Processor Affinity dialog box, select the specific processor that you want the process to execute on and click OK.

> **Local Lingo**
>
> **Multithreaded** Multithreaded processes have distinct units of execution, called *threads*, which can be configured to execute at the same time across two or more processors.

Other Tools

You use the Performance Logs And Alerts node of the Performance Console to collect performance data over time and to configure notification of exceeded activity thresholds. The Performance Console is a preconfigured MMC snap-in that can be found under the Administrative Tools menu. The Performance Logs

And Alerts utility is capable of creating two types of logs—Counter logs and Trace logs—and is capable of generating alerts.

Counter Logs

Counter logs let you record data about system resource usage over time and are a useful tool to help you establish a baseline of system use. Counter logs are configured to collect data at specific time intervals. Chapter 6 takes a much closer look at the Performance Console, including an explanation of just what a *counter* is, so it can be used as a reference point here in our discussion of counter logs.

1. To create a Counter log, right-click the Counter Logs node in the Performance Console and select New Log Settings from the pop-up menu. Then give your log file a name. Click OK.
2. The counter log Properties dialog box appears. You will then click the Add button to begin specifying the counters to be tracked by the log file and how often to track them, as shown in Figure 5-20. When you are finished adding counters that will be monitored in your log, click Close and then OK from the log Properties dialog box.

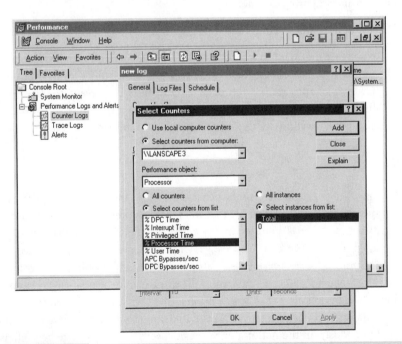

FIGURE 5-20 Set the counters to track from here

3. You will add counters to track from the Properties dialog box's General tab by clicking the Add button and choosing the specific counters.
4. The Schedule tab lets you specify when the log will start and lets you set logging with a minimum of administrative overhead.
5. The Log Files tab lets you set the log file location, type, and size.

Once you have configured the counters, duration, and schedule, the counter log will begin to track data, as will be indicated by green icon in the details pane of Counter Logs. (Notice that there is a System Overview log, which tracks just that, already configured but not running. You can start this log file capturing data by right-clicking the icon and choosing Start from the context menu.)

Trace Logs

Trace logs measure data continuously rather than through specific timed intervals, as is the case with Counter logs. Trace logs are used mainly to track the behavior of the operating system or applications, such as when an application creates or deletes a process or thread.

Trace logs are created using almost the same procedure as described previously when configuring Counter logs.

1. Create a New Log Setting, and then give the trace log a name.

2. Configure the events to trace from the Properties dialog box that will be presented next. The General tab is the only one that will differ from that of the Counter logs process, as you will be selecting the system events to trace from here. For example, you can select the Disk Input/Output And Process Creations/Deletions by clicking the appropriate check box.

Alerts

Alerts are used to generate an event when preconfigured thresholds are tripped. For example, you can create a trace log that will record an event every time processor activity is greater than 80 percent capacity. You can configure alerts so that a message is sent, a program is run, or a detailed log is written when these values are exceeded.

The process for creating an alert is also similar to that for setting Counter logs. But rather than just gathering data, you will be instructing the utility to take a specific action or actions. What action is performed will be configured from the Action tab after you have created a New Alert Setting by the same method as outlined previously. In the Action tab, you can specify that a message be sent, as shown in Figure 5-21.

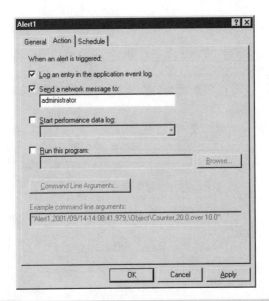

FIGURE 5-21   Giving instructions to the Alerts utility

 **Objective 5.06**

Install, Configure, and Troubleshoot Network Adapters

Windows 2000 Professional supports many network adapter models as well as protocols and services that use the adapter hardware. As you will see, there is really no difference between installing a network interface card (NIC) and installing any other hardware device, other than its importance in network communications. A device driver for a Plug and Play network adapter is installed automatically when the operating system detects the device, and the device driver is contained in the driver.cab file on the Windows 2000 Professional Setup CD-ROM. Installing a device driver for a network adapter that is not Plug and Play compatible is typically done using the Add/Remove Hardware Wizard, as we have discussed earlier. After a device driver is installed for a network card, protocols and services are bound to the adapter so that it can communicate on the network.

Once the network card has been installed, you will manage its behavior through its Local Area Connection Properties dialog box. You can access this dialog box, as shown in Figure 5-22, by right-clicking the Local Area Connection icon in My Network Places and choosing Properties.

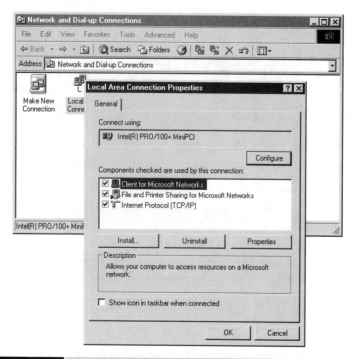

FIGURE 5-22   The Local Area Connection Properties dialog box

If you click the Configure button, you'll see another Properties dialog box, which we will be dealing with here. Figure 5-23 shows you the network card's Properties dialog box, with five tabs displayed: General, Advanced, Driver, Resources, and Power Management. We will talk about each of these in the following section.

As you've seen, there are actually several ways to bring up this dialog box; I have just outlined my personal preference. The same dialog box, for example, can be launched by finding it in Device Manager. Now let's see what is possible from each of these tabs.

- **General**   Displays the name and manufacturer of the network card for quick reference. You can also enable or disable the device from here and run a Troubleshooter on a mutinous device.
- **Advanced**   The contents of the Advanced tab will be specific to the adapter you are configuring. We have seen this before when configuring UPS devices. To make configuration changes from this tab, choose the property you want to modify in the left column and then the value you want to set from the drop-down box on the right.

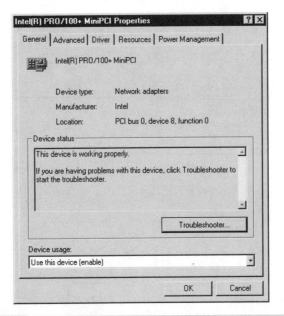

FIGURE 5-23   The network card's Properties dialog box

Travel Advisory

You should not need to make any changes from the network's Properties dialog box unless instructed to do so by the network card manufacturer.

- **Driver**   The Driver tab should look pretty familiar by now. You can view the driver provider, date of manufacture, and the digital signer (the company that provided the digital signature), and upgrade the driver by launching the Update Driver Wizard.
- **Resources**   The Resources tab is most useful in troubleshooting circumstances, when devices are using the same computer resources. Information gathered here includes the IRQ the device is using to get the attention of the processor and the I/O settings, among others. Figure 5-24 shows the Resources tab.
- **Power Management**   Like the Modem's Power Management options, you can configure the network card to be turned off when the computer is in low power mode, or to bring the computer out of a standby state to respond to a network event.

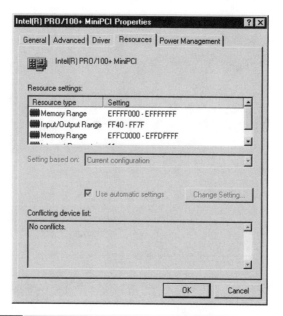

FIGURE 5-24 The resources a device is using is displayed here

---

Travel Advisory

Microsoft does not expect you to memorize IRQ lines of memory addresses, but you should know that when other devices are trying to use the same resource settings, the devices will not work properly.

Troubleshooting Network Cards

When you look at the General tab and find that the device is *not* working properly, what should you do? Microsoft expects you to have the answer, at least to a couple of the more common conditions that affect network card performance. Table 5-2 lists some common problems and solutions that will serve as a good starting point when troubleshooting network cards. Some of the solutions here are fairly intuitive once you know the source of the problem, but that's the hitch— the thorny part in most troubleshooting is pinpointing the cause.

TABLE 5.2	Common Problems and Solutions for Troubleshooting Network Cards
Problem	**Solution**
Network adapter not on the HCL	Contact the vendor for advice or buy a new adapter that is on the HCL.
Outdated driver	Get the most current driver for the card, usually to be found on the hardware vendor's Web site (which you might have to access with another computer).
Adapter not recognized by Windows 2000	The device might not be Plug and Play, and you will have to set it up through the Add/Remove Hardware program in the Control Panel. You should also check for resource conflicts.
Hardware not working properly	Use the diagnostics software that ships with the adapter. Rule out cabling and hub issues by testing with known goods.
Improperly configured network protocols	Configure your protocols properly. See Chapter 7 for details.

CHECKPOINT

✔ **Objective 5.01   Implement, Manage, and Troubleshoot Display Devices.**
We looked at some ways to manage the display of Windows 2000 Professional, including the ability to add video adapters and extend the desktop across multiple monitors.

✔ **Objective 5.02   Implement, Manage, and Troubleshoot Mobile Computer Hardware.** In this section, we noted many of the technologies that make

Windows 2000 Professional an excellent choice for laptop computers. Included in this section was a discussion of the various power management options available. The power saving options of Hibernate and Standby were discussed as ways to help mobile computers conserve battery power.

✔ **Objective 5.03   Implement, Manage, and Troubleshoot Input and Output Devices.** We looked at ways to install and configure input and output devices that are not covered specifically by other objectives. These I/O devices included wireless and USB devices, and even smart card configuration. We also looked at how to get a modem up and running so that a Windows 2000 Professional computer can take advantage of dial-up networking.

✔ **Objective 5.04   Update Drivers.** We looked at the process for updating the device drivers for the many hardware components of our system. We defined what a driver does and then walked through the Update Driver Wizard, which helped us make the driver updates.

✔ **Objective 5.05   Monitor and Configure Multiple Processing Units.** Because Windows 2000 Professional can take advantage of multiple processors, we need to know how this is done should the occasion arise. We looked at issues such as upgrading the HAL and setting processor affinity for currently executing processes.

✔ **Objective 5.06   Install, Configure, and Troubleshoot Network Adapters.** Windows 2000 Professional is an OS that is designed to operate in a network, and as such we must always ensure that the network cards are properly installed and configured. We also spent some time looking at various troubleshooting scenarios. You will be expected to have a general idea of what problems to look for given a set of symptoms on the Windows 2000 Professional exam.

REVIEW QUESTIONS

1. You have assembled a Pentium III computer that has an AGP video adapter. You run Windows 2000 Professional Setup, and the adapter is configured automatically. You later want to change the refresh rate of the display. What do you do?

   A. Use the Refresh Rate node of the Computer Management MMC snap-in.
   B. Use the Monitor tab in the Display Adapter Advanced Options dialog box.
   C. Open Computer Management and access the Device Manager.
   D Refresh rates are set by the video card manufacturer and cannot be changed.

2. You are planning to purchase a new computer that will run Windows 2000 Professional. The motherboard will have an on-board display adapter, and you want to extend your desktop across two monitors. What do you need to do?

   A. Install Windows 2000 after installing the second video adapter.
   B. Install Windows 2000 before installing the second video adapter.
   C. Ensure that the motherboard adapter is multidisplay compatible.
   D. Ensure that the motherboard adapter is configured as the primary adapter.

3. You install Windows 2000 Professional and open the Power Options program in the Control Panel. No APM tab is displayed. Which conditions are most likely to cause this APM tab to be missing?

   A. APM is disabled in the BIOS.
   B. The computer does not have an APM-compliant system board.
   C. The computer has an ACPI-compliant system board.
   D. The computer does not have a smart UPS device connected to the serial port.

4. What three methods can you use to install a modem under Windows 2000 Professional? (Choose three.)

   A. Use Device Manager.
   B. Plug in a Plug and Play modem.
   C. Use the Mail and Fax program in the Control Panel.
   D. Use the Add/Remove Hardware tool in Control Panel.
   E. Use the Add/Remove Modems and Network Devices in the Control Panel.
   F. Use the Phone and Modem Options program in the Control Panel.

5. You have a computer that is running Windows 2000 Professional, and you want to connect a digital camera to one of the USB ports on the system. You do this, but Windows does not install the device. What is the first thing you should suspect?

   A. USB support is disabled in the BIOS.
   B. USB support is disabled by default in Windows 2000 Professional.
   C. The USB port is damaged.
   D. The device is not supported by Windows 2000. You need to try to get an updated driver from the manufacturer.

6. You attach an IrDA transceiver to a serial port on your computer that is running Windows 2000 Professional, but the device is not automatically installed. What should you do to install the IrDA device?

   A. Use the Wireless Link program in the Control Panel.
   B. Use the Add/Remove Hardware program in the Control Panel.
   C. Use the Add/Remove Programs program in the Control Panel.
   D. Windows 2000 Professional does not support IrDA devices connected to a serial port.

7. You are the administrator of a computer that is running Windows 2000 Professional. What will be the main interface used to upgrade a device driver?

   A. Device Manager
   B. The Add/Remove Hardware Wizard
   C. The Installed Drivers program in the Control Panel
   D. The Devices and Drivers node in Computer Management

8. A hard disk on a Windows 98 box fails. You decide to replace the disk and install Windows 2000 Professional on a new hard drive. As you are performing this task, a driver for the system is not automatically installed by Windows 2000. Which conditions might require a manual installation of drivers?

   A. An error occurs during installation.
   B. The driver package is not digitally signed.
   C. The driver installation process requires a user interface to be displayed.
   D. The driver package does not contain all files needed to complete the installation.

9. You have set up a uniprocessor computer that is running Windows 2000 Professional. A few months later, you decide to upgrade to a motherboard that supports two processors. How are you going to now configure Windows 2000 Professional to distribute the processing load across the two processors?

   A. Recompile the operating system components that you want to use the two processors.
   B. Upgrade the HAL from Device Manager.
   C. Windows 2000 Professional does not support multiple processors.
   D. Do nothing. Windows 2000 Professional will automatically start to use the two processors for applications that are multithreaded.

10. What kind of multiprocessing does Windows 2000 Professional support?

    A. Symmetric multiprocessing (SMP)

    B. Asymmetric multiprocessing (ASMP)

    C. Both SMP and ASMP

    D. None of the above

REVIEW ANSWERS

1. **B** You will configure the display settings in the Monitor tab of the Advanced Options dialog box. This tab provides information about the model of monitor detected and the monitor's properties. You configure the refresh frequency from here.

2. **B C** When Windows 2000 is installed on a computer with a single integrated video adapter, a driver will be loaded for the on-board device. To install a second video adapter, first shut down the computer and physically install the second video card in an AGP or PCI slot. After Windows starts again, the second adapter will be detected and the driver will be installed. As long as the BIOS is not configured to disable the motherboard video adapter, you will now be able to configure multiple displays. Some motherboard video adapters, however, do not support multiple monitor displays. Laptop computers, for example, often have video adapters that are disabled when connected to a docking station that has a video card.

3. **B C** A computer without an APM-compliant BIOS, or a computer that supports ACPI, will not have an APM tab in the Power Options Properties dialog box. Windows 2000 can still provide limited power management features, like disk and monitor power control, but there will be no APM tab from which to configure this behavior. ACPI functions are fully controlled by the operating system and are automatic. You can change individual power management settings in the Power Options Properties dialog box, but you cannot enable and disable system ACPI support.

4. **B D F** After connecting a Plug and Play modem to the computer, the Install New Modem screen appears (it is actually part of the Add/Remove Hardware Wizard) and automatically detects the modem. If a modem cannot be detected, you are prompted to select the appropriate model. You will usually have to point to a driver location in this case, and an .inf (information)

file will be read to present the list of devices to set up. From the Add/Remove Hardware Wizard, you can select the Add A New Device option on the Choose A Hardware Device dialog box. After selecting an option and clicking Next, you can either search for new hardware or select one from an existing list. From here, the process will look similar to adding a Plug and Play device. Clicking Add in the Modems tab in the Phone and Modem Options dialog box opens the Install New Modem screen of the Add/Remove Hardware Wizard.

5. **A** This question is a bit tricky, because it asks the first thing you should suspect. It is possible that the device is not supported by Windows 2000, or that the USB port is damaged, but it would be best to start with a check of the BIOS here. As USB is a relatively new interface, Windows 2000 Professional will support most devices that use it. You are more likely to run into problems with older devices.

6. **B** Serial ports are an older interface developed before the days of Plug and Play, so it's unlikely that devices attached to a serial port will be detected automatically and installed. You are more likely to expect this behavior on a USB-connected device (see question 5). In this case, you should use the Add/Remove Hardware Wizard to locate and install the IrDA device.

7. **A** You can update drivers through a variety of methods, but Device Manager is the only valid choice in this question. The last two are fictional utilities. To update a driver, access the properties of the device from Device Manager, and then from the Driver tab, click Update Driver to begin the driver upgrade process.

8. **A B C D** All of these conditions will cause automatic driver installation to be skipped, requiring a manual install of a driver. Some devices use a device driver interface that is separate from the Windows 2000 Professional Setup routine.

9. **B** You are assuming that the computer here is capable of supporting a second processor. To change the installed HAL, start Device Manager, expand the Computer node, and access the Properties dialog box for the Computer node. From there, click the Update Driver button to start the Upgrade Device Driver Wizard.

10. **A** SMP is a multiprocessor architecture in which all permission processors share the same memory containing a single copy of the operating system and one copy of each running application. The Windows 2000 Professional kernel divides the instructions that need to be processed into distinct units called *threads*, and threads can be sent to each processor for execution.

CHAPTER 6

Monitoring and Optimizing System Performance and Reliability

ITINERARY

- **Objective 6.01** Configure, Manage, and Troubleshoot the Task Scheduler

- **Objective 6.02** Manage, and Troubleshoot the Use of Offline Files

- **Objective 6.03** Optimize and Troubleshoot Performance of the Windows 2000 Professional Desktop

- **Objective 6.04** Manage Hardware Profiles

- **Objective 6.05** Recover System State Data and User Data

	NEWBIE	SOME EXPERIENCE	EXPERT
ETA	4 hours	2 hours	1 hour

This chapter deals with issues that will help keep your Windows 2000 Professional computer operating in tip-top shape. One of the first things you can do to make your administrative life easier, and to keep you computer running smoothly, is to automate some of the common tasks that need to be done on a daily, weekly, or monthly basis.

It's also very important to determine exactly the performance level of your system. This is a job that starts with the ability to measure and monitor what's happening with the performance of components such as processors, memory, hard disks, and the like. The performance of these components determines the overall efficiency at which your system is running.

Sometimes, one computer will need to use two or more separate hardware configurations. If this is the case, it is best to create a hardware profile, which will specify that certain hardware will be enabled or disabled, depending on the properties of the profile. As you will see, hardware profiles are most often used with users of laptop computers, a group that will also have the most need for Offline Files. Offline Files ensure that users have access to the same set of files whether they are connected to the network or traveling.

In modern networks, it is common for users to take work with them either on the road or at home. To easily facilitate this, Windows 2000 provides Offline Files, which helps keep documents and other working data in sync whether the user is working on or off the network. Users always have access to the latest updates of a particular file.

In this chapter, we'll talk about how to recover in the event of a system failure. Windows 2000 provides a utility called Windows Backup that makes backing up user data a snap, and it's a utility that can by scheduled to run at regular intervals as well.

Configure, Manage, and Troubleshoot the Task Scheduler

Objective 6.01

Windows 2000 includes two utilities, the Scheduled Task Wizard and the AT command-line utility, that make use of the Task Scheduler service. As you probably have guessed, the job of the Task Scheduler is to allow you to configure operation of tasks to run at specified intervals. You can have Windows 2000 Professional run any program, script, or document at a predefined time—which can be every day, week, month, or even when the computer starts up or when a user logs on. Common uses of Scheduled Tasks include regular backups, virus scans, and disk cleanup. You can even use the Scheduled Tasks utility to run tasks at remote computers.

Starting and configuring a task to run using the Scheduled Task Wizard is straightforward. You launch the program with the applet located in the Control

Panel, or choose Start | Programs | Accessories | System Tools | Scheduled Tasks. The Scheduled Tasks window appears, as shown in Figure 6-1.

1. From the Scheduled Tasks window, you can access a task to configure by double-clicking the Add Scheduled Task icon. The Scheduled Task Wizard will then lead you through the steps to create a scheduled task.
2. Click Next to see the tasks that can be run, as shown in Figure 6-2. You can select a job from the list of applications presented here or Browse for another, even one stored on a remote computer.
3. In the next couple of dialog boxes, you will be asked to specify exactly when you want the task to run. Depending on the frequency of the task, you will be given the options to further modify the schedule as applicable to your time frame.
4. The final dialog box summarizes your Scheduled Task selections. Verify that the information is correct, click Finish, and the task will be saved with a .job file extension and added to your Scheduled Tasks window.

If at any time you change your mind about how and when you want the scheduled task to run, no problem. You can manage the properties of that task whenever you like in the Scheduled Tasks program by right-clicking the task and choosing Properties.

The task's Properties dialog box has three tabs with an optional Security tab that appears only on an NTFS partition. You can use the options on these tabs for managing and modifying how the task is to run, including a tab that lets you specify who can further manage the task. Let's take a look at these configuration options.

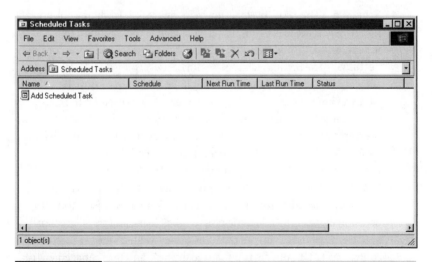

FIGURE 6-1   The Scheduled Tasks window

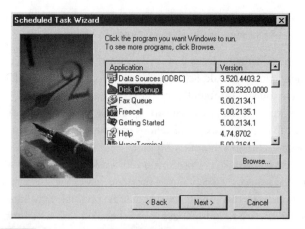

FIGURE 6-2   Choosing which Task to run

- **Task**   Here you configure the command-line program that actually runs
  the task, enter comments for informational purposes (helpful if other
  people will be managing the scheduled task), and add the user name and
  password that will be used to represent this task when the program is
  run. This information is vital because many common administrative
  tasks require a higher level of rights than a normal user account typically
  has. Finally, you can even disable the task without deleting it by clearing a
  single check box. The task will be enabled by default. Figure 6-3 shows
  the Task tab.
- **Schedule**   The Schedule tab, shown in Figure 6-4, is where you can
  modify when the task is run. When you change the option in the
  Schedule Task drop down box, the rest of the options change accordingly.
- **Settings**   The Settings tab assists with housekeeping details such as
  allowing you to delete a task if it is not to be run again or stop the task if it
  takes too long to complete. The Idle Time section is useful if the computer
  must be idle for the task to run. You can specify that the task be stopped if
  the computer is not idle. The Power Management section comes in handy
  if the task runs or may be run on a computer that is battery-powered.
  Figure 6-5 shows the options configurable from the Settings tab.
- **Security**   The Security tab will appear only on an NTFS partition.
  Normally, only administrators can manage Scheduled Tasks. You may
  occasionally want to assign the task to other users, and those users may
  need permissions to run the task. The Security tab contains an access
  control list (ACL) of who can manage the task, and the management of
  this list is no different than managing access to folders and files, as discussed in Chapter 2. Figure 6-6 shows the Security tab.

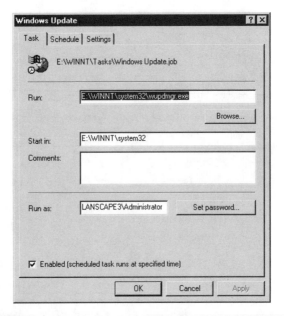

FIGURE 6-3   The Task tab of the Properties dialog box

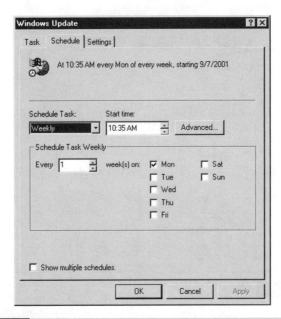

FIGURE 6-4   The Schedule tab

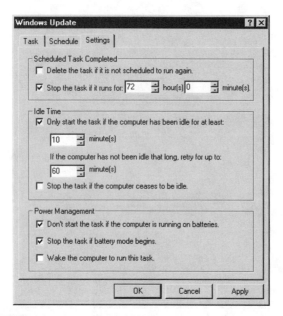

FIGURE 6-5 The Settings tab

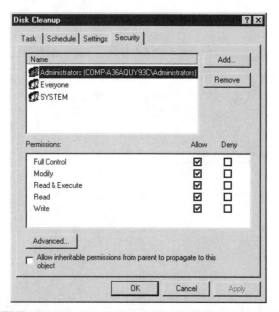

FIGURE 6-6 The Security tab

Tasks can also be scheduled the old-fashioned way, using the AT utility, which literally tells programs or scripts to run AT a certain time. The AT utility is a holdover from earlier versions of Windows and has been carried forward for use in the Windows 2000 environment. You won't be tested on the exact syntax of the AT command, but as a reference the syntax can be reviewed by typing AT /? from the command line. Just typing AT without any parameters lists all the scheduled commands.

The tasks configured this way will also appear in the Scheduled Tasks window, but they are further managed from the command line. You can modify AT-configured tasks with the Scheduled Tasks applet, but be aware of what happens if you do. If you modify a task with Scheduled Tasks that has been originally scheduled with the AT command, Scheduled Tasks will remove the task from the AT job list and make it a Scheduled Task.

Either interface, however, lets you easily schedule, reschedule, disable, or remove a task.

Travel Advisory

It is possible to configure certain jobs to run on a schedule through other interfaces, like the Windows Backup utility. However, understand that even though the jobs are scheduled with a different program, they still rely on the Task Scheduler service to launch successfully. In other words, when you're scheduling a backup job with the Backup utility, you're still using the Task Scheduler.

Management of tasks is done by reviewing which tasks the Task Scheduler service has attempted to start. As mentioned, you can manage an individual task by accessing its Properties dialog box. This places a summary of potential management changes at your fingertips. More detailed results are contained in the Task log, which is stored in the %systemroot% directory and is called SCHEDLGU.TXT. When problems are encountered during scheduled task operation, the log file can be an important troubleshooting aid. The log file is the best tool to help you pinpoint exactly why a task is not running. View a log file, as shown in Figure 6-7, by choosing the View Log command from the Advanced menu of the Scheduled Tasks window.

Other important management tasks can be configured from the Advanced menu, including notification options when a task is missed, pausing and resuming the Task Scheduler service, and configuring the user account context for tasks scheduled with the AT command. The user context configuration is especially

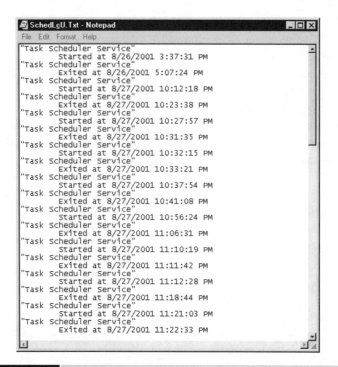

```
SchedLgU.Txt - Notepad                          _ □ ×
File  Edit  Format  Help
"Task Scheduler Service"
      Started at 8/26/2001 3:37:31 PM
"Task Scheduler Service"
      Exited at 8/26/2001 5:07:24 PM
"Task Scheduler Service"
      Started at 8/27/2001 10:12:18 PM
"Task Scheduler Service"
      Exited at 8/27/2001 10:23:38 PM
"Task Scheduler Service"
      Started at 8/27/2001 10:27:57 PM
"Task Scheduler Service"
      Exited at 8/27/2001 10:31:35 PM
"Task Scheduler Service"
      Started at 8/27/2001 10:32:15 PM
"Task Scheduler Service"
      Exited at 8/27/2001 10:33:21 PM
"Task Scheduler Service"
      Started at 8/27/2001 10:37:54 PM
"Task Scheduler Service"
      Exited at 8/27/2001 10:41:08 PM
"Task Scheduler Service"
      Started at 8/27/2001 10:56:24 PM
"Task Scheduler Service"
      Exited at 8/27/2001 11:06:31 PM
"Task Scheduler Service"
      Started at 8/27/2001 11:10:19 PM
"Task Scheduler Service"
      Exited at 8/27/2001 11:11:42 PM
"Task Scheduler Service"
      Started at 8/27/2001 11:12:28 PM
"Task Scheduler Service"
      Exited at 8/27/2001 11:18:44 PM
"Task Scheduler Service"
      Started at 8/27/2001 11:21:03 PM
"Task Scheduler Service"
      Exited at 8/27/2001 11:22:33 PM
```

FIGURE 6-7   Viewing the Scheduled Tasks log

important because everything that happens in the Windows 2000 operating system—*everything*—happens in the context of a user account.

Exam Tip

A task cannot be scheduled, run, or modified if the Task Scheduler service is stopped. (Check the Services running from Computer Management; the service runs by default.) It must be either running or paused.

Manage and Troubleshoot the Use of Offline Files

One of the design objectives of Windows 2000 Professional was to bring the performance and security of the NT platform to a laptop computer, and make it a whole lot easier to manage and configure on laptops than NT. Offline

Files is one of the tools that help achieve this goal, and it's a welcome departure from the previous iteration of Offline Files, an albatross you may remember called My Briefcase.

The Offline Files feature in Windows 2000 Professional synchronizes files from a network to a local hard disk, ensuring that the files are always available, even if either server or client computer is disconnected from the network. It is especially useful for mobile computers for obvious reasons, but it's also well-suited for networked desktop computers for less obvious ones. For example, Offline Files can increase the performance of the network because users work on a local copy of the file instead of accessing files over the network.

Offline Files are made available the same way that other file resources are made available, through folder sharing. Because the Offline Files mechanism is built on the technologies of sharing, it is probably useful here to jog your memory about some of these fundamental concepts:

- On a Microsoft Windows 2000 network, the computer that hosts the share does so because it runs the Server service (called File and Print Sharing for Microsoft Networks on Windows 9x).
- The computer that accesses the share is the client, running the Workstation service, which is the client redirector on 2000 machines. (It's called Client for Microsoft Networks on Windows 9x computers.)
- Now here's the really important part, because it has to do with how computers in a Microsoft network exchange files. Both the Server service and the Workstation client redirector are using the same file sharing protocol, Server Message Blocks (SMB), for network communication. This combination of Microsoft networking components is worth mentioning again because it is the only one that supports the use of Offline Files. You cannot set up offline files with a Novell NetWare Network, although you can synchronize folders that are shared from Windows NT 4 or 9x computers. Novell computers use NetWare Core Protocol (NCP) as their file and print sharing protocol.

After sharing a resource, the Offline Files feature is either enabled and configured centrally using Group Policies, or it is configured independently on each computer that needs the ability to access files when not connected to the network.

Setting Up Offline Files

Configuring Offline Files is a two-step process. The first step is done through the Offline Files tab of the Folder Options dialog box, as shown in Figure 6-8. Once you locate this tab, verify that the Enable Offline Files box is checked. This gives your computer the ability to use offline files. This checkbox is enabled by default.

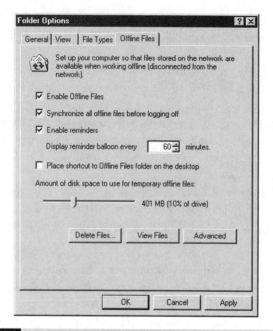

FIGURE 6-8   The Folder Options dialog box

The second step in this process is telling your computer exactly what shares you want available offline. This can be done one of two ways: performed on the server or performed on the client side. Client side configuration is the more common practice, so we'll explain it here.

1. Right-click a network share, and choose Make Available Offline, as shown in Figure 6-9. This launches the Offline Files Wizard, which runs the first time you create an offline file or folder.

2. The Wizard asks you questions about how you want the synchronization of the Offline Files to behave, and asks if you want a shortcut placed on your desktop.

3. When you are done answering these, the offline files are copied to your local machine, and you see that the share has been enabled for offline access by the new double-arrow icon (it looks like a Yin/Yang symbol, sort of). From now on, you won't be led through the Offline Files Wizard when you make additional files available offline.

Enabling and configuring Offline Files initiates an upgrade of the %system-root%\Csc folder with offline file cache information. The Client Side Cache (CSC) is the database for the cached offline files. You see several folders there when

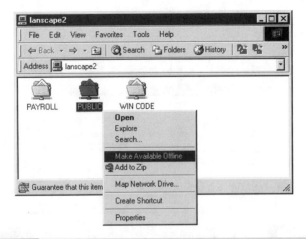

FIGURE 6-9 Making a share available offline

Offline Files are enabled, but Windows names them with cryptic names, so looking through this folder structure won't do you a lot of good.

There are also two ways in which copies of Offline Files can be created at the client computer. One of these ways is from the Server, where connections made to the share will initiate that an offline copy be made. The other way is from the client, which lets a user specify what Offline Files will be made available.

Automatic Caching

Files are not automatically synchronized as a result of enabling and configuring Offline Files. Instead, files are made available offline through either automatic file caching or manual file caching. Automatic file caching copies any files selected or opened to the client cache. Automatic file caching is configured from the server side, at the share level, so that files below the share are also configured for automatic file caching. This is a bit of a fascist take on offline files, as you are not giving any choice to the clients about the files available offline. The files will be available whether the client likes it or not.

In the Caching Settings dialog box, which you access from the Sharing tab of the folder (refer to Chapter 2 for how to access this dialog box), the default setting on the share is for Manual Caching of Documents. This must be changed to support automatic caching, as shown in Figure 6-10. The cache size on the client is set by default to be 10 percent of the total logical disk capacity on the

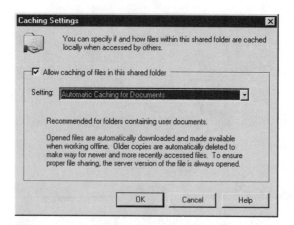

FIGURE 6-10   Setting automatic caching in the Caching Settings dialog box

drive holding the \Csc folder, but this parameter is adjustable. Files automatically cached are not guaranteed to be available on the cache for this reason, as cached files are automatically deleted on a First In, First Out (FIFO) basis when the cache approaches the maximum configured size.

Manual Caching

Files are made permanently available offline through manual file caching, which is done from the client side of things and is a little bit more of a democratic approach. It lets users choose what they want offline. Use the Offline Files Wizard to make files permanently available offline. Launch the Offline Files Wizard by selecting a share and then choosing Make Available Offline from the File menu (or right-click to access the context menu and choose the command from there). The share must be located on a remote computer and it must be configured for caching, or the Make Available Offline option will not appear on the menu.

Certain file types cannot be cached, such as .pst (Microsoft Outlook personal store files) and .mdb (Microsoft Access database files). You can modify this, however, by changing the exclusion list through the Files Not Cached Group Policy setting.

No matter what type of file synchronization you have configured, it will be carried out according to one of the following events: logon, logoff, idle time, or a fixed schedule. To accomplish manual synchronization, in Windows Explorer, choose Tools | Synchronize to open the Items To Synchronize dialog box. Then click the Synchronize button. To configure synchronization settings, click the Setup button in the Items To Synchronize dialog box.

Travel Advisory

I always get the same question in class: What happens if more than one user is synchronizing a file? Whose copy gets saved? The answer is that the last one to make the sync wins. Preventing this really has nothing to do with Offline Files, however. If you don't want users overwriting each other's files, don't give them all change permission to the same file.

Here are a couple of other notes about situations where conflicts can arise between the network version of a file and the copy you are working with offline:

- If someone else makes changes to the same network file that you have updated offline, you can keep your version, keep the one on the network, or keep both. To save both versions of the file, give your version a different file name, and both files will appear in both locations.
- If you delete a network file on your computer while working offline but someone else on the network makes changes to that file, the file is deleted from your computer but not from the network.
- If you change a network file while working offline but someone else on the network deletes that file, you can choose to save your version onto the network or delete it from your computer.

As you can see, the tendency is to ensure that a file is not accidentally deleted, or that someone does not delete a file even though you would rather keep a copy.

Objective 6.03

Optimize and Troubleshoot Performance of the Window 2000 Professional Desktop

Before optimizing the performance of Windows 2000 Professional, you need some way of measuring current performance. You should be able to measure and quantify your performance observations, at least to the people who are responsible for releasing the funds so that upgrades can occur.

Two tools that ship with Windows 2000 Professional help track system performance: the System Monitor and the Performance Logs and Alerts utility. You access both of these tools through the preconfigured Performance snap-in on the Microsoft Management Console (MMC), which can be found by choosing Start | Programs | Administrative Tools. This section takes a look at the use of these two tools and what they can be used for, and then spends some time with how you will use either or both to measure specific areas of Windows 2000 desktop performance.

Before you can accurately measure abnormal use on your system, you have to go about defining normal use. This process of appraising normal use is also known as establishing a *baseline*.

Local Lingo

Benchmarking   Sometimes establishing a baseline is described as *benchmarking* a system. No matter what you call it, the question answered by the process is the same: what is normal for this machine?

In real-world use, there is probably no great need to establish baselines for each and every one of your enterprise's computers. You should certainly do this, however, on any servers that will form the backbone of your network, because if these machines perform poorly, so will your entire network. You should especially measure baselines at the following times:

- When the computer is first brought online and begins operation
- When any changes are made to the hardware or software configuration

The reason that baselines are useful for the above-mentioned situations is self-evident: when any changes are made to the system, you will have something to which you can compare the changes. Like a weight-loss advertisement, you will create a "before" snapshot that you can compare to the "after." Good administrative practice is to make sure baselines have been created before making any changes to your Windows 2000 Professional computer.

Another way these two tools are used is to identify a bottleneck. A bottleneck is any system resource that causes slowdowns to the computer system as a whole. Bottlenecks cause slowdowns by causing other resources to sit around while the source of the bottleneck completes its task. The thing you need to keep in mind about bottlenecks is that there's *always* a bottleneck. The computer won't operate at the speed of light. (Not for now...but they will someday. Scientists have been able to send music from one place to another faster than the speed of light. But that is another book, by a different author...)

So, upgrading a component to resolve a bottleneck in one area can shift the focus of a bottleneck to another area. It's just a matter of finding and resolving the ones that are causing a noticeable degradation of performance. Same thing happens when you buy a new pair of shoes: as soon as you throw 'em in your closet, your old ones in there don't look so great anymore.

The other monitoring duty you have is to proactively find *trends* that are occurring on a system. This job goes hand in hand with the creation of baselines and is really nothing more than comparing multiple baselines against one another to determine whether usage patterns emerge. For example, suppose you are taking snapshots of normal usage for one day a month, and the log files show that CPU usage is increasing by about 5 percent each time you measure. You can then assume that within eight months' time, your CPU usage will increase by 40 percent, and you're going to have problems. By tracking trends, you can proactively take steps to ensure that certain performance problems never occur. (Steven Covey would be proud. That's a *Seven Habits of Highly Effective People* reference, which I doubt many computer books contain.)

System Monitor

A picture is worth a thousand words, and the System Monitor helps you create pictures from the data that is collected during monitoring. The System Monitor is part of the Performance Console that lets you easily display data generated from either real-time activity or from log files. When you first open System Monitor, you'll notice that nothing is tracked by default. To start making use of the tool, you must tell the System Monitor exactly what to track. You do this by adding *instances of counters* of certain *objects* to the current graph in the Add Counters dialog box, as shown in Figure 6-11. To access this dialog box, either right-click any area in System Monitor graph and choose Add Counters, or click the plus-sign icon above the System Monitor graph.

Local Lingo

Object   The individual system resource that can be monitored.

Counter   A unit of performance of that object that can be quantified numerically.

Instance of a counter   A further subdivision of a counter. For example, on a system with two processors, there can be three instances of the %Processor Time counter: one for processor 1, one for processor 2, and a third instance for Total processor time.

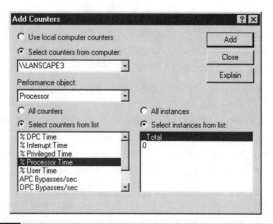

FIGURE 6-11   The Add Counters dialog box

When you start using System Monitor, the options available can be a little overwhelming. Don't worry; nobody outside of Redmond has a thorough understanding of every single counter that can be tracked with System Monitor. You won't be able to memorize every aspect of the System Monitor, so don't try. The important thing to remember, both for exam purposes and for real-world use, is which counters are most effective for measuring everyday usage of a system. You will have to experiment with the System Monitor, of course, to get comfortable with this tool, but one nice feature is a detailed description of what each counter does that pops up when you click the Explain button from the Add Counters dialog box as you go to add a counter. You can see what happens when you click this button in Figure 6-12.

To further explain what I mean about *getting a handle* on the System Monitor, think about the areas that have the greatest impact on the vast majority of systems. What are they? In the order of importance, the resources that have the greatest impact on performance are *memory, processor, network,* and *disk*. It's the old 80/20 rule (20 percent of your work takes 80 percent of your time) at work, and we've just considerably whittled down our list of objects to which we need to give our day-to-day attention. Of the possible counters for these objects, some are going to be more helpful than others when taking performance snapshots. In the following sections, the most common counters that are measured on the most important objects will be noted.

Memory Performance

Consider the metaphor of the desktop as it applies to the computer. Windows has been using this metaphor for years because it is an *anchor,* a link to something that we are

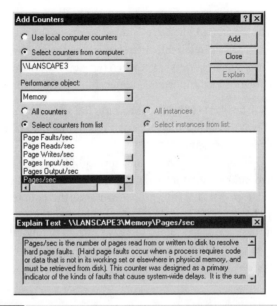

FIGURE 6-12 The contents of the Explain button

already familiar with, and something we've had an understanding of for years—a desk—that helps us relate to this entirely new tool, a computer operating system.

You can also extend this metaphor to help you understand most computer hardware. If you think of your brain as the CPU, all the stuff on your office desk is the area of memory. It is the place you first look when you want to "process" more information. If the information you are looking for is on your desk, that's great, and you can access it quickly. If not, you have to go to the filing cabinet to retrieve the information you want. The bigger the desk space you have, the more things will quickly be at your fingertips when you want to work with them.

Memory is the most common cause of system bottlenecks. There is virtually no way for a system to have too much memory, and it is a great starting point as you begin to look for bottlenecks. To find out how much memory your system is using, you need to examine two main areas: physical memory and the page file.

Physical memory is the physical sticks of RAM that hold all the 1's and 0's that make up the instructions of an application, an operating system, or a hardware device. Each location in memory is given a memory address, which is how the CPU keeps track of what application is placing instructions where. So to applications, RAM is simply a long list of numbers that it sees as available. Again, you can't have too much and it's next to free.

The page file is logical memory that exists in a file called pagefile.sys located on the root of the drive Windows has been installed on. Like physical RAM, the page file is a list of addressable locations. In fact, applications have no idea whether or not the instructions it is sending to memory are kept on the page file or in physical RAM. The one who can tell the difference is you, the user, who will notice a considerable slowdown in performance when the page file is accessed frequently.

Following are the most important counters for monitoring memory:

- **Memory—Available MBytes**   Measures the amount of available memory that is available to run a process. If this number is less than 4MB, you should add more memory.
- **Memory—Pages/Sec**   Shows the number of times that the processor requested information that was not in physical memory and had to be retrieved from disk. For optimal performance, this counter should be set at around 4 or 5.
- **Paging file—%Usage**   Indicates how much of the allocated page file is currently in use. If this number is consistently larger than 99 percent, you may need to add memory.

Exam Tip

Because of the page file, systems that are short on memory will often report high disk usage. This is because the disk is being asked all the time for instructions that should be living in physical memory. See the exam tip in the "Disk Performance" section. Fix the memory problem and the high disk usage problem disappears.

Processor Utilization

It's a rare case that a processor is the source of a bottleneck. Most people buy much more processor than they really need. Then again, people buy SUV's and drive to their own block parties. After all, how fast do you need that e-mail to open anyway?

However, if you suspect that your processor is cause for concern, you should monitor the following counters:

- **Processor—%Processor Time**   Measures the time that the processor is busy responding to system requests. If this value is consistently above 80 percent, you may indeed have a processor bottleneck.
- **Processor—Interrupts/Sec**   Shows the average number of times each second the processor is interrupted by hardware requests for attention.

This number should generally be below 3500. However, problems in this area indicate a problem with hardware that may be malfunctioning and sending unnecessary interrupts.

Disk Performance

Disk access is the amount of time it takes your disk subsystem to retrieve data that is requested by the operating system. You can monitor two objects when measuring disk performance. The PhysicalDisk object is a sum of all logical drives on a single hard disk, and the LogicalDisk object represents a single logical disk. The following counters can be tracked for both the PhysicalDisk and LogicalDisk object; the PhysicalDisk is used in this example:

- **PhysicalDisk—%Disk Time**   Shows the amount of time a disk is busy responding to read and write requests. If the disk is busy more than 90 percent of the time, you can improve performance by adding another disk channel and splitting the I/O requests between the channels.
- **PhysicalDisk—%Current Disk Queue Length**   Indicates the number of outstanding disk requests that are waiting to be processed. This value should be less than 2.

Exam Tip

High disk counter measurements can result from high usage of your paging file, which is an indicator of low memory, not of a disk that needs to be upgraded. Just wanted to remind you.

Network Performance

The measurement of network performance is usually done by looking at the network as a whole, not the performance of an individual computer. Windows 2000 Professional does not include a tool for monitoring the entire network, but you can monitor the traffic that is being sent and received on the local network card, as well as the performance of any protocols bound to that card. Here are the network counters that you will find most useful:

- **Network Interface—Bytes Total/Sec**   Measures the total number of bytes sent and received from the network interface card (NIC). It does not specify which protocol, instead looking at total traffic. You can compare this number against the total bandwidth capacity of your card. You should not exceed 30 percent of your card's total Megabits per second (Mbps) rating for extended periods.

- **TCP—Segments/Sec**   Filters and measures the number of bytes that are sent or received from the network interface that are TCP-specific.

By the way, how does one go about fixing these problems when bottlenecks are detected? In a word, *upgrade*. In other words, add more memory, swap out to a better processor if the motherboard allows, use faster drives or a striping array, and get a faster NIC of at least 100Mbps.

Application Performance

If you are consistently running multiple applications concurrently on your Windows 2000 Professional system, there are a couple of ways to optimize performance.

To configure application performance, from the Control Panel, double-click the System icon and select the Advanced tab. (You can also right-click My Computer and choose Properties.) From there, click the Performance Options button to display the Performance Options dialog box, as shown in Figure 6-13.

The Performance Options dialog box allows you to configure application response so that foreground applications are always given a higher performance priority, which is the default, or so that foreground applications and background services are given the same priority. You might want to consider changing the application response option to background services if your Windows 2000 Professional system is frequently accessed as a file or print server.

You can also set the paging file (virtual memory) size and location from here. To review, the page file is the physical location of logical memory—memory that exists on the hard drive. Windows manages virtual memory, and it would be rare

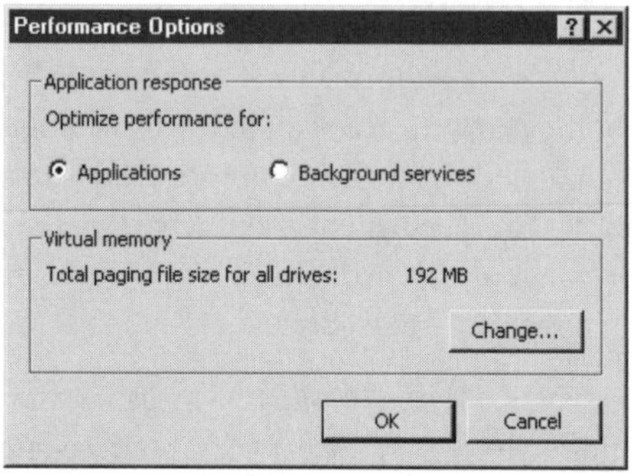

FIGURE 6-13   The Performance Options dialog box

for an administrator to change any of the virtual memory settings on a Windows 2000 Professional computer. It is possible to improve virtual memory slightly by moving the paging file, pagefile.sys, to a faster hard drive. You can configure this by clicking the Change button on the Performance Options dialog box. Then, from the Virtual Memory dialog box, as seen in Figure 6-14, you can change the location of the page file by selecting the desired drive, choosing the Initial Size and the Maximum Size settings, and clicking Set. You can also improve virtual memory performance by setting the paging file's initial size and maximum size to be the same. This step will greatly reduce fragmentation of the swap file, thus making virtual memory access more efficient. Keep in mind, however, that these steps will only produce incremental increases in memory performance.

Of course, the best way to optimize the use of virtual memory is not to use it—install more physical memory instead, which is approximately 1000 times faster than virtual memory.

Objective 6.04   Manage Hardware Profiles

When you set up hardware profiles, you specify different hardware configurations to be used when Windows 2000 Professional is started. You manage

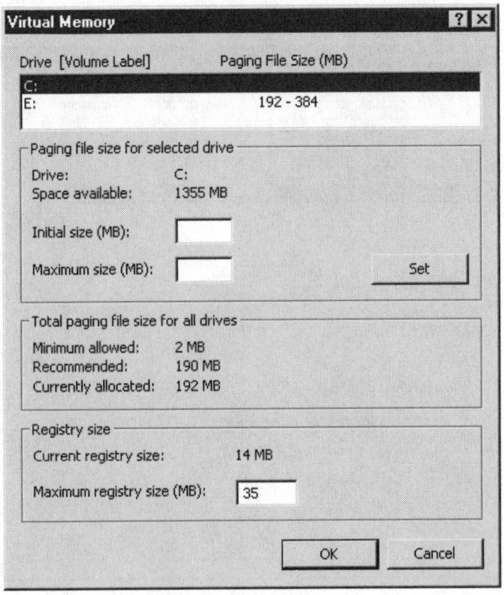

FIGURE 6-14   Altering the default Virtual Memory Settings

hardware profiles through the Hardware Profiles dialog box, which is accessed by launching the System program in Control Panel. In the System Properties dialog box, click the Hardware tab and then click the Hardware Profiles button. You see the dialog box shown in Figure 6-15.

The default hardware profile is created when you install Windows 2000 and is made up from the devices that are attached to your computer at the time. The name of this first profile will always be Profile 1, but this can be changed if you feel the need. (Renaming might make the profile a little more user friendly if you plan to configure additional hardware profiles in the future; otherwise it won't make any difference because you won't be presented with the option to choose a profile.)

The actual contents of a hardware profile can be set and edited using Device Manager. You can use Device Manager to either enable or disable the use of certain hardware devices. On the General tab of the device's Properties dialog box, select the Device Usage drop-down box to specify whether the device is enabled for all profiles, disabled for the current profile, or disabled for all profiles, as shown in Figure 6-16.

What's more, you can also configure the behavior of certain services as part of the hardware profile. For example, you might not want the Messenger service to run as a part of an offline profile.

You can open the Services MMC snap-in from the Administrative Tools section in the Start menu. To access the Properties of a particular service, simply

FIGURE 6-15   The Hardware Profiles dialog box

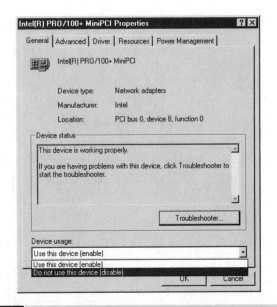

FIGURE 6-16   Disabling a device in Device Manager

double-click the services name in the details pane. From the Services program, access the properties of the Messenger service. Then, on the Log On tab in the service Properties dialog box, select the hardware profile appearing in the You Can Enable Or Disable This Service For The Hardware Profiles Listed Below list box, as shown in Figure 6-17. Then click Enable or Disable to change the state of the service for the selected profile.

The results of the changes made in either Device Manager or the Services applet are saved to the current hardware profile upon shutdown and are used again the next time the hardware profile is selected. For example, suppose you disable the network card on your laptop and shut down. The next time you boot up, your network card will be disabled. Why? Because you're using a hardware profile that has the network card disabled.

As mentioned, most users will never need a second hardware profile, because on a desktop computer there is little need for a device to be enabled one day and disabled the next. A common use for hardware profiles is on laptop computers, especially those with a network card that will not be needed when the computer is used without network connectivity.

To create a second hardware profile, access the Hardware Profiles dialog box (shown in Figure 6-15) and click Copy to copy an existing profile. Once you have the second hardware profile configured, the bottom half of the Hardware Profiles dialog box comes into play. From the Hardware Profiles Selection section, you can

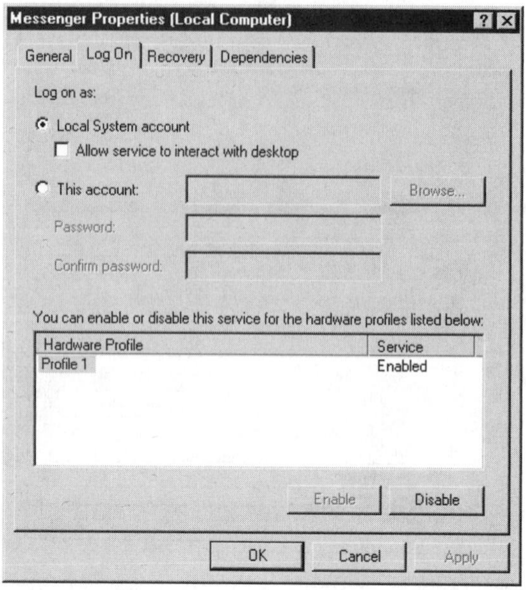

FIGURE 6-17   Disabling a service as a part of a hardware profile

tell Windows to either wait until you specify a hardware profile or select the first profile after a given time interval, which is 30 seconds by default. The first profile in the list is what Windows 2000 considers the default profile.

You can then choose either profile at startup time and configure away with the Device Manager and the Services applet. Additionally, you can specify whether or not the computer is portable and whether or not a docking station is used by looking at the Properties dialog box of a profile. To open this dialog box, shown in Figure 6-18, simply double-click a Profile name in the Hardware Profiles dialog box.

Travel Advisory

Windows 2000 Professional automatically creates a Docked Profile and an Undocked Profile for a laptop computer if the following conditions are met: it must be fully ACPI compliant, and it must run only Plug and Play compatible device drivers. If these two conditions are met, you should not manually tamper with these two hardware profiles. You probably won't be tested on this information, but you should be aware of this for real-world laptop use.

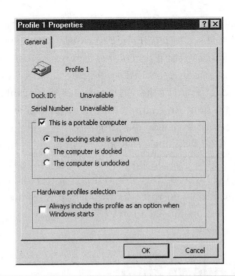

The individual profile Properties dialog box

Recover System State Data and User Data

Objective 6.05

Windows 2000 Professional includes a powerful set of tools and utilities that can help you recover a failed system and the data contained therein. These tools include the Windows Backup, the Advanced Options menu, and the Recovery Console.

Windows Backup

The Windows 2000 Backup utility, as first introduced in Chapter 3, backs up all selected data to a single file that is named with a file extension of .bkf. The destination of this file can be any device that stores files, such as tape devices, removable disks, and even network locations.

The Windows 2000 Backup utility can make use of tape devices just like its predecessor utility in NT 4. But unlike NT 4's Backup utility, the Windows 2000 version can also back up to other media, such as hard drives or even writable CD-ROM's. The Backup utility's executable is called ntbackup.exe, and it can be run from the command prompt or by choosing Start | Programs | Accessories | System Tools. For help using ntbackup from the command line, don't forget the / ? switch, which will guide you in the use of the command line version of this tool.

Windows 2000 Backup is also used to create an Emergency Repair Disk (ERD), which will be used to repair and restart Windows 2000 in the event that your computer will not start or if system files have become corrupt. Good administrative practice is to create an ERD right after a successful installation of Windows 2000, and then update the ERD any time a significant change is made to the system configuration. An example of this would be when you change or upgrade any vital device drivers on the computer.

There are two things you need to know about an ERD right off the bat: the ERD, by default, does not back up any data (there is an exception to this—see the section "Creating the ERD," a little later in this chapter) and it is not a bootable disk. To access the ERD, you must first boot the computer using either the Windows 2000 Professional installation CD-ROM or the setup floppies that can be created from the Setup CD.

Creating Windows 2000 Professional Setup Boot Disks

So how do you make those bootable setup floppy disks? You have to run the command

```
makebt32.exe
```

from a 32-bit client like Windows 2000 or Windows 9x, or run the command

```
makeboot.exe
```

from Windows 16-bit clients such as DOS or Windows for Workgroups 3.11.

Exam Tip

The Windows NT 4 utility to create bootable floppies is called winnt32.exe, which is also the utility that launches installation of the operating system. Microsoft expects you to know the new commands to make bootable floppies.

You can then use these floppy disks to boot to the Windows 2000 Professional OS in the event that your system is not bootable to the hard drive, and able to access the CD-ROM drive. From these floppies, you can perform the following:

- Reinstall the Windows 2000 operating system.
- Use the recovery console.
- Use the ERD.

You will need four floppy disks to make the bootable set. These four Windows 2000 Professional setup disks will not be specific to any one computer—they can be used to boot all computers running Windows 2000 Professional. It is not necessary to keep multiple copies on hand for every computer.

> ### Exam Tip
>
> The setup disks created for Windows 2000 Professional will not work with Windows 2000 Server, and the disks created for Server will not work with Professional.

Remember, though, that you will usually not need the setup floppy disks. Provided your computer supports booting from the CD (and most computers capable of running Windows 2000 do), the Windows 2000 Professional CD-ROM will let you boot the computer and get to the place where you can use the ERD. So you need to use the four setup boot disk only on systems that do not allow you to boot from the Windows 2000 Professional CD.

Creating the ERD

Now, back to using the Backup utility. To create an ERD, click the Emergency Repair Disk button when the Backup utility opens and displays the Welcome screen. This button will bring up the Emergency Repair dialog box, which will prompt you to insert a blank, formatted floppy disk. At this point, you can specify whether you want to back up the Registry as a part of your ERD creation (here's that exception about backing up data, by the way). If the Registry can fit onto the floppy, you should select this option. When you then click OK, the system data will be copied onto the ERD.

Here's what gets saved when you create an ERD:

- The system files
- The partition boot sector
- The startup environment
- The Registry (if you've selected that option)

These items can also be repaired with your new ERD after you've booted the system with the Windows 2000 Professional CD-ROM or startup floppies created, as described above.

Backing Up Data

Now let's get to the core task of using the Backup utility: backing up vital information for the purposes of disaster recovery. You can start this process in two ways. The Backup Wizard, accessible form the Welcome tab of the Backup utility, will walk you through a series of questions that will help you configure backup jobs. You can also set backup jobs manually from the Backup tab.

When you click the Backup Wizard button of the Backup utility's Welcome dialog box, the Backup Wizard will launch and take you through all the steps necessary for a successful backup.

1. Click Next on the Welcome To The Windows 2000 Backup and Recovery Tools dialog box, and you will see the What to Back Up dialog box, as shown in Figure 6-19. This lets you quickly back up everything on your computer, selected files, or the System State. The System State data will be discussed later in the section "Backup Types."

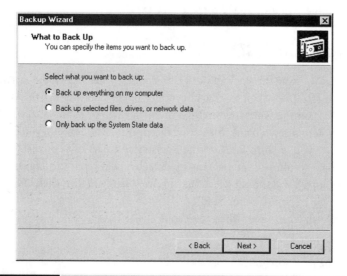

FIGURE 6-19   Selecting what to back up

2. If you choose the Back Up Selected Files, Drives, Or Network Data radio button, the next dialog box to appear is the Items To Back Up dialog, which is really just another way of getting to the Backup tab of the Backup utility tool.
3. After you decide what to back up, click Next to bring up the Where To Store The Backup dialog box. Here you can either type the backup media drive letter and filename or click Browse to navigate to the location.
4. After you've made your selection, the Completing The Backup Wizard dialog box will summarize your choices. If the information is to your satisfaction, click Finish and the backup job will begin.

You can further configure your backup jobs by selecting from several backup options. The Backup Options dialog box, as seen in Figure 6-20, can be accessed by choosing Tools | Options.

Backup Types

To make an informed choice from the Backup Type tab of the Options dialog box, it is important that you understand the differences between the backup types. Furthermore, an understanding of the different backup types requires that you know the significance of the *archive bit*, or *backup marker*, and how different backup types treat this marker. You will set the default backup type from the Backup Type tab, as shown in Figure 6-21.

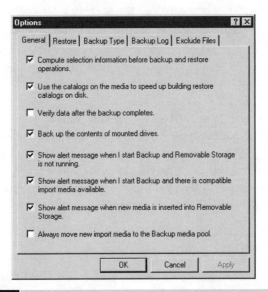

FIGURE 6-20 The General tab of the Backup Options dialog box

FIGURE 6-21 The Backup Type tab

Local Lingo

Archive bit A bit that is set on a file when the file has changed and is removed by certain backup types to "'flag" the file as having been backed up. Some backup types "care" about this flag and some don't.

As you will see in Table 6-1, backup types differ mainly in how they treat the archive bit. Which backup type you choose will depend on factors such as how much data is being backed up and how often, how quickly you want the backup to be performed, and how many backups you ware willing to apply in the event of a restore. For example, differential backups will take longer than incremental backups, but differential will be easier to restore.

Exam Tip

You shouldn't see a lot of questions about the actual use of the Backup utility, but you will likely see a question that requires that you understand the significance between the different backup types.

Table 6-1 shows a summary of the different backup types. Pay special attention to how each treats the archive bit.

TABLE 6.1 Types of Backups	
Backup Type	**Description**
Normal	Backs up all files selected and marks each file as having been backed up; easy to restore.
Copy	Backs up all files selected and does not mark them as being backed up; easy to restore.
Differential	Backs up only the selected files that have changed since the last backup and does not mark them as having been backed up. At restore time, these backups require that the last normal backup be applied before the differential backup is applied.
Incremental	Backs up selected files that have not been marked as archived and sets the archive bit. To perform a restore, requires the last normal backup and all of the incremental backups be applied.
Daily	Backs up only the selected files that have changed today and does not set the archive bit. Requires each daily backup and the last normal backup for a successful restore.

Exam Tip

Users with Administrator or Backup Operator–level privileges can back up and restore any files on the system, even those they cannot otherwise access. Individual users can back up files that they own.

The Windows Backup utility also provides a System State backup option that's used to restore the operating system back to its original state in the case of a catastrophic system failure. (This would usually be applied to a clean OS install to retrieve all configuration changes quickly.) This option appears in Windows Backup as a selection on the Backup tab, and backs up the following on a Windows 2000 Professional installation:

- The Registry
- The Windows 2000 boot files
- System files on the boot partition
- The COM+ Class Registration database

Performing a Restore

A carefully planned backup policy, thorough understanding of the backup types, and all the backups in the world are useless if you are unable to restore your data to its original state. Your most important line of defense in this effort is *a consistent testing of the restoration process.* To ease the restoration procedure, you can use the Restore Wizard to guide you along the way to a successful restore.

To use the Restore Wizard, you should take the following steps.

1. From the Welcome tab of the Backup utility, click the Restore Wizard button.
2. Click the Next button from the wizard's Welcome screen, which will bring up the What to Restore dialog box, as shown in Figure 6-22. This is the heart of this wizard. Click the filename of the backup job you want to restore and click the Next button.
3. After you have selected the backup you want to restore, you can choose to restore the entire session or selectively restore individual drives, folders, or files.
4. The Completing the Restore Wizard dialog box then appears, summarizing your chosen restore options. When you are certain of your selection, click the Finish button to proceed with the restore.

The Removable Storage Service manages tape backups for Windows Backup. File backups to fixed or removable disks are managed directly by Windows Backup. The target of a compressed file backup can be a local disk or a network-accessible share. Windows Backup supports a number of backup types: Normal, Differential, Incremental, Copy, and Daily.

Safe Mode

When you press the F8 key during startup, you will see the Advanced Startup Options menu. From this menu, you can select from three different versions of

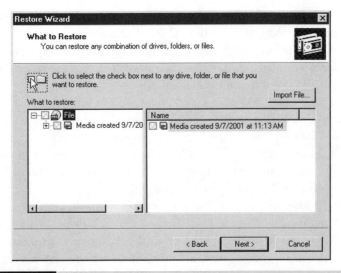

FIGURE 6-22   The What to Restore dialog box

Safe Mode: with networking support, without networking support, and command prompt only. You can use the Safe Mode startup commands to resolve device driver conflicts, system service failures, and even application autostart problems. When the computer is started in Safe Mode, boot logging is automatic. Boot logging can also be configured to occur during normal startups from this Advanced Options menu. You will be able to resolve incompatible display settings using the Enable VGA Mode command. You can also solve system configuration changes that have prevented the operating system from starting by selecting the Last Known Configuration. Troubleshooting the system with a kernel debugger starts by choosing Debugging Mode from the Advanced Options menu.

Recovery Console

If problems persist even after some of the procedures available from the Advanced Options startup menu have failed, you may want to consider using the Recovery Console. The Recovery Console runs a Windows 2000 command interpreter to provide access to the local disk. You start the Recovery Console in one of two ways: either from the Windows 2000 Setup routine or from the local disk. To start from the Setup routine, press R when prompted by the appropriate installation screen; doing so will display the Repair Options screen. From the Repair Options screen, press C to start the Recovery Console.

If you would like to select the recovery console from the Advanced Startup menu, you must keep in mind that the Recovery Console is not installed by default. To install the Recovery Console, open a command prompt window and locate the \i386 folder on the Setup CD-ROM and type `winnt32 /cmdcons`. This local installation will be an easy way to launch the Recovery Console, but often it is needed when local disk access is impossible. In this case, running it from the Setup CD-ROM is the only viable option.

All file systems that Windows 2000 Professional uses are accessible from the Recovery Console. This console includes a number of disk utilities, such as ChkDisk, DiskPart, Fixboot, and Fixmbr. You can also run several file manipulation utilities such as Expand, Md, Rd, and Ren. And if you need help using the Recovery Console, simply type **help** for a list of available commands. To learn about a specific utility, type the utility name and then `/?`.

Using the Recovery Console is a better way to restore a damaged Registry than running an Emergency Repair. This is because the Registry files in the %systemroot%\Repair folder are from the original installation of Windows 2000 Professional, so any changes made after the initial operating system installation are lost when you use the Emergency Repair. Conversely, the Registry data from the %systemroot%\Repair\Regbak folder is the current one.

CHECKPOINT

✔ **Objective 6.01   Configure, Manage, and Troubleshoot the Task Scheduler.** In this objective, we looked at the two utilities that can be used to automate certain tasks. This automation will ease the overhead of day-to-day administration, especially on larger networks.

✔ **Objective 6.02   Manage and Troubleshoot the Use of Offline Files.** This objective looked at the use of Offline Files, which are most often used to keep files synchronized between laptop computers and network servers. We looked at the steps needed to configure a client for Offline Files and ways to automate Offline File usage by changing the server's configuration.

✔ **Objective 6.03   Optimize and Troubleshoot Performance of the Windows 2000 Professional Desktop.** In this objective, we examined two tools that are used in conjunction with a benchmarking and monitoring policy. These tools are the Performance Console and the Task Manager. Each is used to achieve similar, yet distinct, monitoring tasks and are often used in tandem to keep a computer running smoothly.

✔ **Objective 6.04** **Manage Hardware Profiles.** We gained an understanding of hardware profiles and looked at the steps involved in creating additional hardware profiles for a single computer that uses multiple hardware configurations. We also identified some of the instances where this might be most beneficial.

✔ **Objective 6.05** **Recover System State Data and User Data.** This objective looked at the important recovery task of backing up and restoring data on a Windows 2000 machine. We looked at options here that included the different types of backups available, and what those backup types recovery implications were. We also learned about the significance of backing up System State data.

REVIEW QUESTIONS

1. What two methods can you use to create a scheduled task on Windows 2000 Professional?

   A. Open the Control Panel and double-click the Scheduled Tasks program.

   B. Open the Control Panel and double-click the Administrative Tools folder.

   C. On the Start menu, choose Programs | Administrative Tools, and click Scheduled Tasks.

   D. On the Start menu, choose Programs | Accessories | System Tools, and then click Scheduled Tasks.

2. You want to configure a task to run at a specified interval. Additionally, you want to specify how the task will behave. Which of these properties will you not be able to configure as you manage that task?

   A. That the user account will be used to run the task

   B. That the task will not run if the computer is running on batteries

   C. That the task will be run only one time

   D. Whether another task will be run if certain conditions trigger the secondary task

3. You are the administrator for a network of Windows 2000 computers. Most of your data is kept on a Windows 2000 Server, and you want to use Offline Files to synchronize your laptop while you are away from the office. Which computer do you need to configure?

A. Both server and laptop

B. The server

C. The laptop

D. Neither server nor laptop. When Windows 2000 Professional is installed on a laptop, default behavior for the laptop is to enable caching on all shares accessed.

4. Which of the following statements is true about Offline Files?

A. You can use offline files on any computer that is running the SMB protocol.

B. Offline files are available only between computers running a version of Windows 2000.

C. You can access files offline when the sharing computer is on the local network, but not when traffic must cross a WAN connection.

D. Once the Enable Offline Files option is set on the client, any connection to a share is automatically cached.

5. You administer a small peer-to-peer network of Windows 2000 Professional computers. Many of the users have laptops because the nature of their work requires that they be working out of the office quite often. The users need to update offline files kept in a folder on your computer. You want to set things up so that any opened files in this folder are automatically downloaded each time a user connects to the folder. The clients have already configured Offline Files from the Folder Options dialog box. How should you configure the share for automatic download?

A. Share the appropriate folder. From the Shares node of Computer Management, set the Share Properties to Automatically Cache Accessed Files.

B. Share the appropriate folder. On the Sharing tab of the folder's Properties dialog box, click the Caching button and select the Automatic Caching for Documents setting.

C. Share the appropriate folder. On the Sharing tab of the folder's Properties dialog box, click the Caching button and select the Automatic Caching for Accessed Files setting.

D. Share the appropriate folder. On the Sharing tab of the folder's Properties dialog box, click the Caching button and select the Manual Caching for Documents setting.

6. Everything is working properly at your laptop computer, and you have just finished configuring two hardware profiles—one docked, and one undocked. As the name suggests, the docked profile is on the network and the undocked

profile is not. You reboot the computer and then turn away to check your voice mail for the next five minutes. When you return to the computer, you cannot use the company network. What is probably going on?

A. Your network card has just gone out.

B. You have been disconnected by a failure at the hub.

C. The undocked profile has been set as the default hardware profile.

D. The DHCP scope has run out of IP addresses.

7. You have checked out a laptop from your company for out of town meetings. Your laptop is running Windows 2000 Professional, and you want to configure a separate profile that will apply when the computer is used away from the office. What steps should you take before configuring this second hardware profile?

A. Back up the System State data and reboot the computer.

B. Make a copy of the default profile, reboot the computer, select the copied profile, and make changes.

C. Make a copy of the default profile, switch your Current Configuration to the copied profile, and make changes.

D. No preparation is necessary. Two profiles will be created automatically for a Windows 2000 Professional laptop.

8. How many hardware profiles are created on a Windows 2000 Professional by default?

A. None

B. One

C. Two: one for networked and one for standalone

D. Two: one for default user and one for Administrator

9. What methods can you use to repair a Windows 2000 Professional installation that will not start?

A. Use the Recovery Console.

B. Use the Emergency Repair process.

C. Use Directory Services Restore mode.

D. Use the Local System Restore option from the Advanced Options startup menu.

10. What command is used to install the Recovery Console?

A. `Winnt32 /cmdcons`

B. `Winnt32 /console`

C. `Setup.exe /cmdcons`

D. `Setup.exe /console`

11. You are planning a backup strategy for a Windows 2000 Professional computer at a Web design firm. Several graphics files that are regularly changed are stored on a share, and that share, with all its subfolders, can be several gigabytes in size. You want backups to be done every day in the least amount of time possible, but you want the restores to be performed quickly as well. What will your strategy be?

   A. Normal backups

   B. Incremental

   C. Differential

   D. Normal and Differential

   E. Normal and Incremental

12. Cori has just made several changes to the hardware configuration of her Windows 2000 Professional computer, and now she wants to update the Emergency Repair Disk. What utility should she use to do this?

   A. Winnt32 /makebt32

   B. The ERD command line utility, with appropriate switches

   C. The Windows 2000 Backup utility

   D. The RDISK command line utility

REVIEW ANSWERS

1. **A** **D** Double-clicking the Scheduled Tasks in Control Panel opens the Scheduled Tasks window, where you can create or modify scheduled tasks. This Scheduled Tasks window can also be launched from the System Tools program group.

2. **D** This question requires you to have explored a bit beyond the text of the book and taken a peek at the Scheduled Tasks Properties tabs. This option cannot be specified from the task management tools. **A**, **B**, and **C** are incorrect because all of these things can be configured about a given task.

3. **D** Both the server and the laptop. A share must be configured at the server. Caching is automatically enabled and set to Manual Caching For Documents. The client then accesses the share and makes the data available offline by choosing Make Available Offline from the context menu.

4. **A** You can use Offline Files on any computers that are running the SMB protocol, the Microsoft file sharing protocol, regardless of the title of the OS. **B** is wrong because of this; Offline Files are not limited to the 2000 operating system. **C** is wrong because the physical connectivity component is not a concern, just as it is not with sharing. **D** is also incorrect because the client usually has to specify exactly what resources will be available offline by running the Offline Files Wizard.

5. **B** After a folder is shared, it is enabled for manual caching only. Clicking the Caching button opens the Caching Settings dialog box. From there, in the Setting drop-down box, select Automatic Caching For Documents. After a client computer is configured for Offline Files access to this share, opening any file automatically downloads it and makes it available offline.

6. **C** The question asks what is most likely, and **C** is the troubleshooting step you should take first. The default hardware profile will be used after a countdown, which is by default 30 seconds. Answers **A**, **B**, and **D** could all be the cause of lost network function, but none is as likely as the profile problem mentioned here.

7. **B** These are the necessary steps to create and modify a second profile. **A** is incorrect because, while necessary sometimes, backing up the System State will not help in this matter. **C** is incorrect because you cannot switch to the second hardware profile unless you reboot the computer. **D** might be correct if the laptop devices fully support Plug and Play and are ACPI compliant, but no mention of such a configuration is made, so you can't assume this in the scenario. (And you know what happens when we assume.)

8. **B** One hardware profile is created, called Profile 1, containing all of the hardware detected at setup time. Any changes are made to that default profile until a second hardware profile is created. **A** is incorrect because a profile is needed for the computer to start. **C** is incorrect because only one profile is created. **D** is something that would apply to user profiles, not hardware profiles.

9. **A** **B** The Recovery Console provides access so that recovery commands and utilities can be run—for example copying a known good copy of a boot.ini file. The Recovery Console is also the preferred method of restoring a damaged Registry. The Emergency Repair process returns the computer to the state it was in when the operating system was first installed. This is not to say that data is harmed, but any configuration changes that were made to the Registry will be reset. **C** is a valid option from the Advanced

Options Start menu, but only on domain controllers, and the Windows 2000 Professional computer is not one. **D** is incorrect because this is not a valid recovery option.

10. **A** This is the command to install the Recovery Console, which is not installed by default. Choices **B**, **C**, and **D** do not exist, except in my imagination.

11. **D** There's some room for argument here, but combining these two backup types is the best way to balance these two goals. A nightly Differential would backup any changes to the share and could be applied quickly to the last Normal Backup in the event of a restore. **A** is wrong because the Normal backup would back up the whole share, taking too much time. **B** is wrong because there would never be a reference point for the Incremental backup to look for. **C** is wrong for the same reason. These backup types need to be combined with a Normal backup. **E** is wrong because while backups would be a breeze, you would potentially have many Incremental backups to apply in the event of a restore, taking up too much time.

12. **C** The ERD is created through the Windows 2000 Backup utility. **D** was the utility used in NT 4, but it does not work in 2000. **A** is not a viable option. **B** is wrong because there is no ERD command line utility.

Implementing, Managing, and Troubleshooting Protocols and Services

	NEWBIE	SOME EXPERIENCE	EXPERT
ETA	5 hours	3 hours	1.5 hours

247

The focus of this chapter is to explore in detail the mechanics of how Windows 2000 Professional participates in a network. We'll look at the languages spoken and rules followed when computers are exchanging information. We'll also examine how computers establish connections to one another and share information.

We will explore the Transmission Control Protocol/Internet Protocol (TCP/IP) and how it relates to networked computing. Make no mistake: The material presented in this chapter is not optional. You will need to know how TCP/IP works, no matter where your next step in the computer field takes you.

The services of TCP/IP have evolved with the explosion of computer networks, and more specifically with the development of the largest computer network on the planet, the Internet. Al Gore's one-time claim notwithstanding, TCP/IP was originally developed during the 1970s by the Department of Defense for the same reason that the interstate highway system was developed: to get things across the country quickly using many possible routes in case one of those routes was bombed. Since then, the TCP/IP protocol suite has been improved and added to by the open standards community. So because no one really owns the protocol, and because hundreds of programmers are constantly looking at ways to improve its performance and flexibility, it has become an excellent way to connect dissimilar networks, as in the case of the Internet.

The design of Windows 2000 tightly integrates with these dependable, tested, and open-standard Internet technologies. Therefore, knowledge of how to configure and maintain a TCP/IP network is knowledge of how Windows 2000 operates in a network environment.

Services like dial-up networking and virtual private networks (VPNs) allow us to extend a local TCP/IP network across wide geographic boundaries, without any change in how the network functions. Dial-up networking and VPN support are key technologies to operating Windows 2000 Professional in a wide area network (WAN) computing environment.

Finally, this chapter will look at how we access resources once the underlying network architecture is in place. Some of these access methods have been discussed in Chapter 2, so we will turn our attention to other ways to find out what's available and how to establish a connection in a Windows 2000 environment.

Objective 7.01   Configure and Troubleshoot the TCP/IP Protocol

A *protocol* is the "language" a network interface card (NIC) uses to communicate with other NICs on the network. The principle used is much like human-to-human communication: network cards that want to exchange information must both "speak" the same language, or there must be a translator between the two. Windows 2000 Professional supports several network protocols, including TCP/IP, NWLink (Microsoft's version of Novell's proprietary network protocol, Internetwork Packet Exchange/Sequenced Packet Exchange, or IPX/SPX), Data Link Control (DLC), and AppleTalk protocols.

The most widely used protocol is TCP/IP, which has really become a *de facto* standard for network communications because of its use as the core protocol of the Internet. In addition to the advantage of support by almost all network operating systems, it also offers the following advantages:

- It is scalable for use in networks large and small.
- It is *routable*, which means that the data being delivered may leave the physical network using this protocol. The network device that sends information from one network to another is called a *router*, and a routable protocol has the ability to cross that router.
- It works with companion services like Dynamic Host Configuration Protocol (DHCP) and Domain Name System (DNS) to offer additional functionality and ease of use. These companion services can further be developed and improved independently of the TCP/IP protocol.

Each protocol, however, shares the following characteristic: they are designed to communicate with other network-accessible devices that are running the same protocol.

Today's networking protocols are implemented as protocol *suites*, a combination of several pieces of networking software and services that work in tandem to provide network functionality. Protocol suites precisely define the series of steps that are applied to a chunk of data that is to be sent over the network wire. For example, let's take a look at Web site browsing and the protocols involved: the TCP/IP suite contains Hypertext Transfer Protocol (HTTP) services to support TCP/IP file transfer, which can be sent over an Ethernet network. If you were to diagram it schematically, the HTTP protocol lives on top of the transport services of the TCP and IP protocols. As represented in Figure 7-1, below TCP/IP lives the Ethernet protocol, which defines how the network wire is accessed. Each layer of the protocol suite performs specific actions to a packet of information before the data is either sent from a Web server or received by a Web browser.

Protocols must be configured on each computer for each computer to operate on the network properly. In fact, most troubleshooting of network protocols comes down to fixing improper configuration of a particular protocol. For example, for TCP/IP to work, a network card must be configured with an IP address. There are a couple of ways that this address can be configured: manually, by typing a number

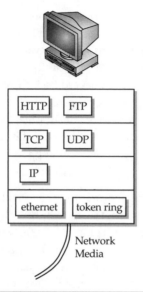

FIGURE 7-1 Representation of the TCP/IP stack

into dialog boxes, or dynamically, through the services of either DHCP or Automatic Private IP Addressing (APIPA). (Both DHCP and APIPA are discussed later in this chapter in the section "Configuring TCP/IP.")

Another critical software component that runs on client computers that use file and print services is the *redirector*. The job of the redirector is to play traffic cop: it decides whether a request for a resource is to be serviced *locally* by one of the disk device drivers or *remotely* on a network server. Just like protocols, the redirectors in a network must be compatible. For example, the Microsoft redirector in Windows 2000 is called the Workstation service (also known as Client for Microsoft Networks), and it's used to request file and print resources from the Microsoft operating systems running the Server service. You can see both of these services running when you look in the Services console under the Administrative tools.

If you want a Microsoft client to access a NetWare server, you must install another redirector that is compatible with NetWare. The redirector for accessing a NetWare server is called Client Services for NetWare (CSNW), which also relies on the installation of the NWLink transport protocol. It is important to know that these two redirectors (client software) can live happily side by side; this is practical because a lot of organizations are running both Windows 2000 and NetWare servers to provide network resources. The Workstation service will be used to access the Microsoft servers, and the NetWare client will be used to access resources from the Novell servers.

Exam Tip

Since the exam focuses on Windows 2000 Professional, it is best to focus on the redirector's role in network interoperability as opposed to server components.

Just as Microsoft clients cannot talk to a NetWare server by default, a NetWare client cannot talk to the Microsoft Server service. Neither can the Macintosh client software. For these clients to interact with a Microsoft Server service, additional software components must be installed on the Windows 2000 server. These components include File and Print Services for NetWare and File and Print Services for Macintosh, respectively. They exist to "fool" non-Microsoft clients into thinking they are talking to non-Microsoft servers, as illustrated in Figure 7-2.

TCP/IP Fundamentals

To help you understand TCP/IP, let's start by illustrating with a more simplified protocol, one that people already use every day: the telephone system. When you

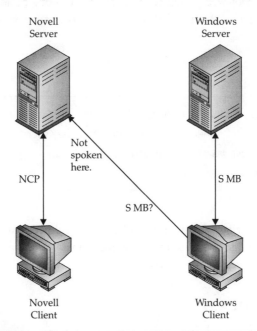

FIGURE 7-2   Clients and servers must speak the same language to exchange data

place a phone call, you must dial the area code first (for long distance, that is, unless you live in a 10-digit dialing city; there are exceptions to everything but it's just an illustration, so just stay with me). Your call won't connect with the desired recipient if you decide to dial the area code *after* you dial the seven-digit number. Why? Because dialing the area code first, not last, is part of the set of rules, or the protocol, of telephone communications. The area code must be dialed first and is three digits in length, and everyone who uses the Public Switched Telephone Network (PSTN) follows this standard. If you were to dial an imaginary four-digit area code, the phone system would get confused about your request, and communication would fail. These same concepts hold true for the protocols used in computer communication.

We also use a protocol when sending data along a computer network, and as mentioned, TCP/IP is one of the most commonly used network protocols. It, too, defines the steps that are taken when computers communicate with one another. On a clean installation of Windows 2000 Professional, TCP/IP is the default networking protocol installed.

What follows is the condensed version of TCP/IP. Entire books have been devoted to exploring TCP/IP, and with good reason. Microsoft used to teach it in a five-day class. There is *no way* that this chapter can do anything other than present an overview of what is needed to acquire a thorough understanding of TCP/IP. As mentioned, Microsoft assumes by now that you have already gained this understanding.

Travel Assistance

If you don't have a good idea of what an IP address is, you need to begin your studies elsewhere, such as *Networking: A Beginners Guide, Second Edition* by Bruce Hallberg (Osborne/McGraw-Hill), and then come back to this chapter.

When configuring TCP/IP, an IP address and a subnet mask are absolutely required. You can, and often will, configure many other optional parameters, such as the default gateway and DNS server address.

The IP Address

Computers speak to each other using numbers, and the *IP address* is the number that uniquely identifies your computer on the network. Further, the IP address identifies what network your computer is living on. The IP address is a 32-bit binary address—a string of 32 1's and 0's—that humans work with by breaking up into four octets (each octet being made up of 8 bits) that are then converted into decimal equivalents and separated by periods. In other words, the IP address to a human is going to look something like this:

192.168.2.200

but to the computer, it's just a string of 32 1's and 0's:

11000000101010000000001011001000

Every IP address comprises two parts: the *network* ID and the *host* ID. The network ID represents the network the computer belongs to, while the host ID uniquely identifies the computer on that network. Every network ID on a TCP/IP internetwork (like the Internet) must be unique—kinda like every zip code in the U.S. must be unique. Further, every host ID on each network must also be unique—kinda like every house on a street must have a different number. So there must be a way to separate the IP address into a network portion and a host portion. But how does IP do this? How does the computer know which part of the IP address is the network identifier and what part is the host identifier? Read on.

The Subnet Mask

The *subnet mask* is used to divide the IP address into the network portion and the host portion. It is a required TCP/IP setting. Without the subnet mask, the computer has no idea what network it belongs to. The subnet mask is also a 32-bit binary number broken into four octets for easy human consumption. A subnet mask might look like this to us:

255.255.0.0

and the interesting thing to note about the subnet mask is how it looks to the computer, as shown in Figure 7-3.

Notice anything about the binary number shown in Figure 7-3? That's right; it's a string of **contiguous** 1's followed by **contiguous** 0's. Note also that the decimal number 255 octet is a string of eight binary 1's. The decimal 0 octet is a string of eight binary 0's. The job of the 1's, then, is to *mask* out the network number—they identify which of the 32 1's and 0's in the IP address are used as the network ID; everything else—everything that lines up with the 0's in the subnet mask—is the host ID. If we use the IP address with the subnet mask here, we are able to determine which 1's and 0's of the IP address are the network ID, and which 1's and 0's are the host ID. The subnet mask tells us that the first 16 binary numbers are the network number, which when we convert back to decimal is 192.168. The next 16 binary numbers are the host ID, which translate into 2.200.

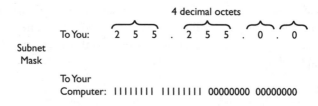

| FIGURE 7-3 | The subnet mask displayed in decimal and in binary |

If any of this is confusing, think back to the example of the telephone proto-col. Part of the telephone number you dial represents a big grouping of phone lines (the first three numbers), and part represents an individual line within that larger grouping (the last four numbers). You can think of this as the network ID and the host ID in IP communications.

So why is this determination of network ID and host ID important? Why is a subnet mask *required* for a valid IP address? It is needed for the successful delivery of information to the proper network, and it helps make TCP/IP a *routable* protocol.

Each and every packet of TCP/IP communications has a *source* address and a *destination* address. And once TCP/IP determines the network ID of the source and destination computers, an important decision is made about how to deliver the packet to its destination. If the network IDs match, the packet is delivered to the local segment of computers. But if the network IDs of source and destination do not match, the packet must be *routed* to a remote network via a default gateway

The Default Gateway

Here's another key ingredient in IP configuration. Although it is not technically required, your network communication would be limited without a default gate-way. A default gateway is the IP address of the router, which is the pathway to any and all remote networks. To get a packet of information from one network to another, the packet is sent to the default gateway, which helps forward the packet to its destination network. In fact, computers that live on the other side of routers are said to be on *remote* networks. Without default gateways, Internet communi-cation is not possible, because your computer doesn't have a way to send a packet destined for any other network. On the workstation, it is common for the default gateway option to be configured automatically through DHCP configuration.

Local Lingo

Router We tend to think of a router as a big box with the letters C-I-S-C-O etched on the front, but it can be any device that simply passes information from one network to another. A Windows 2000 Server with multiple network cards can be configured to act as a router.

Configuring TCP/IP

After you install and bind TCP/IP to a LAN or a WAN adapter (remember that this will be done automatically by Windows 2000 Setup), the core tasks for configuring TCP/IP include the assignment of an IP address, the configuration of name resolution, and the configuration of TCP/IP security.

A client can get an IP address *statically* or *dynamically*. Static addressing is accomplished through the Internet Protocol TCP/IP Properties dialog box by an administrator who manually types in the IP address, the subnet mask, and the default gateway, as shown in Figure 7-4.

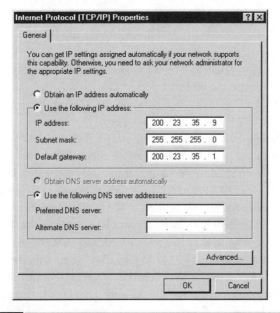

FIGURE 7-4   Configuring TCP/IP

To open the Internet Protocol TCIP/IP Properties dialog box,

1. Right-click My Network Places and choose Properties.
2. Right-click Local Area Connection and choose Properties
3. Select Internet Protocol (TCP/IP) and click the Properties button.

Rather than typing all this information on hundreds or thousands of computers in your network, you can let DHCP do it for you by selecting Obtain an IP Address Automatically. As one of the companion services of TCP/IP that can run on a Windows 2000 server, DHCP's job is to hand out valid IP addresses to computers on the network at boot-up time. It will always assign the two required IP address components—the IP address and the subnet mask. It can be, and usually is, configured to assign configuration information about the default gateway and name resolution servers. By using this vital component of modern TCP/IP networks, you can automate the IP address allocation to network computers to reduce confusion, administrative overhead, and problems related to human error.

Travel Assistance

You will be tested heavily on the DHCP server topic—but not on the Windows 2000 Professional exam! You cannot set up a Windows 2000 Professional computer as a DHCP server.

By default, when TCP/IP is installed on a Windows 2000 Professional computer (which is always the case with default installation), the computer is configured as a DHCP client. This configuration can be done at any time from the Internet Protocol TCP/IP Properties dialog box.

And although it's counterintuitive, a DHCP client does not even need a DHCP server to get an IP address. A DHCP client that cannot locate a DHCP server will assign an IP addresses to itself through a mechanism called *automatic private IP addressing* (APIPA). APIPA is not new to Windows, as it was used beginning with Windows 98, but it is new to the NT family. Here's how it works.

When a DHCP client is unable to locate a DHCP server, the client picks out a random IP address from the private APIPA address range of 169.254.x.y, with a subnet mask of 255.255.0.0. The 169.254.x.y IP range is *private* because that network number is not in use on the Internet; it is *random* because the client generates an arbitrary host number for that network. Let's say the client picks the host ID of 100.23. The client will then announce to the network that it wants to use the IP address of 169.254.100.23. If no other computer announces, "You'll get this IP address when you pry it out of my cold, dead, silicon chipset," or words to that effect, the client registers that IP address and binds it to the network card.

The significance of APIPA is that DHCP client computers that cannot find a DHCP server can still be assigned an IP address and communicate with other computers on the same subnet that also cannot find a DHCP server. It allows communication when the DHCP server is down, or just plain not there. Note, however, that APIPA does not assign a default gateway, and therefore it cannot communicate with any computers that live on the other side of a router.

At times you might prefer this behavior, as it can be an effective method for easily administering TCP/IP in a small network. Keep in mind, however, that the addresses assigned will not be able to communicate with Internet hosts or with a host that exists on any other network, because APIPA assigns an IP address and subnet mask but not a default gateway.

Exam Tip

Here is at least one test question you can expect: something that requires you to know that an APIPA address looks like (169.254.x.y), what its significance is (the DHCP server is down or nonexistent), and what its symptoms are (computers on a segment can communicate with one another, but not with remote computers).

Name Resolution

Computers identify each other using numbers, because that's what computers do—they crunch numbers. Humans, however, like to give computers names, because that's what people do. After all, humans invented computers so that we wouldn't have to work with the numbers. The upshot of these anthropological considerations is that computer communication, at least when humans are involved, usually relies on name resolution to translate names to IP addresses.

A quick example to illustrate: When you log on to a domain, you use a domain name, not a number. That request is sent to another computer, in this case a domain controller. But how does your client computer know to which domain controller to send the request? And how does it actually send your logon request to a domain controller? It does this through a name resolution mechanism that resolves the name of the domain into a number of domain controllers that can answer your logon request. Which name resolution mechanism is used depends on how the network is configured. Again, several mechanisms' *raison d'etre* is to resolve names to IPs. These methods include using files such as HOSTS and LMHOSTS and DNS and WINS (Windows Internet Naming Service) servers, which we'll discuss next.

HOSTS and LMHOSTS files are simple text files that contain name-to-IP address mappings. The HOSTS file maps host names, or fully qualified domain names (FQDN), to IP addresses. A sample HOSTS file is shown in Figure 7-5.

The LMHOSTS file maps NetBIOS names, or computer names, to IP addresses, as shown in Figure 7-6. This can be a bit confusing because the host name and the computer name are often the same, but the distinction again is that the LMHOSTS file maps computer names, or NetBIOS names, and the HOSTS file maps host names, which are Internet-style names. Figure 7-6 is a section of the LMHOSTS file, as it includes extensive instructions about how to use the file. What's important is to note the difference in syntax between the HOSTS and LMHOSTS files. The location of these files is \%*systemroot*%\system32\drivers\etc.

You won't be using these files too often because of their limitations. One of the drawbacks of using the HOSTS file or the LMHOSTS file for name resolution is that they are created manually, which can be a pain and is prone to human error. The other big drawback of the HOSTS and LMHOSTS files is that they are static and do not adapt well to an environment in which the IP addresses of machines is changing constantly. For example, what happens if a client grabs one IP address one day and you manually update the HOSTS file to reflect this, and then the next

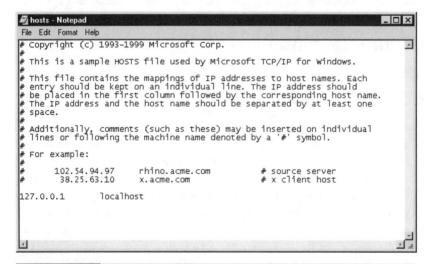

FIGURE 7-5   The sample HOSTS file

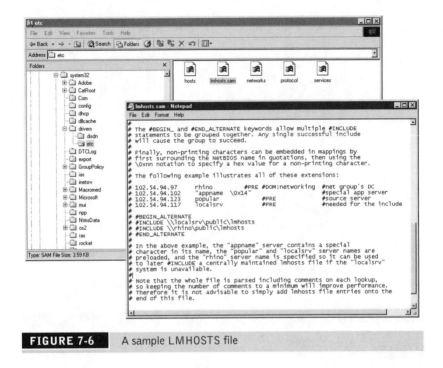

FIGURE 7-6 A sample LMHOSTS file

day the client grabs another IP address? The HOSTS file would then contain an incorrect address mapping, and you would have to edit the HOSTS file again. In such a case, you should consider using a name resolution server solution where the entries are updated automatically.

Domain Name System Servers

Domain Name System (DNS) Servers are used to resolve host names, or FQDNs, to IP addresses. They perform the same function as the HOSTS file, but the database of DNS name-to-IP address mappings can be updated automatically. As clients obtain new IP addresses, their mapping information is updated so that name resolution to IP addresses is always current.

DNS serves as the core name resolution service for Windows 2000; as you will learn, Active Directory domains are not possible without a DNS server. You configure a Windows 2000 Professional client to use a DNS server for name resolution in one of two ways: by setting it as optional configuration information in DHCP, or by manually pointing the client to the IP address of a DNS server in the Internet Protocol TCP/IP Properties dialog box, as shown in Figure 7-7.

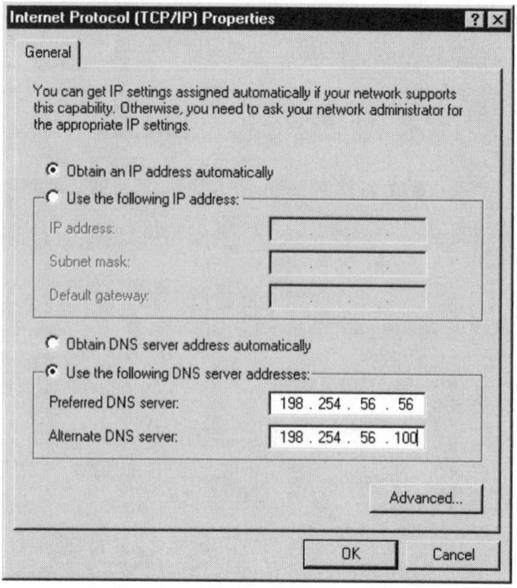

FIGURE 7-7 Configuring the DNS server for a Windows 2000 Professional client

WINS

WINS servers are to DNS servers as LMHOSTS files are to HOSTS files. They are used to resolve NetBIOS names to IP addresses, which can be an important function for backward compatibility with Windows NT 4. NT 4's default networking protocol and naming scheme was NetBIOS. The WINS database of computer name to IP address mappings is also capable of being updated dynamically, just like Windows 2000's version of DNS. This makes WINS another excellent choice for clients when DHCP is used in a network.

You may configure a Windows 2000 Professional system for WINS by having DHCP hand out the address of a WINS server as part of automatic IP address configuration, or you can configure the Windows 2000 Professional computers with a WINS server address manually. To configure this manually, you access the WINS tab after clicking the Advanced button from the Internet Protocol TCP/IP Properties dialog box. The Advanced TCP/IP Settings dialog box is shown in Figure 7-8.

Other Protocols

Earlier in this chapter, we discussed how multiple client redirectors can be installed on the same Windows 2000 Professional computer. This lets a client access resources kept on different types of servers. Likewise, multiple networking protocols

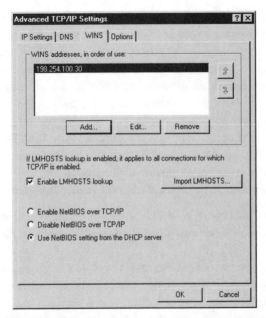

FIGURE 7-8 Configuring Windows 2000 Professional for WINS

can be installed on the same computer, which is also a necessary step in enabling communication between different networks. In fact, when you install certain client components, such as Client Services for NetWare (CSNW), you also install the networking protocol needed for communication, such as NWLink.

NWLink

NWLink, as mentioned earlier, is the Microsoft implementation of Novell's IPX/SPX, used as a transport protocol for Novell networks. Like TCP/IP, its job is to deliver packets of information from one computer to another. Also like TCP/IP, it is a routable protocol. When installed by itself, however, the NWLink protocol does not allow you to access file and print resources on a Novell server; you will also need to install the CSNW redirector to access a file on NetWare servers. You can even run Microsoft networks using the NWLink protocol alone, but you will not be able to access Internet resources.

NetBEUI

The NetBIOS Extended User Interface (NetBEUI) protocol was developed in the 1980s for peer-to-peer workgroup communication. It is easy to install, easy to configure, and it uses less overhead than TCP/IP or IPX/SPX, making it a smaller and faster protocol than its cousins. NetBEUI sends communications from computer to computer using NetBIOS computer names in a *flat naming* space. (In a flat naming space, computer names cannot be reused because the name space where they live contains no subdivisions. Conversely, in a hierarchical naming space, like the one DNS uses, computer names can be reused all the time, as long as they exist in separate parent name spaces. For example, I can have a SERVER1 in the lanscapecomputer.com name space and also use SERVER1 in the bc.org name space.) The drawback of NetBEUI is that it is not routable and is therefore not a solution for routed networks, like the Internet.

To install either of these protocols, you will follow these steps.

1. Click the Install button on the Local Area Connection Properties dialog box. (The procedure for opening this dialog box was described earlier in the section "Configuring TCP/IP.")

2. The Select Network Component Type dialog box appears, as shown in Figure 7-9. Specify that a protocol will be installed, and then click Add.

3. In the Select Network Protocol dialog box, select the manufacturer from the left side and then select the Network Protocol you wish to install from the right side. Then click OK.

Travel Advisory

You will *not* need to know how to configure NetBIOS or NWLink for the Windows 2000 Professional exam. However, if you will be working with either of these protocols extensively, you will need further study. For further information, see *Networking: A Beginners Guide, Second Edition,* by Bruce Hallberg (Osborne/McGraw-Hill)— particularly Chapters 7, 15, and 16.

Binding Order

If you are using multiple protocols on your client computer, an important performance setting for your computer is the *binding order* of the protocols. On a system with only one protocol (as is the default, TCP/IP), you can't set a binding order. When running multiple protocols, though, the binding order determines what protocol is used first when establishing network communications. What's important to understand when setting binding order is that the *client* determines the protocol used in information transfer, not the server. Therefore, setting binding order on

FIGURE 7-9   Selecting the network component type

the server does not have a significant impact on network performance, but setting it on the workstation can have considerable effects. You will set the binding order from the Advanced Setting dialog box shown in Figure 7-10, which you access from the Network and Dial-Up connections window by choosing Advanced | Advanced Settings.

How will the binding order of protocols make a difference when networking computers together? Let's say, for example, that your network connection has both

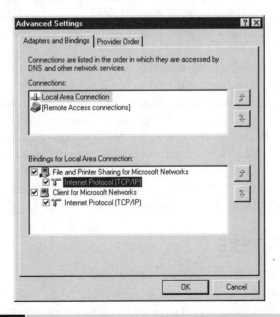

FIGURE 7-10   Setting the binding order for network protocols

IPX/SPX and TCP/IP installed and bound, but you rarely use the IPX/SPX protocol because you rarely access NetWare servers. In this case, you would make sure that the TCP/IP protocol was at the top of the list of bound protocols to ensure best performance. This would tell the computer to try TCP/IP first when establishing a network connection. Again, because the client, not the server, is initiating the conversation, the binding order on the client is of greatest import.

Troubleshooting TCP/IP

Many things can go wrong in network communication, and you will spend a great deal of your administrative time making sure computers can get information back and forth. As with all troubleshooting, you will gain more expertise by doing than by reading. However, you should be familiar with a few tools and techniques.

The first line of any communications efforts should be to check the physical connections. Is everything turned on and attached? One of the old saws of network troubleshooting is that the top 10 reasons that networks break are at the ends of your arms. People mess with things, sometimes unknowingly, and they break. Cables get kicked, tripped over, cut by construction crews, and just generally moved, and cleaning crews have been known to unplug devices to plug in their vacuum cleaners. Companies have exposed cable close to radio transmitters, acting as antennas that attract excess network traffic. The more time you spend in the field, the more things you will see that can interrupt network communication, none of which call on your actual knowledge of operating systems or network protocols.

If, however, you determine that everything is attached properly, but a network adapter is not able to communicate on the network, check the Device Manager to verify that the driver is installed and operational. If everything then checks out, you can get down to the business of checking and testing your network protocols. These are the utilities that you need to be familiar with for the exam.

TCP/IP is a complex and mature protocol suite, and it includes as a part of the protocol stack a robust set of utilities for troubleshooting and diagnostic purposes. To diagnose whether the TCP/IP stack is loaded properly, you can use tools such as IPCONFIG.EXE, PING.EXE, and TRACERT.EXE.

IPCONFIG.EXE

The IPCONFIG.EXE command-line utility displays IP configuration information. When it is run without any switches, it will show the configured IP address, subnet mask, and default gateway. It can also be used with one of several switches that can be listed by running `IPCONFIG` with the `/?` help switch. Table 7-1 shows a few of the more common IPCONFIG switches you will use.

TABLE 7.1	Common IPCONFIG Switches
Switch	**What It Does**
`/all`	Shows information about your IP connection, including any DNS and WINS servers used and whether the address is dynamic or static, and shows the host name.
`/release`	Releases the IP address that has been assigned through DHCP. You cannot release a leased IP address through the TCP/IP Properties dialog box.
`/renew`	Renews a DHCP address. Not possible through the TCP/IP Properties dialog box.
`/registerdns`	Re-registers the DNS name with the configured DNS server. Can be useful for troubleshooting name resolution problems.
`/flushdns`	Clears the contents of the DNS resolver cache located on the workstation. A client will check its DNS resolver cache before checking a DNS server. This will clear out an incorrect entry made by an improperly configured DNS server.

PING.EXE

The Packet Internet Groper (PING) command-line utility is used to send a packet of information that is used to verify that a computer can communicate with other devices on the network. You can think of it as sonar for computer communication. If a PING is successful, the computer is on and can send and receive TCP/IP packets with a remote host. Therefore, other types of communication should work as well.

The syntax of the PING command is this:

```
ping IP Address or computername
```

The PING command can be used with a series of modifiers, such as changing the size of the PING packet. Use the /? switch to see a list of these modifiers. You won't see test questions on any of these modifiers, though.

When communication is failing, the general flow of PINGing to verify TCP/IP connectivity from a computer is as follows:

1. PING the loopback address of 127.0.0.1.
2. PING the local computer's IP address.
3. PING the default gateway.
4. PING the remote computer you are trying to reach.

This can also be done in reverse order to try to isolate the cause of broken network communication.

Furthermore, you can PING other computers using IP addresses or by using host names. This is a good way to troubleshoot name resolution problems. If a PING is successful using the IP address of a computer but not its host name, you should check your name resolution methods for problems. (This might be a good time to run ipconfig /flushdns.)

If PING is unable to resolve an IP address on the network but PINGing the local loopback adapter address of 127.0.0.1 works, type ipconfig to verify that an address has been assigned to the network adapter. Configuration and protocol testing varies from one protocol to the next.

TRACERT.EXE

The TRACERT.EXE utility is used to follow the path a packet takes as it tries to reach its final destination. This utility uses PING packets with progressive time-to-live (TTL) values, starting with a TTL of 1. Each time a packet hits a router, the TTL value is decremented by at least 1. When the TTL value reaches 0, the packet is dropped. This prevents all undelivered traffic on the Internet from still being out there, passing from one router to another in a never-ending attempt to reach its destination.

In the case of tracert, a TTL of 1 means that the packet will die at its first stop. When it dies, another companion protocol will report back that the packed has, indeed, expired and will also report the IP address of the device that dropped the packet. The next PING packet is sent to the destination has a TTL value of 2. It dies two hops away from its source. The TTL keeps incrementing until the PING reaches its destination, at which time the route from sender to receiver has been reconstructed.

The tracert utility, because it steps through the path a packet takes, is useful for identifying slow or broken links in the chain to get information from point A to point B. The syntax of the command is similar to PING:

```
tracert IP Address or computername
```

The tracert should begin reporting the route taken by the packet, along with performance indicators for each stop along the way. You will be able to see where the slow links are in the network.

Travel Advisory

It is possible that you will be able to browse a Web site even though you cannot PING the Web server, because many firewalls on the Internet filter out the type of packets used for PINGing (Internet Control Message Protocol, or ICMP, traffic). This is a security measure, because one easy, effective hack is to flood a Web server with continuous "fat packet" PINGs from one or more computers, which try to overwhelm a server with repeated, large PING packets. One way to combat this is to have a firewall block all ICMP traffic. You can experience this firsthand by surfing to a site like **www.microsoft.com** and then opening a command prompt and trying a PING to the same site.

Other Troubleshooting Notes

Following are a few other troubleshooting notes, in no particular order. Much of your troubleshooting effectiveness is predicated on a thorough understanding of the technologies that let computers communicate with one another.

For example, if clients are set up as DHCP clients, check to ensure that the DHCP server is available. Remember that Windows 2000 Professional DHCP clients that cannot locate a DHCP server will choose an IP on their own using APIPA. What would be the result of an IP address chosen from APIPA? Your ability to recognize this problem will depend on your understanding of this technology. One of the common symptoms of such a condition is that these computers will all be able to talk to each other on their own subnet (because they will *be* on the same 169.254.x.y IP subnet), but they will be unable to communicate anywhere else, such as the Internet. When troubleshooting, remember that APIPA does not assign a default gateway.

As mentioned in the discussion, every IP address must be unique. If a computer tries to use an IP address that is already in use on the network, the IP address will not bind to the network adapter. This avoids disruption of network communications. Fortunately, Windows 2000 is kind enough to inform you when a duplicate address is detected. You will see a dialog box explaining that an IP address conflict has been detected, usually before you are able to log in. If you run the IPCONFIG utility, the subnet mask will be 0.0.0.0.

To troubleshoot name resolution problems, determine whether the problem is related to NetBIOS name resolution or host name resolution, and check the corresponding files and/or services. If NetBIOS name resolution is the problem, review the LMHOSTS file and conduct a check of WINS. If host name resolution seems to be the trouble, check the HOSTS file and the DNS service. You can also generate a summary status report of network activity with the Network Diagnostics utility (NETDIAG.EXE).

Objective 7.02   Connect to Computers Using Dial-Up Networking

So far, the focus of networking has been on a LAN—computers in a room or office building that communicate with one another using networking components such as network interface cards (NICs), CAT 5 cabling, and hubs, with maybe a router separating floors of an office. But what if you want to extend that network to include computers in other cities, in other countries, even. Well, you can't very well string cable between computers from, for example, Athens, Georgia, to Atchison, Kansas. Fortunately, however, other companies do lay this wire so that information can be carried over long distances. One of those networks of wire is the Publicly Switched Telephone Network (PSTN), built by companies like Ma Bell for the express purpose of enabling telephone communications. With different equipment and different communication protocols, computers, too, can take advantage of this existing infrastructure to get data from point A to point B.

So while it may seem difficult, complex, and even mysterious, at its heart, dial-up networking behaves exactly the same as a local network set up in your office: computers send information to one another in the form of an electrical signal, which is carried over a wire connecting the two computers. It's incredible to think about, but every Web page you view as you are surfing is a result of a physical connection (there are a few wireless exceptions) of wire between the sender and recipient. All that's different with dial-up networking are the wires and the protocols. When we dial-up, we are connected to every other computer on the Internet. We have become the Borg.

The purpose of dial-up networking is to allow you to connect to and access remote network resources such as an Internet service provider (ISP) or your corporate network. You will accomplish this by creating a connection in the Networking And Dial-Up Connections window. Each connection object in this window is a logical object and can contain settings unique to that connection.

When you dial-in to a remote access service (RAS) server, you are making a direct connection to your private network, as illustrated in Figure 7-11. RAS is a technology that allows remote users to connect to the network using a modem and dialing the phone number of the RAS server. Once the RAS server answers, the remote user has a connection to that server and can access the network resources as if the user was on the network. The RAS server takes data it receives from one network interface (the modem), and routes it to the LAN using another network interface (the network card). The RAS server acts as the outside boundary between the mobile user and the corporate network, enabling the LAN to be extended over other wires. The RAS client can connect using several dial-up technologies, but a plain old modem is by far the most common way.

Note that the RAS server and the dial-up client must be using the same connectivity option; the client can't dial-up with a regular modem and the server has an Integrated Services Digital Network (ISDN) modem installed.

You will configure a dial-up connection from the Network and Dial-up Connections window by double-clicking the Make a New Connection icon. This launches the Network Connection Wizard, which will ask you a series of questions so that it can configure your connection. Figure 7-12 shows you the available options.

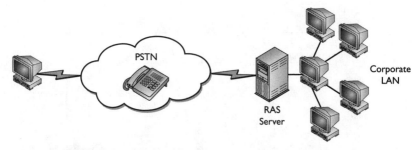

FIGURE 7-11   The RAS server receives your remote request to access the LAN

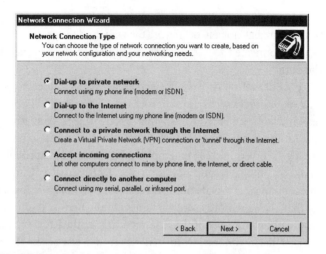

FIGURE 7-12 The Network Connection Type dialog box

As you can see, five connection options appear.

1. Select the first one, Dial-Up To Private Network, because it is the focus of our discussion. Click Next.

2. Now tell the wizard what number to dial, as shown in Figure 7-13. Keeping the Use Dialing Rules box checked means that you will dial a 1 to make a long distance call, or dial a 9 to get an outside line, for example. Unchecking this box will prevent access to the area code field.

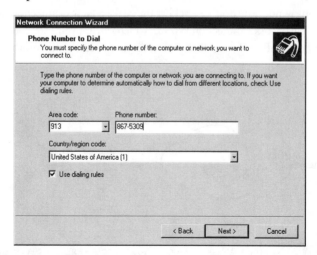

FIGURE 7-13 Giving the client the number to dial

3. Click Next, and then specify whether to make the connection available for all users or just yourself in the Connection Availability dialog box shown in Figure 7-14. Make your choice and then click Next.

4. The next dialog box lets you change the default name of the connection and/or create a shortcut from the desktop if you wish. To save the dial-up connection, click Finish.

5. Because Windows will assume that you are champing at the bit to establish this newly created connection, the next thing you see will be the Connect Dial-Up Connection dialog box shown in Figure 7-15. Here you specify the user name and password that will be submitted to the RAS server when the connection is made. You can also change the Dialing Rules directly from this dialog box.

6. After the dial-up connection has been established, another dialog box will tell you whether the connection is successful.

Because different wires are used in dial-up networking for carrying data across long distances, different protocols are used to help the packets along their way. The Windows 2000 Professional dial-up client can use two protocols to transmit information over long-distance serial (phone) lines. The Serial Line Internet Protocol (SLIP) can be used to connect to legacy dial-up servers such as UNIX servers running SLIP. You cannot use SLIP to dial up to a Microsoft Windows NT or Windows 2000 server, because the SLIP protocol is not supported on the Microsoft RAS server side. The dial-up client can also use the Point-to-Point Protocol (PPP) for dial-up connections, which is the preferred method for establishing serial connections. Most

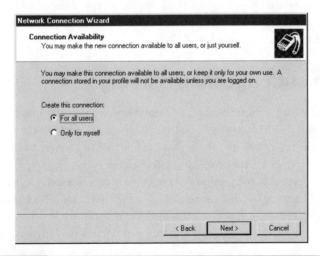

FIGURE 7-14   Who gets access to the connection

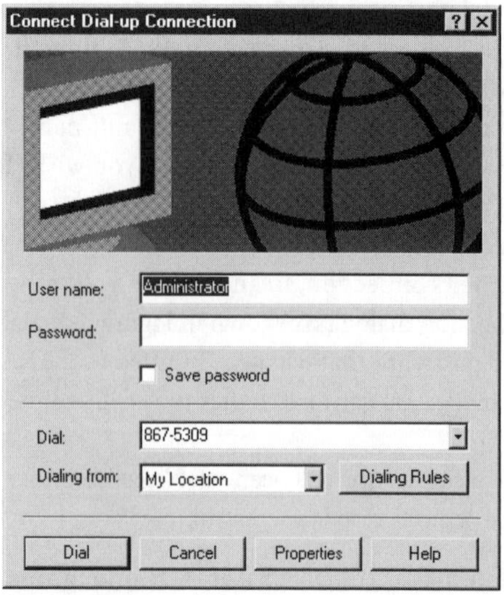

FIGURE 7-15 Establishing your connection

modern dial-up servers support PPP, and as mentioned, Microsoft servers support *only* this protocol for incoming connections. It is recommended that PPP always be used when you have a choice.

Why not SLIP? In a word, because it's unsafe. Unlike PPP, the SLIP protocol (yes, that's redundant) transmits passwords in clear text. PPP, on the other hand, encrypts passwords before sending them over the wire. Additionally, PPP supports other security features such as mutual authentication, data encryption, and call-back, which are not supported by SLIP.

Internet Connection Sharing

The Internet Connection Sharing (ICS) feature makes a dial-up Internet connection available to other computers on the network, and it functionally behaves the same way as folder sharing. It allows a small office to connect to the Internet through a single connection, as illustrated in Figure 7-16.

To configure ICS, you need to share out the logical connection object from the Properties dialog box of that connection, as shown in Figure 7-17. The other network computers who will be using this shared connection for Internet access need to configure their ICS through a LAN as they step through the Internet Connection Wizard.

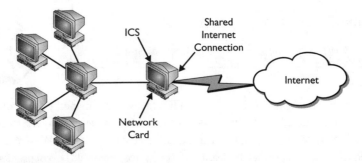

FIGURE 7-16   Internet Connection Sharing

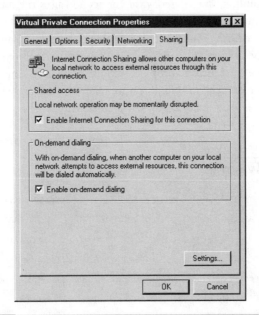

FIGURE 7-17   Sharing the Internet connection

Similar to the services of DCHP, ICS allocates IP addresses and subnet masks to computers in the network. Also, the ICS computer sets a default gateway on these computers that is the same IP address as the computer performing ICS. That way, any packets destined outside the local network are routed to the ICS computer. The default gateway in this case is the network adapter of the computer configured for ICS, which now performs the services of a dedicated router.

Travel Advisory

To set up ICS, you must be in the Administrators group.

Demand dialing is an enhancement of ICS that will automatically dial a connection when required. This eliminates the need for the computer running ICS to maintain an open connection, and it can be an ideal solution when WAN access is infrequently needed or when the leasing of a dedicated line would be cost prohibitive.

Another feature enhancement of ICS is *Multilink*, which allows for the bandwidth of multiple dial-up connections to be combined. When a connection is configured for Multilink, the single *logical* connection uses the multiple *physical* connection components (that is, modems and phone lines) to establish the link to the dial-up server. All the connections are combined and load-balanced to improve performance. Multilink is also dynamic. As bandwidth requirements decrease, Multilink can be configured to drop the number of physical connections to save on connection costs. The Multilink feature relies on the Bandwidth Allocation Protocol (BAP), and both the dial-up server and client must be configured to support Multilink.

Travel Advisory

For several reasons, Multilink is not a practical real-world solution for connectivity. If you have two modems and configure Multilink, but the dial-up server is not configured to support your two inbound connections (for instance, because it has only one modem installed), you are simply wasting a phone line and a modem. Moreover, the reduction in cost and availability of broadband Internet connectivity means that you can get 10 to 20 times more bandwidth for as much as—and maybe less than—the cost of an extra phone line and modem. Increased availability of broadband access means that configuration of virtual private networks is now imperative. Read on.

Virtual Private Networks

A VPN extends the scope of a company's private LAN across a non-private WAN— namely, the Internet. It works by having a remote client establish a connection to the public Internet—doesn't matter how…dial-up, cable modem, DSL—and then, using that networking infrastructure, establishing a *tunneled* connection to the corporate LAN. Figure 7-18 is a conceptual representation of this tunneled connection. Note that a VPN connection requires a Windows 2000 Server computer configured as a VPN server to serve as the endpoint of the tunnel.

Because of the tunneling protocols involved, the communication sent to the remote network remains completely confidential, even though the medium used to transmit the data is completely public. In other words, the network communication is *virtually* private. Get it? To the end user, there is no difference between working locally at the private LAN or remotely through a VPN. Everything's the same to the end user—same shares, same permissions, same access to network printers. The VPN connection just uses different protocols and different wires. VPNs have become an ideal choice for companies to implement WAN connectivity at a dramatically reduced cost.

Authentication Protocols

Several protocols are used by Windows 2000 that give you many authentication and encryption options. These protocols are used in conjunction with the existing network protocols (TCP/IP, for example) to scramble user names and passwords, encrypt the data that is being transmitted, or both. These additional protocols define the level of security that your dial-up or VPN connections have, and they are configured via the Security tab of the Virtual Private Connection Properties dialog box, as shown in Figure 7-19.

If you need to configure specific security protocols, select the Advanced radio button on the Security tab and then click on the Settings button to open the Advanced Security Settings dialog box shown in Figure 7-20.

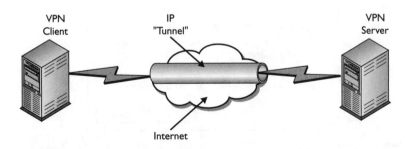

FIGURE 7-18 Representation of a tunneled connection

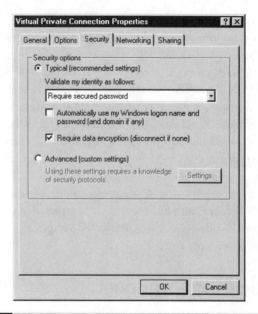

FIGURE 7-19 The Security settings of a dial-up or VPN connection

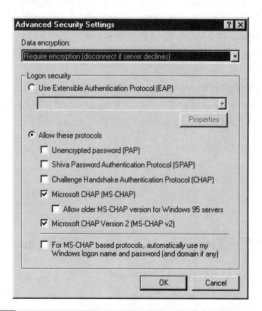

FIGURE 7-20 Additional security configuration

From this dialog box, you can configure the type of encryption that will be used for the VPN connection and whether or not logon security will use the Extensible Authentication Protocol (EAP). As the name suggests, EAP lets you *extend* the functionality of logon security with the use of other devices, such as smart cards or certificates. It also lets you select from the following protocols for logon security:

Protocol	Function
Password Authentication Protocol (PAP)	Uses a plain-text password and is the least secure for this reason
Shiva Password Authentication Protocol (SPAP)	Used for dial-up into Shiva servers
Challenge Handshake Authentication Protocol (CHAP)	Negotiates a secure form of encrypted authentication
Microsoft CHAP (Microsoft-CHAP)	Uses one-way encryption with challenge-response method; can be used by 2000, NT 4 and 9x clients
Microsoft CHAP version 2 (Microsoft-CHAP v2)	A more secure form of Microsoft-CHAP

Exam Tip

One authentication method you need to be especially aware of is the Extensible Authentication Protocol-Transport Level Security (EAP-TLS), which provides certificate-based encrypted authentication. It is the authentication protocol you would need to enable smart card support.

With VPN's, a remote access client connects to a remote private network using either the Point-to-Point Tunneling Protocol (PPTP) or the Layer Two Tunneling Protocol (L2TP) with IP Security (IPSec). A VPN connection allows you to tunnel packets securely using standard networking protocols such as TCP/IP, IPX/SPX, or NetBEUI.

Data encryption is supported between remote access clients and RAS servers using either the Microsoft Point-to-Point Encryption (MPPE) or IPSec. IPSec is a set of security protocols and cryptographic protection services that ensure private communication over IP networks and can be applied to any TCP/IP connection, including the LAN connection. IPSec provides L2TP with encryption services so that data is transmitted securely from the remote access client to its final destination on the remote network. L2TP is a tunneling protocol; with IPSec, L2TP operates as a VPN. IPSec ensures that data sent through the L2TP connection can only be read by its intended recipient.

Travel Advisory

You must choose an authentication protocol that meets or exceeds your security requirements and that is supported by the client and the remote access server.

Troubleshooting Dial-Up Networking

Several troubleshooting aids help solve configuration problems with the dial-up facility. One of these is PPP logging, but you must first enable it on a client, as it is not enabled by default. To enable PPP logging on a client, use the Netsh dial-up scripting utility. Type Netsh /? at the command line for information on using this utility.

If you are able to establish a connection with the remote network but you are unable to communicate with remote resources, run Netdiag to review a summary report of network communications. If a dial-up device is unavailable for configuration in the Network and Dial-Up Connections window, check the dial-up hardware in Device Manager and use the Add/Remove Hardware Wizard to install the device.

Objective 7.03

Connect to Shared Resources on a Microsoft Network

In the first two objectives, we looked at the ways and means that computers use to send information to one another. We've been examining the physical connection components and the languages used to send packets of data over these connections. Now we turn our attention to the end result of getting these computers to talk to one another. What is being accessed when we enable communication?

We touched on many of these topics in Chapter 2 as we set up what was being shared and how we could then secure those resources. So just to review, and so you're not flipping back and forth for a point of reference, following are several methods for connecting to a shared resource:

- Browsing through My Network Places
- Mapping a network drive through Windows Explorer
- Using the NET USE utility from the command line

These methods require that you understand an important syntax for identifying resources on a network: the Universal Naming Convention (UNC) syntax. The UNC syntax locates the resources in the network, and the servers they live on, like this:

```
\\servername\sharename
```

This syntax is used by the NET USE utility and when mapping a drive, and it is also used under My Network Places.

Another method of making resources is available, however, and we haven't yet talked about it, except for a brief mention in Chapter 2. But it's one that you already are familiar with on some level: Web sharing.

Web Sharing with Peer Web Services

Web sharing, put simply, is publishing files using the HTTP protocol, as opposed to the Server Message Blocks (SMB) protocol for Server service sharing. Windows 2000 uses two software components to accomplish HTTP publication: *Internet Information Services* (IIS) and *Peer Web Services* (PWS). These are actually the same software; they just install differently on different operating systems. When you install IIS on a computer running Windows 2000 Professional, you are installing PWS. IIS installs only on a 2000 Server installation. PWS is designed to act as a small-scale Web server for a small intranet or Internet site with limited traffic.

Exam Tip	
Know that your computer must be running TCP/IP to install IIS or PWS.	

You install PWS by choosing the Add/Remove Programs icon in Control Panel and then choosing Add/Remove Windows Components. You then check the Internet Information Services (IIS) checkbox, as shown in Figure 7-21.

After IIS is installed, you will see new program items in Administrative Tools called Personal Web Manager and Internet Information Services Manager. You will use these tools to configure and manage your Web site by right-clicking the node you want to manipulate and choosing Properties. Figure 7-22 shows you how the Internet Information Services Manager will look.

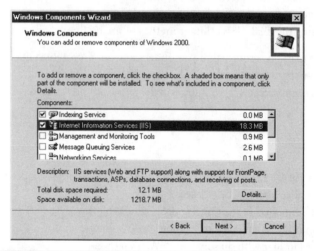

FIGURE 7-21 Installing PWS

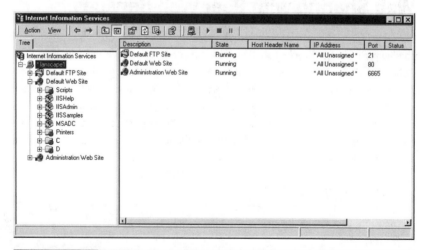

FIGURE 7-22 The Internet Information Services Manager utility

> ### Travel Assistance
>
> For more information on IIS, see *Windows 2000: The Complete Reference*, Chapters 23 and 24, by Kathy Ivens and Kenton Gardner, from Osborne-McGraw-Hill.

Browsing

Now, back to regular sharing. File system resources are made available to network users by creating shares. We do this (unless you're a command-line devotee) by using Windows Explorer, but there are two services working behind the scenes that are key ingredients in making shares available to network users: the Server service, which we've discussed, and the *Computer Browser* service. To review, the job of the Server service is to publish files using the SMB protocol so that clients running the Workstation service can access them.

The job of the Computer Browser service is to make everyone on the network aware of all the shares that have been published and which computers are publishing them. The Computer Browser service exists to manage lists. It all works through a series of browser roles that different computers play on a network. On every subnet is a Master Browser that keeps the list of all computers running the Server service. Each time a computer boots up on the subnet and is running the Browser service (all NT and 2000 computers do), it contacts the Master Browser and gives it the updated information. The Master Browser then compiles this and other announcements from the subnet's computers into a Master Browse List and sends copies of the latest edition to backup browsers on the subnet. The backup browsers then do most of the dirty work of browsing the network. Browse clients, when they want to find out what resources are out there, first contact a Master Browser, who sends a list of backup browsers. The client contacts one of the backup browsers and retrieves the browse list, as shown in Figure 7-23. The client then selects one of the computers from the browse list and retrieves directly from that computer the list of resources that are being shared.

I could go on for several pages about the mysteries of the Browser service. For example, it can take up to 30 minutes for a computer that has been turned off to be removed from the browse list. It can also take a while for your computer to show up on a browse list in the first place, especially if servers in the network are being rebooted (the Master Browser role can shift). Fortunately, this is not something that you will have to know volumes about for your 70-210 test, or even in a working network for that matter, because its self-configuring and self-managing. Just keep this canned answer handy when users ask you about why they don't see

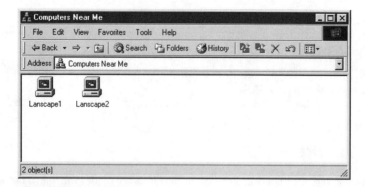

FIGURE 7-23   The browse list for a subnet

certain computers on the network from time to time: "The Browser service is just
is a little weird sometimes. If it's not there in a half an hour call me back."

Finally, this test objective requires that you know how shared resources can be
protected when network connections are made. See? I told you back in Chapter 2
that it wouldn't be the last time you would come across these topics. They will
overlap throughout your studies.

I've mentioned it before, but the topics are so important that a review is mer-
ited here: file system resources are protected by the Server service using share permissions, and they can be further protected on an NTFS partition using NTFS
permissions. Share permissions do not apply locally, but only when a resource is
accessed over the network. NTFS permissions, however, do apply locally.

All permissions, both share and NTFS, are inherited unless inheritance is specifically blocked. The default behavior for permissions is that the Everyone group is
granted the Full Control share permission when a share is created. If a folder or file
is created on an NTFS partition, the object inherits the local permission of its parent folder. What's more, if local permissions are not modified on an NTFS partition
or parent folder, the default local permission is Full Control to the Everyone group.

CHECKPOINT

✔ **Objective 7.01   Configure and Troubleshoot the TCP/IP Protocol.** In
this objective, we looked at the central components of TCP/IP and the ways
that Windows 2000 Professional clients can be configured to receive an IP

address. We examined the significance of the DHCP server and the default gateway in day-to-day network operation. We also examined what utilities can be used to troubleshoot TCP/IP and some common problems that may occur.

✔ **Objective 7.02   Connect to Computers Using Dial-Up Networking.**
This objective focused on how we could extend the networking functionality of Windows 2000 Professional computers across different networks, such as the Internet. We looked at dial-up considerations to Remote Access Servers and looked at how to implement virtual private networks. Finally, we looked at some of the security protocols that can be used in conjunction with these dial-up and VPN technologies.

✔ **Objective 7.03   Connect to Shared Resources on a Microsoft Network.**
This objective is a continuation of the topics first explored in Chapter 2, when we looked at network sharing and ways we could secure shared resources. We examined how a Windows 2000 Professional computer could be set up to host a Web site. We also looked at how Windows 2000 participates in network browsing, which is an easy, point-and-click way to find out about available resources on the network.

REVIEW QUESTIONS

1. Which of the following services must be configured on a Windows 2000 Server for a Windows 2000 Professional client to obtain IP addressing configuration automatically?

   A. DNS
   B. DHCP
   C. WINS
   D. None of the above

2. You are the administrator of a small network of 20 Windows 2000 Professional computers, and you have negotiated a deal with an ISP wherein it will lease you 20 IP addresses. You decide that it will be easiest to assign these 20 IP addresses to all of your clients manually. One of the computers on the network is reporting communication problems. You investigate, run the IPCONFIG utility, and this reports back an IP address with a subnet mask of 0.0.0.0. What's wrong?

A. The NIC has failed.

B. A duplicate IP exists on the network.

C. The computer is a DHCP client that has not been able to contact a DHCP server.

D. Nothing is wrong; you have accidentally configured the subnet mask this way.

3. Which protocols are installed by default on a Windows 2000 Professional clean installation? (Choose all that apply.)

A. TCP/IP

B. NetBIOS

C. NetBEUI

D. NWLink

E. AppleTalk

4. Your company's only means of getting Internet access is through a 56Kbps modem connection to an ISP. However, every computer on the network must occasionally access the Internet to research certain issues. You install the modem in one of the computers running Windows 2000 Professional and create a new logical connection object in the Network and Dial-Up Connections window that uses the modem. What do you now need to do to accomplish your objective?

A. Enable ICS on the computer where the modem resides.

B. Enable ICS on all computers running Windows 2000 Professional.

C. Manually assign IP addresses on all computers.

D. Configure all the computers to obtain an IP address automatically.

5. You are the administrator for a small network, and all of the computers are running Windows 2000 Professional. You want to connect to a shared folder on a computer called Davis1. The path to the shared folder on that computer is D:\Public\Data\Region1\Sales\March. The March folder has been shared out as Monthly. What do you type in the Run dialog box to connect to the share?

A. \Davis1\Monthly

B. \\Davis1\Public\Data\Region1\Sales\Monthly

C. \\Davis1\March

D. \\Davis1\Monthly

6. Which TCP/IP parameters must be configured during a manual configuration? (Choose all that apply.)

   A. IP address
   B. Subnet mask
   C. Default gateway
   D. DNS address

7. Kim Manning is head of an international accounting firm. She is at a meeting in Tel Aviv and needs to connect to the home office back in Dallas to retrieve some of the company's financial statements. Which kind of connection will she not be able to create from the Network Connection Wizard?

   A. Dial-up to a private network
   B. Dial-up to a VPN server
   C. Dial-up to the Internet
   D. Connect directly to another computer

8. You are a part of the IT department and have just been involved in a project that moved large groups of computers from one subnet to another. The next day, one of the users calls and reports that she cannot access Internet resources, even though she can PING servers on her own subnet. Beth runs IPCONFIG and gets back the following information:

   ```
   IP Address:   55.100.10.16
   Subnet Mask:    255.255.192.0
   Default Gateway:   55.100.210.1
   ```

   What is likely the problem with this user's connectivity?

   A. TCP/IP is not bound correctly to the network card.
   B. The IP address is incorrect.
   C. The subnet mask is invalid.
   D. The default gateway is wrong for her subnet.

9. During a study of network traffic, you discover that 80 percent of all packets carried are using the TCP/IP protocol, and the other 20 percent of traffic is split evenly between NWLink IPX/SPX packets and AppleTalk packets. During a spot check of client workstations, you further discover that the

binding order of the TCP/IP protocol is at the bottom of the list. How should you modify this situation with the least administrative overhead?

- **A.** Change the protocol binding order on the domain controllers, since they are accessed at startup time.
- **B.** Change the binding order at all of the client workstations.
- **C.** Change the binding order at the domain controllers, member servers, and client workstations.
- **D.** Do nothing; the lowest listing in the binding order is tried first.

10. You are running a small company made up of 2 Windows 2000 servers, 20 Windows 2000 Professional computers, and 10 Windows 98 computers. You are using the services of one of your local servers for DHCP. Your existing dial-up Internet solution is becoming expensive and slow, and the local cable company suggests that you install a cable modem and use its DHCP server for IP address allocation. However, you have more clients wanting Internet access than the cable company is willing to give you IPs for. You decide, however, to get an additional NIC for one of your Windows 2000 Professional computers, install the cable modem on that new NIC, share out the connection, and disable your existing DHCP service. What will this change in network configuration provide?

- **A.** The internal workstations will get their IP addresses automatically.
- **B.** The number of IPs needed by your company will not be exceeded.
- **C.** All workstations will have access to the Internet.
- **D.** All workstations will be able to resolve Internet names without further configuration.
- **E.** All of the above.

REVIEW ANSWERS

1. **D** OK, this is a bit of a trick question. Here's my e-mail address for complaints: brian@youhavetocarefullyreadthequestion.com. You might have been leaning toward answer **B**, but in reality none of these services are *required*; Windows 2000 Professional clients can still obtain automatic IP addresses from APIPA if there is no DHCP server running. **A** and **C** are wrong because these are name resolution and registration services and are not used for IP configuration.

2. **B**   The Windows 2000 Professional TCP/IP protocol stack checks the network to see if the IP address it is assigned is already in use on the network. If a duplicate address is detected, the operating system displays a dialog box explaining that an IP address conflict has been detected. If you run IPCONFIG, the subnet mask will be 0.0.0.0. **A** is incorrect because no information would appear for the failed adapter when running the IPCONFIG utility. **C** is incorrect because the client would have an IP address and subnet mask, one from the APIPA subnet of 169.254.x.y, with a subnet mask of 255.255.0.0. **D** is also incorrect because Windows will not let you configure an illegal subnet mask, such as 0.0.0.0. You're welcome to try.

3. **A**   Only TCP/IP is installed on a clean installation. If any other protocols are present after installation, Windows 2000 Professional has been installed as an upgrade. All other protocols are optional, with the exception of AppleTalk, which is available only on a Windows 2000 server.

4. **A** **D**   After the modem is installed, access the properties of the connection, and from the Sharing tab, select the Enable Internet Connection Sharing For This Connection check box. Then configure all the other computers to obtain an IP address automatically. The DHCP allocator in ICS assigns IP addresses based on the 192.168.0.x subnet and assigns a default gateway of 192.168.0.1, which will be the new IP address of the computer running ICS. Additionally, on-demand dialing and the DNS proxy are enabled. **B** is incorrect because only one computer on the network will be running the ICS service; all others will be pointed to that computer for Internet access. **C** is incorrect because ICS runs the DHCP allocator service to hand out IP addresses, and manual configuration is not required.

5. **D**   This is the correct syntax to connect to a share. **A** is incorrect because the syntax is missing a second backslash to indicate the computer name. **B** is incorrect because this looks like the MS-DOS pathname. The server services just makes shares available, no matter what drive they live on or how deep in the folder hierarchy. **C** is incorrect because the folder, March, has been given the share name of Monthly, and you want to connect to the share. Again, this illustrates the difference between accessing something locally and over the network.

6. **A** **B**   These two parameters are required for TCP/IP communication. The IP address uniquely identifies a computer on a network, and the subnet mask divides the IP address into a network section and a host section. **C**

and **D** are wrong because they are not required. They will most likely be configured for any fully functioning network, but they are not necessary to get data from one IP host to another.

7. **B** There is no option to dial-up to a VPN server. To establish a VPN connection, she would choose to Dial-up To A Private Network Through The Internet from the wizard. All the other choices are available from the Network Connection Wizard.

8. **D** The default gateway here is an address that is not on the user's subnet. Any default gateway will be just another host (a network card with TCP/IP bound to it) on the same subnet. This host will have the ability to forward packets to other network cards that live on other subnets. **A** is incorrect because the user can PING successfully on her own subnet, indicating that TCP/IP is installed and working properly. **B** and **C** are incorrect because both the IP address and subnet mask are valid addresses. The decimal 192 in binary is 11000000, which adheres to the rule that subnet masks must be a string of contiguous 1's followed by contiguous 0's. This example's subnet mask would look like this in binary: 11111111111111111100000000000000.

9. **B** The binding order at the clients is the determining factor in network communication performance, since the clients initiate the conversation and the servers just respond. **A** is incorrect because the server binding order is irrelevant. **C** is wrong because you are doing more than required, causing additional administrative overhead. **D** is incorrect because the top listing is used first, not the lowest. It's used last.

10. **E** This is an ideal situation where ICS can be a solution. Through its implementation, all of the listed changes will occur.

Implementing, Monitoring, and Troubleshooting Security

CHAPTER 8

	NEWBIE	SOME EXPERIENCE	EXPERT
ETA	5.5 hours	3.5 hours	2 hours

289

By the time you've reached this, the last chapter, you might be thinking, "Hey, I've come this far, how important can the last chapter be, anyway? If this really mattered, the author would've put it in the beginning, right? I've already gotten 90 percent of this stuff, so what if I don't carefully study the last part?" That's what all the voices in *my* head might say, anyway.

A word of advice: *Don't skip or skim through this chapter.* Something has to come last, and in this case, it's last but definitely not least important. (In fairness, many books put troubleshooting sections in the last chapter, and you can skim most of those, because there's no way you can recall from a book chapter everything you will need to effectively troubleshoot anyway.) But as I mentioned in the book's introduction, I've tried to arrange chapters according to how you will *use* the operating system and not by any particular ranking of topic importance. There are no wasted sections here; all material presented maps directly to a Microsoft 70-210 exam objective. In this book, *everything* is important.

Most of the content in this chapter deals with the security of a computer running Windows 2000 Professional. We will start with a discussion of data encryption, and how Windows 2000 makes that possible for drives formatted with NTFS (NT file system). We will turn our attention to managing local users and groups, which is crucial to understanding and determining who will get access to the resources on a computer.

Objective 8.01 Implement, Configure, Manage, and Troubleshoot Local User Accounts

We've spent the greater portion of this book discussing the *whats* and *hows* of the Windows 2000 Professional environment. Another important consideration, though, is *who* gets access to the system in the first place. Setting up your user accounts and then managing them with groups can be one of your simplest yet most effective lines of defense in an effort to secure your computer.

If you want to allow multiple users access to a standalone or workgroup computer, you first need to create user accounts for them. This objective looks at managing *who* gets to use the Windows 2000 Professional computer and examines some tasks that can be performed to monitor their activities.

Creating and Managing Local Users and Groups

You will complete most local user account administration from the Local Users and Groups snap-in, which you access from the Computer Management console, as shown in Figure 8-1. This snap-in contains the Users and Groups subfolders, which are the container objects for your users and groups, respectively.

On Windows 2000 Professional machines only, you can also use the Users and Passwords program in the Control Panel to complete user administration tasks. If you use the Control Panel, Wizards will walk you through the process of creating the local accounts. You should know, however, that the Users and Passwords program will not be quite as robust as the Local Users and Groups Microsoft Management Console (MMC) snap-in. For example, from the Users and Passwords interface, you won't be able to set the path to a user's home folder (profiles and home folders will be discussed in the section "Domain Accounts," later in

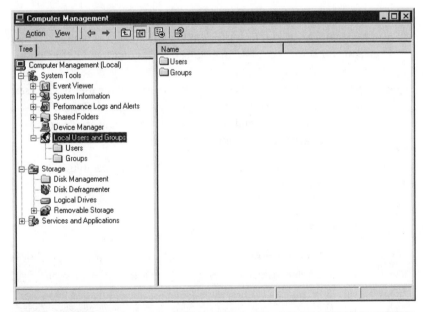

FIGURE 8-1   Accessing Users and Groups from the Computer Management console

this chapter). In fact, if you click around the Users and Passwords utility, when you try to perform advanced user management, you'll be steered to the Local Users and Groups MMC snap-in!

The Users and Passwords program on the Control Panel is meant for users with little to no administrative experience or for users setting up an account or two for standalone use. Since you have seen many wizards by this time, you should have a good idea of how this one works, so I won't cover it here. The Microsoft MCSE exams will assume that network administrators will use MMC snap-ins exclusively to manage the Windows 2000 environment. So it pays for you to learn how to use the MMC methods whenever possible.

Managing Built-In Accounts

From the Users folder of the Local Users and Groups node of Computer Management, you can create, modify, and delete local user accounts. By default, the Users folder contains two *built-in* accounts that are created at Windows 2000 Professional installation time:

- **Administrator**   A special account with full control over all resources on the system. This account has the right to perform all system tasks, such as creating other user accounts, managing the file system, and setting up printers.
- **Guest**   Allows a user to access the computer even if the user has no user name and password listed in the computer's accounts database. This account is disabled by default as a security measure, and even when enabled, the Guest account has few system privileges.

You can rename these accounts (see "Renaming an Account" later in this chapter), but you cannot delete them.

Travel Advisory

You can bet that every hacker worth his or her port scanner program knows that the Windows 2000 Administrator account is always enabled. For this reason alone you should rename the Administrator account as one of your first tasks after installation. This ensures that hackers won't have one-half of the combination they need to *completely* wreak havoc on your network.

You cannot disable the Administrator account; this provides a safeguard against accidentally disabling the only account with management privileges. And, in case you're wondering, there is no safeguard against forgetting the Administrator password.

> **Travel Advisory**
>
> Don't leave the Administrator account blank, and don't configure it with a password of *password*—I've seen this in plenty of production environments. Talk about leading with your chin...

Creating a New User Account

Because you have limited management capabilities over the built-in accounts, any additional accounts that the administrator creates mark the starting point of account management. Creating new user accounts with the Users and Groups snap-in is pretty straightforward:

1. In the Computer Management Console, right-click the Users folder and choose New User. You will then see the New User dialog box, as shown in Figure 8-2.

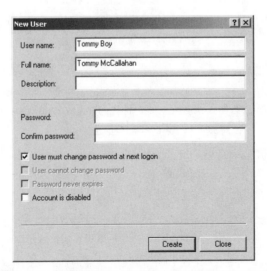

FIGURE 8-2 Creating a new user account

2. Add the User Name. This name must be unique in the Users folder and must follow certain naming rules:

- It must contain between 1 and 20 characters.
- It cannot match the name of Group accounts in the Groups folder.
- It cannot include the following reserved characters, which have special meaning to Windows 2000: / \ [ ] ; : | + = , ? < > "
- It cannot contain all spaces or periods.

3. Add other information in the dialog box as you wish. Table 8-1 helps decipher the configuration options possible when configuring a new local account.

TABLE 8.1 User Account Configuration Options

Option	Description
User Name	The only required field; user names are not case sensitive when used to log on
Full Name	Lets you provide more information about the user; defaults to the User Name if left blank
Description	Lets you provide more information about the account
Password	Assigns the initial password for the account; passwords are case sensitive
Confirm Password	Confirms that you have typed the password correctly
User Must Change Password at Next Logon	Forces users to change passwords upon first successful logon; selected by default to ensure that password is individual user responsibility
User Cannot Change Password	Prevents a user from changing a password; useful for accounts accessed infrequently by many users, such as the Guest account
Password Never Expires	Specifies that a user's password never expires; overrides any settings that have been configured with Group Policies
Account is Disabled	Specifies that account will not be used for logon purposes; helps keep inactive accounts from being used to breach network security

Using this process, you have configured a *local* user account, which will be stored in the Windows 2000 Professional's local Security Accounts Manager (SAM) database. If you use local user accounts in a Windows 2000 setting, you will most likely be working in a workgroup environment. A local user account is needed on each computer that a user needs to access in the network.

More important to the operating system, when you are creating a new user account, you are creating a new *Security identifier* (SID), which is a unique number stored in the system's SAM database. This SID has many attributes, including the user name you just specified. In other words, the SID *is* the account as far as the operating system is concerned. Understanding this important aspect of account creation will help you appreciate what's going on under the hood when accounts are renamed, disabled, and deleted.

Creating and Managing Domain Accounts

Now let's contrast the method for the creation of a local account with the creation of a *domain* user account. (Although you don't need to know *all* the specifics of domain accounts for this exam, you will need to know this for other exams, so it helps to get a background now.) You create a Windows 2000 domain account in the *Active Directory* database, which is the central repository of account information in a domain environment. Because the account is stored in a central location, the account needs to be created only once, and it allows users to access network resources from any computer in the domain.

Travel Advisory

Although not a recommended practice, you can create a local account on the local machine's SAM database even if a user has a domain account. However, doing so violates many of the tenets of domain creation and can be confusing because a single user might have many user accounts, each with different sets of permissions assigned. It is important to keep the two types of accounts straight when working in a Windows 2000 network. It's especially important to keep them straight when you're troubleshooting.

Renaming an Account

After an account has been set up, you can rename it at any time. When you rename an account, you are simply changing one of the descriptors associated with the SID. The account still retains all its settings and group memberships. This is an ideal administrative step to use, for example, when an employee is leaving a company and is being replaced by another person who will be performing the same job and will need the same security group access.

Renaming a user account is simple:

1. Right-click the account you want to rename and choose Rename from the context menu.
2. Type in the new name for the account and press ENTER.

Deleting an Account

You should delete a user account only if you are sure that it will never be needed again, because when you delete a user account, you are 86-ing the account's SID. If you were to then create a new account with the same name, an entirely new SID would be created, whose properties would need to be completely reconfigured. Because this is such a drastic action, you are warned with the dialog box shown in Figure 8-3 when trying to delete a user account.

To delete a user account, right-click the account name and choose Delete.

Disabling a User Account

You can disable an account when the account won't be needed for a while—such as when a user is away from the office on a leave of absence. When a disabled account is re-enabled, the user resumes normal network activity with minimal administrative overhead.

You might also disable an account for security reasons. Say, for instance, your dot-com is doing another round of layoffs while managers figure out a way to make money on products they don't currently charge for. In such a case, you could disable the soon-to-be ex-employees' accounts before handing out the bad news. That way, disgruntled users could not do any harm to the network on their way

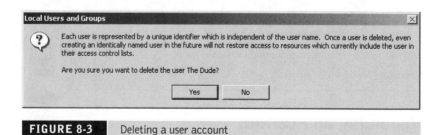

FIGURE 8-3   Deleting a user account

out the door. (However, their first call could be to Microsoft to have you audited for software piracy!)

You disable a user account from the account's Properties page. On the General tab, as shown in Figure 8-4, checking the Account Is Disabled checkbox will disable the account.

Changing a Password

At times, believe it or not, users forget their passwords. When this rarest of circumstances happens, the administrator cannot simply look at the Properties page to see what the password is. The password must be changed.

1. Right-click the user's account from the Local Users and Groups snap-in.
2. Choose Set Password.
3. Type in the new password and then confirm to reset.

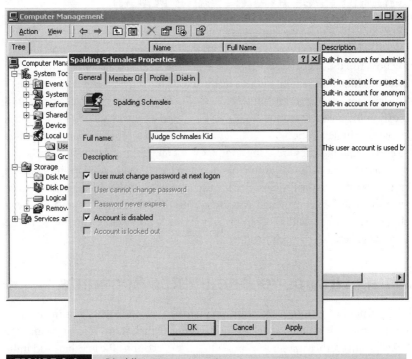

FIGURE 8-4 Disabling a user account

Using Logon Scripts

Logon scripts have done for years what user profiles do in Windows 2000 Professional. Logon scripts set the user environment, including setting up drive mappings or specifying that certain executables, such as a virus check, run every time a user account logs onto a computer. Logon scripts are also useful in configuring compatibility for clients that do not support Windows 2000 profiles but still want to maintain consistent environment settings with their native operating systems. Logon scripts aren't heavily emphasized in Windows 2000 because their function has been largely replaced by user profiles. In a pure Windows 2000 environment, logon scripts should not be necessary.

That doesn't mean you don't have to know where and how logon scripts would be configured for an account. Logon scripts can be specified for a user by accessing the Properties page of the account and entering the name of the script in the Logon Script text box from the Profile tab.

Storing Files in the Home Folder

Users can store their working files in a private network location called a *home folder*. This setting is also configured from the Profile tab of a user's Properties dialog box. You'll notice in this tab that the home folder can also be located on the local machine for the user, but this really defeats the purpose of a home folder.

When you set up home folders for your network's users, you set up a central location for file storage by using a shared folder. This way, all you have to do is back up a single location, rather that having to travel around to many computers to ensure that backups are being completed for all working data.

To specify a path to a home folder, enter a UNC pathname in the Connect textbox located on the Profile tab in the user account's Properties dialog box. Make sure that the folder to which you are connecting already exists and has been shared. (If you're wondering about User Profiles, flip back to Chapter 4, where they are covered in painstaking detail.)

Using Groups to Administer Accounts

The purpose of groups is to streamline permission and rights administration. Groups simplify your life as an administrator; it's much more efficient to manage a few groups rather than many individual user accounts. Rather than add individual accounts to an access control list (ACL), you can add members to a group and then add the single group to the ACL entries page. Any permissions given to the group affect all members of that group.

Groups are also used to manage what *permissions* and *rights* a user has on the system. Although you were exposed to these concepts back in Chapter 3, it might be beneficial to define the terms a litter further here: A *permission* defines the *level of access* a group (or user) has to a resource. An example of permission would be the Change permission that allows users to change or delete the data in a file. *Rights* provide the user with the ability to *perform some action*, to interact with the operating system. A right might include the authority to shut down the system. It's important to understand the distinction between these two concepts, as groups are instrumental in administering each.

In Local Users and Groups, you use the Groups folder to create, modify, and delete group accounts. Groups are container accounts—a SID to the operating system, just like user accounts—that contain other accounts. To illustrate this point, try creating a group (the steps are outlined later in "Creating a Group") with the same name of an already existing user account. You'll get an error message notifying you that an *account* already exists with the same name. Just a little insight as to what work all those mice are doing in your computer case as we continue.

And just like user accounts, a few Group accounts are created at installation time. At setup, the following Groups are created on a Windows 2000 Professional machine:

- **Administrators**   Have full permissions and rights to the system. Membership in this group is like having an American Express card; it has its privileges. Members of the Administrators group, as we have seen, can take ownership of any object on the computer and then manage that object. To list just a few of the other tasks Administrators can do, they can install device drivers, configure audit policies, manage disk quotas, configure password policies, and install service packs. For reasons that after seven chapters should be obvious by now, membership in this group should be most carefully guarded.
- **Backup Operators**   Have the right to back up and restore all files and folders on a system. This right is significant because the Backup Operators also have the right to back up files they would not normally have any access to. However, members of this group can access the system only through the Backup Utility. No members are included in the Backup Operators group by default.
- **Guests**   Have limited access to the computer. This group is built-in so that its members have occasional access to the computer, even if they are

not regular network users. One account is a member by default—the Guest account.

- **Power Users**   Have almost every right that Administrators do, but not quite. Members of the Power Users group can create local users and groups, set up local printers, change the system clock, and stop and start services. Unlike the Administrators group members, they do not have the power to take ownership and manage anything they want. Power Users come in handy when distributing administrative work in a workgroup environment.
- **Replicator**   Supports directory replication (*directory replication* is used by domain servers to synchronize directory information). There are no members by default.
- **Users**   The accounts of any users that are created outside the built-in Guest accounts. The settings of this group generally keep users from harming themselves, as they cannot tamper with the operating system or program files. Any user that is set up automatically becomes a member of this group.

Special Groups

Membership in special groups is automatic and will be determined based on how a user account is interacting with the computer. Accounts become members of these groups based on operating system activity.

Several of these special groups are built into Windows 2000, but as mentioned, administrators cannot manage the membership of each special group. The one special group most administrators need to be cognizant of on a day-to-day basis is the Everyone group, as mentioned in Chapter 2.

The Everyone special group includes anyone who can possibly access the computer. Compare this with the built-in group Users. What's the difference? The Users are the accounts that you create, while the Everyone group includes all of those plus any accounts that you did not create.

Travel Advisory

Because you cannot influence the membership of the special groups, you will not see them listed in the Local Users and Groups utility. To verify that these groups exist, you must access the ACL for a file folder and then add a group to the list.

Creating a Group

When creating a group, many of the same rules apply as for creating User accounts. To create a group, you must first be logged on as a member of the Administrators or Power Users group.

1. Right-click the Groups folder (found in Local Users and Groups) and choose New Group.
2. In the New Group dialog box, shown in Figure 8-5, specify the name and description of the group.
3. As with user accounts, the only required part is the Group name, and it must be unique.
4. You can modify the membership of the group you are creating by clicking the Add button and then choosing the accounts you wish to make part of the group.
5. When you're happy with the configuration of the group, click Create and you're done.

If you change your mind later, you can always make changes by double-clicking the group in the Groups folder of the Local Users and Groups snap-in and adding user accounts from the General tab. You can also access the Properties of a user account and add the user to a group or two on the Member Of tab.

FIGURE 8-5   Creating a new group

Deleting and Renaming Groups

Because groups are accounts in the computer's local security database, the renaming and deleting considerations for group accounts are exactly the same as they are for user accounts. You can rename a group by right-clicking the group name and choosing Rename. Because you are changing only an attribute of the SID, renaming a group does not affect the group's membership in any way.

Deleting a group is a permanent action, as you are deleting that all-important SID. If you delete a group and then create another later with the same name, you will still have to repopulate the group with user accounts. However, the deletion of the group has no effect on the user accounts it contains. They will still reside in the SAM database.

Exam Tip

Groups cannot be disabled, as user accounts can. You cannot delete a built-in group account.

 **Objective 8.02**

Implement, Configure, Manage, and Troubleshoot Local User Authentication

This section covers in more detail what was touched on in the preceding objective. It looks at the support of user authentication using the local security accounts store and the Active Directory data store.

Account Settings

It sounds like something out of a James Bond movie: To access anything in a Windows 2000 environment, you must first obtain the proper credentials to be authenticated. These credentials are obtained through the logon process, and you can do this in a couple of ways. You are probably most familiar with entering a user name and password combination at the Logon dialog box, but you can also insert a smart card and PIN to be authenticated if your computer supports it.

One of the most fundamental security measures in controlling access to resources on a Windows 2000 computer is through user account configuration. A user account is the first line of defense on a Windows 2000 computer and one of the core differences between the Windows 9*x* user experience and the Windows 2000 (as well as Windows NT 4.0) experience. Without a valid user account, use of the Windows 2000 operating system does not begin.

Local User Accounts vs. Domain User Accounts

The valid user account can be stored in two locations: in the *local* security accounts database or in a *domain* security accounts database. The local database, as the name implies, is stored on the local machine. Local accounts can access the operating system on the computer. The domain database is stored on a domain controller, in the Active Directory data store. The domain database defines which user accounts have access to the domain, including which of the domain's computers the user may log onto.

Travel Advisory

One of the chief benefits of an Active Directory domain is that you have to create only one account for each user to access the domain. In a workgroup setting, you have to set up multiple accounts for the same user if that user is going to access several machines.

Two separate logon processes are used when accessing resources in a Windows 2000 network. You first log on interactively to a computer (if you have the proper user rights to do so) to gain initial access to the network. Logging on *interactively* means that you are sitting down at the machine and using it, even if your account is being submitted to a domain controller over the network. For instance, as I write this book, I am logged on interactively to the computer in front of me. Logging on interactively can be done by entering a user name and password, and then selecting the domain or computer name to which you are logging on.

The chapter file I am working with does not need to live at this computer, however; it can be accessed on another computer on my network. So after the interactive logon process is complete, I access network resources using a *network* authentication method. When I am establishing a connection to the server that the aforementioned chapter files lives on, I am actually submitting a user name and password. The user name submitting account will be the same account used to log on interactively, and these credentials will be checked against the ACL of the resource I am trying to access. In most cases, this will be transparent to the user logged on. Several security measures can be applied to this network logon process. The network authentication method used by default in Windows 2000 networks is called *Kerberos* version 5.

If you log on locally, you must provide separate network authentication credentials to access network resources. When you are logging onto a domain, the interactive logon credentials are used transparently to authenticate you to network resources.

If you intend to log on interactively to a standalone or workgroup computer with a user name/password combination, you will choose the name of the computer in the Log On To textbox in the Logon dialog box when the computer starts up. After a computer joins a Windows 2000 domain, the Log On To textbox is populated with the name of the domain of which the computer is a member, as well as all of the domains that are trusted. On a Windows 2000 Professional computer, the local computer name will appear there as well.

A cool little logon "trick" will keep a user from having to select the appropriate logon domain from the drop-down list in the Log On To textbox. Windows 2000 domain users can log on using their User Principal Names (UPN), which, if you need to jog your memory, is *username@domainname*, where *username* is the account name and *domainname* is the fully qualified domain name defined in the Active Directory store. In other words, domain logons can be sent to domain controllers the same way e-mails are sent. The only difference between an e-mail and a domain login is which records are searched for in the Domain Name Service (DNS) hierarchy: rather than searching for a Mail Exchange (MX) record to find the address of a mail server, a search is made for a Service (SRV) record that identifies a domain controller in the domain where the logon request is being sent. Easy? It will be, if you understand DNS, which you will by the time you pass the Network Infrastructure exam. You won't be able to pass that exam without a thorough understanding of DNS.

Exam Tip

If what I just mentioned leaves you saying "huh?" like when NFL commentator and comedian Dennis Miller throws in one trivial reference too many, you can be comforted that you really *don't* need to know DNS that extensively for now. As long as you recognize that you can log into a domain just like you are composing an e-mail, you should be fine.

To logon to a Windows 2000 domain using a smart card, you begin the process by inserting the smart card into a smart card reader. This prompts the user for a PIN, which is used to authenticate to the smart card (it is the "combination" to the smart card), not to the domain. A public key certificate is stored on the smart card, and that key is used to authenticate to the domain using the Kerberos version 5 protocol. To use smart card logon over Point to Point Protocol (PPP)—in other words, to log on remotely—Extensible Authentication Protocol-Transport Level Security (EAP-TLS) must be used.

The security protocols available consist of the following. Take special note of which authentication forms use encrypted passwords and which do not:

- **Unencrypted Password Authentication Protocol (PAP)** Uses a *plain-text* password and is the least secure authentication type.
- **Shiva Password Authentication Protocol (SPAP)** Used to dial into and be authenticated by Shiva servers.
- **Challenge Handshake Authentication Protocol (CHAP)** Negotiates a secure form of encrypted authentication.
- **Microsoft CHAP (MS-CHAP)** Uses one-way encryption with challenge-response method. This protocol was designed for Windows NT4 and Windows 2000, but it can be used by Windows 9*x* as well.
- **Microsoft CHAP version 2 (MS-CHAP v2)** A more secure form of MS-CHAP.

Objective 8.03

Implement, Configure, Manage, and Troubleshoot a Security Configuration

So far, the objectives in this chapter have dealt with all the security policies save one: those contained in the Security Options folder. Guess which one we're going to talk about now?

On a standalone or workgroup computer, the Security Options are located under the Local Policies node, as shown in Figure 8-6. Just like all other local group policies, the policies configured here apply to the local computer only but affect all users who access the computer. Some are extensions of other policies, such as the Audit Use of Backup and Restore Privilege policy settings. You can also add supplementary events that can be audited from this node.

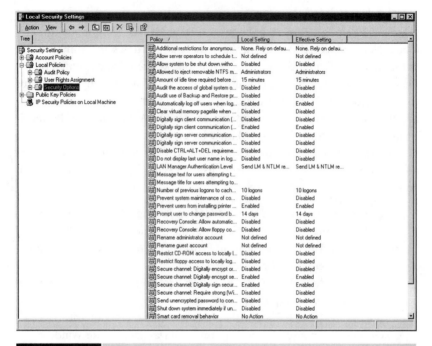

FIGURE 8-6   The Security Options node

As you've realized by now, learning the sheer volume of policy settings that are configurable from the Group Policy tool and configuring security on a computer can be and usually are complex tasks. I won't waste trees or risk carpal tunnel generating a hypnosis-inducing listing all of the possible configuration settings, and you won't have to memorize all the settings for the exam. But you will have to spend some time getting comfortable with some of these settings. Start clicking around to see what the dialog boxes say.

Table 8-2 shows a few of the Local Security settings that you are likely to change most often.

Security Templates

A neat little MMC snap-in makes the application of multiple security settings much easier. The *Security Configuration and Analysis tool* allows you to test and apply wholesale changes to the security settings with just a few clicks of your mouse through the use of *security templates*. The predefined security templates were designed to cover common requirements for security and include four basic

TABLE 8.2	Some Local Security Settings
Setting	**What It Does**
Message Text For Users Attempting To Log On	Displays a message, such as a legal notice or welcome message, to users even before users are presented with the Logon dialog box
Restrict CD-ROM Access To Locally Logged-On User Only	Prevents unauthorized software from being installed on the system
Unsigned Driver Installation Behavior	Prevents the installation of unsigned drivers, even if the user has said it's OK with the driver signing options
Rename Administrator Account	Sets the Administrator account to the name you specify
Allow System To Be Shut Down Without Having To Log On	Can eliminate the requirement that allows a user to first log on with a valid account before shutting down the system

security levels: basic, compatible, secure, and high. The predefined security templates are as follows:

- **Basic workstation, server, and domain controller**   Defines the default security level for Windows 2000. These templates can be used as a base configuration for security analysis and should be applied to any upgraded computer.
- **Compatible workstation**   Provides a higher level of security but still ensures that all the features of standard business applications will run.
- **Secure workstation or server**   Provides an additional level of security, but does not ensure that all the features of standard business applications will run. Some applications might need a lower level of security to operate properly.
- **Highly secure workstation or server**   Ensures the maximum level of security on a Windows 2000 machine, without any regard to application functionality.

838

308 MIKE MEYERS' MCSE WINDOWS 2000 PROFESSIONAL PASSPORT
A security template is an .inf file containing security configuration settings, and Microsoft includes a number of them in the *%systemroot%*\Security\ Templates folder. You can apply a security template directly to a local computer policy when the computer is not part of a domain. You do this to a standalone or workgroup computer by first *importing* the template into a database of Group Policy security settings. To apply a security template to a local computer, you need to perform the following tasks:

1. In the Security Configuration and Analysis snap-in, right-click Security Configuration and Analysis and choose Open Database. This will be your working database of settings that will be either analyzed or applied.
2. Name the database, and then select the security template you wish to apply to the database. Click Open.
3. Now that the database of settings has been created, you can use this database to either configure or just *analyze* your system's security settings, as seen in Figure 8-7. To Configure the system with the template's settings, right-click Security Configuration And Analysis and then select Configure System Now.

The first time you use this tool, tips appear in the details pane that will help you apply a security template for analysis. When you use the tool for analysis, Windows 2000 will compare the database settings against the currently configured settings and then display progress with a series of icons. When the processing is complete, any discrepancies between the local computer settings and the database settings will show up marked with a red flag. Settings that match will show as a

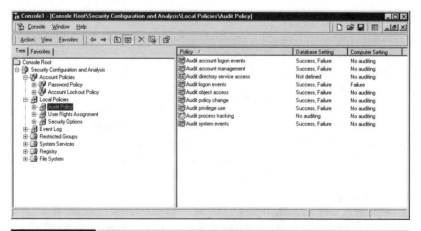

FIGURE 8-7   The Security Configuration and Analysis tool

green checkmark. Settings that do not have either are not configured in the database you have created with the template.

Exam Tip

You should be aware that the security templates can be applied only to Windows 2000 computers. What's more, some of the security settings configured involve encryption technologies not available on earlier versions of Windows. As a result, applying secure or highly secure templates should occur only for communication among Windows 2000 computers.

When you apply the secure or highly secure templates, communication attempts that do not conform to the rules of the template are rejected, and some of these connection and encryption rules are not even available on Windows 9*x* or NT 4 systems. To ensure compatibility with these operating systems, you should use either the Compatible or Default security templates.

You can also use the Security Configuration and Analysis snap-in to import more than one security template. This tool allows you to merge multiple security templates to create a composite template and apply event log, restricted group, system services, and file system configurations. You can also use this snap-in to analyze a computer's security configuration against an existing security template or a composite template.

If you determine that none of the predefined security templates meets your needs, you can create your own templates using the Security Templates MMC snap-in. With this snap-in added, you can start with a new template and modify away, or save a copy of a preexisting template and make changes to the copy.

To modify the predefined templates in Security Templates,

1. Right-click the template you want to modify, and choose Save As.
2. Name the template, and then expand the new template to select the policies you want to configure.
3. Double-click a policy name in the details pane to configure the policy, and then click OK to save changes to the template. The new template will then be immediately available for import into a security configuration.

You can also make changes to existing security templates by selecting an existing policy from the Security Templates snap-in as outlined in step 3, and then making the desired configuration changes.

Command-Line Security Configuration

Windows 2000 Professional includes a tool that you can use to perform security configuration and analysis using script files as opposed to the graphical tools mentioned previously. Further, you can use the secedit.exe utility from the command line, which will provide you with several features that are not available with the graphical tools.

Exam Tip

Secedit.exe is the command-line equivalent of the graphical tool Security Configuration and Analysis.

Five general functions are provided by the secedit.exe utility, with each function performed with different switches used after the `secedit` syntax. As always, don't forget the `/?` to reference the full syntax when first getting comfortable with this tool:

- `/analyze`, `/configure`, and `/export` correspond to the equivalent tasks that are possible through the Security Configuration and Analysis graphical tool. These switches require that you specify a database to analyze with the `/dialog` box switch.
- `/refreshpolicy` forces a Group Policy update event, which by default occurs every time the computer restarts and then every 60 to 90 minutes thereafter. You can use this switch to immediately apply any changes made to a Group Policy. The switch also requires that you specify where the Group Policy will be refreshed. You will usually specify the `machine_policy` with this option.
- `/validate` verifies the syntax of a template created by using the Security Templates tool.

Exam Tip

Know the syntax to refresh a Group Policy immediately with the `secedit` command, namely `secedit /refreshpolicy machine_policy`. You will be sure to see a question about this.

Objective 8.04

Encrypt Data on a Hard Disk Using Encryption File System

Until now, it has been drilled into your head that if you want to restrict access to files and folders locally, you will store them on an NTFS partition and protect them with NTFS permissions. Well, I've got good news and bad news. Start with the bad news? Fine. Local NTFS permissions can be compromised when resources are accessed locally by operating systems other than NT or Windows 2000. That's right, it is possible for a user booted into an OS other than NT or 2000—say, an installation of Windows 98—to bypass NTFS permissions. It takes third-party tools, like NTFSDOS, to do this, and most users have no idea that this is possible, but such tools are accessible to a determined user. Remember that your first line of defense against a potential NTFS security breach is that under normal conditions, a Windows 9*x* user can't even *see* an NTFS partition.

Travel Advisory

Many times ignorance is one of your best lines of defense, and that's not a bad thing. There are lots of ways to wreak havoc on computer networks—just ask any of the brilliant people who code viruses. It's just that most people don't have the time or energy to bother learning all these ways of being destructive. If no one knows what steps are involved in formatting a drive, you don't have to spend much time worrying about it. Of course, the flip side is that knowledge is dangerous—witness the way network administrators are treated when they either leave or are fired from most companies.

Now the good news: Microsoft includes Encrypting File System (EFS) support with Windows 2000 to counter this security vulnerability. EFS provides file encryption services by using a security algorithm and a file encryption key. And, somewhat ironically, you must be running NTFS version 5 (the one that comes with Windows 2000—you can't use EFS on an NTFS partition that was formatted with NT 4) to support encryption. In this way, encryption is simply another attribute that is assigned to a resource on an NTFS partition, no different from a compression attribute or the List Contents attribute. Functionally, encryption behaves like the NTFS Deny permission to a file or folder and is totally transparent to the end user. That's not to say that it *is* the NTFS Deny permission, because a user could very well have Full Control permissions to a folder that has been encrypted by another user. But when the user tried to access the encrypted file, he or she would see an Access Denied message, without further explanation.

A user with the proper access key (either the user who encrypted the file or the Recovery Agent, as explained in its own section later) can open and use encrypted files. Any other normal user will get an Access Denied error when trying to access the same file, and Windows 2000 will not tell the user the reason for the error.

You can set encryption for a file or folder on an NTFS partition in two ways: either from Windows Explorer (as we examined earlier in Chapter 3) when setting the compression attribute, or by using the CIPHER.EXE command-line utility.

To enable encryption from Windows Explorer, open the Properties dialog box of a file or folder and then click the Advanced button from the General tab to open the Advanced Attributes dialog box. As shown again in Figure 8-8, you can choose either to encrypt or compress the resource. Remember that these two operations are mutually exclusive—it's either/or.

An installation of Windows 2000 includes the CIPHER utility, which is more flexible than Windows Explorer. The utility allows you to view the encryption settings on files and folders as well as encrypt and decrypt them. Also, with the CIPHER utility, you can force encryption and create a new encryption key.

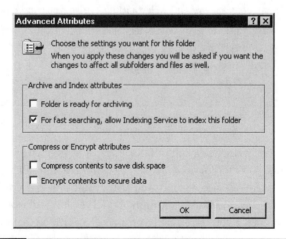

FIGURE 8-8   The Advanced Attributes dialog box

The syntax of the CIPHER utility is

```
cipher /[command parameter] [filename].
```

Table 8-3 shows some of the command parameters of the CIPHER tool and how each one modifies CIPHER's behavior.

TABLE 8.3	Command Parameters of the **CIPHER** utility
Parameter	**Description**
/e	Encrypts files and folders
/d	Decrypts files and folders
/s:dir	Specifies that subfolders and files should also be encrypted or decrypted
/I	Causes any errors to be ignored
/q	Quiet mode displays only the most important information

When you set the encryption attribute, you will have the option of encrypting just the folder or all of its contents, including subfolders. If you encrypt a folder, any new files created in that parent folder are automatically encrypted.

Moving and Copying

Here's where EFS behaves a little different from other NTFS attributes. The rule of thumb is that *encryption is sticky*. That is, encrypted files remain encrypted almost everywhere they go. That makes sense, because you wouldn't want a file to be decrypted if it were copied—that would defeat the purpose of encryption. Really, the only concern is if the destination folder is on a partition that does not support encryption, such as a FAT32 partition or a floppy drive.

Travel Advisory

If an encrypted file is copied to another computer running Windows 2000, the other computer must support at least an equal level of encryption to preserve the encryption attribute.

The Recovery Agent

Windows 2000 requires that at least one user account be configured as the *recovery agent*. This account will be configured with a recovery agent certificate and a copy of the private key. On a standalone or workgroup computer, the user account created during the installation of Windows 2000 Professional is designated as the recovery agent.

You can add recovery agents to a workgroup or standalone computer from the Add Recovery Agent Wizard.

1. To start the wizard, open the Local Security Settings MMC snap-in by clicking the Local Security Policy icon in Administrative Tools.
2. Under Public Key Policies, right-click Encrypted Data Recovery Agents and choose Add. Figure 8-9 shows this.
3. The Add Recovery Agent Wizard will then request that a certificate file be created for recovery. You must use the Certificate Services running on Windows 2000 Server to create additional recovery agent certificates.

If a computer is a part of a Windows 2000 domain, the Domain Administrator account becomes the recovery agent. The Domain Administrator account is designated as the data recovery agent in the Default Domain Policy Group Policy Object (GPO). Additional recovery agents are added to any domain-based GPO's such as an organizational unit (OU) GPO.

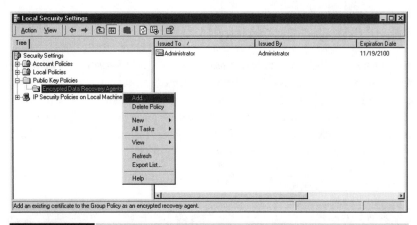

FIGURE 8-9 Adding a recovery agent

Implement, Configure, Manage, and Troubleshoot Local Security Policy

W indows 2000 offers a new way to manage user environments: *Group Policies.* Group Policies are a powerful, flexible, granular way to administer your network environment, and they allow you to manage a wide variety of computer and user settings ranging from software distribution to password restrictions to the appearance of the desktop. Group Policies will be the focus of many lessons that you learn about Windows 2000, especially when discussing Active Directory.

Most of the time, when you work with Group Policies, you will be working with them at the domain level in Active Directory. Policies at the domain level can be applied to sites, domains, and OUs. These objects represent logical and physical structures within an Active Directory enterprise that can be used to break apart an Active Directory installation into separate administrative entities.

However, the focus of Group Policies on the Windows 2000 Professional exam is only at the local level, which means that the policies we will discuss here apply to the local machine alone. You apply local Group Policy to a workgroup or standalone computer that does not use Active Directory to apply security settings.

You configure the Group Policy on an individual Windows 2000 computer using a *local security policy,* which you configure and view from the Local Security Settings console.

Four categories of local security policies exist: *account* policies, *local security* policies, *public key* policies, and *IP Security* policies. We looked at one of these policies earlier in the previous section when we examined the EFS recovery policy, which is a public key policy. By administering the public key policies, for example, we could configure additional recovery agents on a system. This objective covers the other three policy categories.

- *Account policies* are categorized by *password* policy and *account lockout* policy.
- *Local security* policies are categorized by *audit* policy, *user rights* assignment, and *security* options.
- *IP Security* (IPSec) policies are categorized by types of IPSec rules.

Account Policies

Account policies are used to indicate the user account properties that are specific
to the logon process, such as settings for passwords and account lockout options.
To implement account policies, you need to configure the Local Group Policy for
a particular machine by adding the Group Policy snap-in to the MMC.

From the MMC, access the Account Policies folders, as shown in Figure 8-10.
You can see two sub-folders: Password Policy and Account Lockout Policy.

Password policies ensure that security requirements are enforced on the computer, and they apply to *all* users who access that computer; they are not set on a
per-user basis. The policies here are all fairly self explanatory.

The account lockout policies are used for specifying how many invalid logon
attempts should be tolerated before the account is disabled. This is a good way to
prevent possible security compromises by a password-guessing user or program.
You configure the settings of account lockout so that an account will be locked out
after a specified number of unsuccessful logon attempts. You may also configure
how long the account is locked based on a duration of several minutes—or indefinitely until the Administrator unlocks the account. The account lockout policies
are shown in the right pane of Figure 8-11.

As always, it is important to note the defaults. The default Account Lockout
Threshold is 0, which means that accounts will not be locked out no matter how
many bad logons are attempted. Once you set *any* Account Lockout Threshold,
the default time an account will be locked out will be 30 minutes, which means
that a user could come back and try again after waiting 30 minutes. If you reset
this Account Lockout Duration to 0 (after enabling an Account Lockout

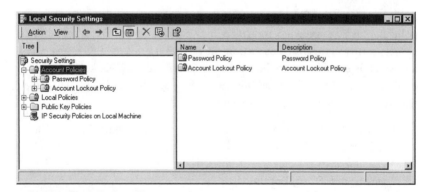

FIGURE 8-10   The Account Policies node

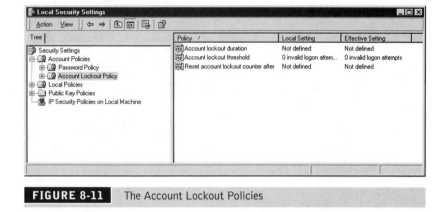

FIGURE 8-11   The Account Lockout Policies

Threshold), the account will be locked out indefinitely until an Administrator unlocks it.

Local Security Policies

To configure most policy settings, you select a node or folder object in the Local Security Settings console. Then double-click the security setting you wish to configure to set the properties of that setting. For example, to deny the local Guest account the ability to log on locally to the computer, open the Local Policies node and select the User Rights Assignment folder. In the details pane, double-click the Log On Locally setting, and to the right of *computername\ Guest*, clear the Local Policy Setting checkbox. Figure 8-12 shows you what this will look like.

User Rights

User rights assignments dictate what a user is able to *do* on a computer. As discussed earlier in this chapter, rights are different from permissions, which define *access* to a resource. A good deal of the function of built-in groups is that members of these groups have predefined rights, which makes rights administration easier. For example, the Backup Operators have the right to back up and restore any file on any file system, regardless of the permissions assigned to the operator. This does not mean, however, that the backup operator has *access* to open the files he is backing up—just that he has the *right* to back them up. Administrators can easily delegate the administrative task of regular backups to a user or users without extensive rights assignment.

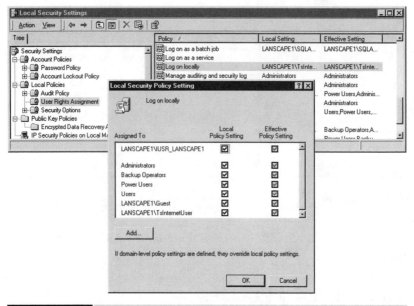

FIGURE 8-12 Configuring a Local Policy Setting

Travel Advisory

One of the hallmarks of the Administrators group is that its members have virtually every possible right on the computer. This is one reason you must carefully guard the membership of this group.

While certain rights are granted to certain groups by default, no rights are explicitly granted to any user accounts. This includes the Administrator account, which is assigned its rights by virtue of its membership in the Administrators local group. You will configure user rights from the User Rights Assignment folder under the Local Policies node, as shown in Figure 8-13.

Auditing

By implementing auditing, you can get an Orwellian ability to monitor what users are doing on the computer. You configure audit policy from the Audit Policy folder under the Local Policies node in the Security Settings console, as shown in Figure 8-14.

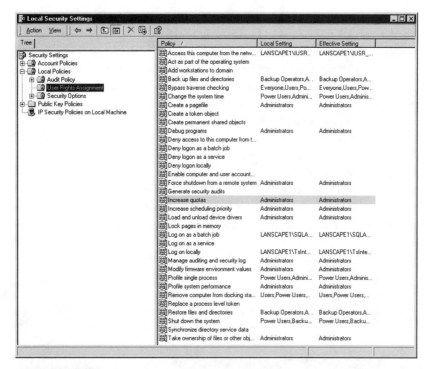

FIGURE 8-13 Local user rights

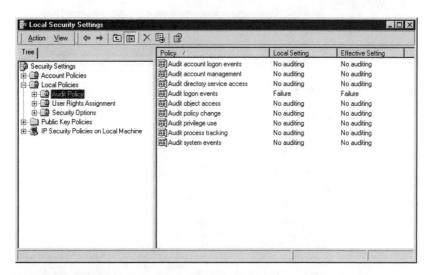

FIGURE 8-14 The audit policies

When you define an audit policy, you get to choose what events to track and whether to track the success or failure of those events. Whether you track success or failure events depends on the activities you are trying to capture. Keep in mind that auditing does generate overhead on the computer, so unnecessary auditing can be a drag on performance. For example, do you really want to audit each and every successful logon? Probably not. Do you want to audit failed logon attempts? In a secure environment, you likely do.

By default, nothing is audited, so you must configure auditing manually, and it is done on a per-computer basis. It can also be a two-step process, as in the case where you would want to audit who is accessing a confidential file. You would first audit the *success* of object access, and you'd then set the auditing on an individual resource by accessing the Properties dialog box of that resource and configuring auditing on a per-group or per-user basis through the Advanced button, as shown in Figure 8-15.

Exam Tip

You can only audit access to resources on NTFS partitions.

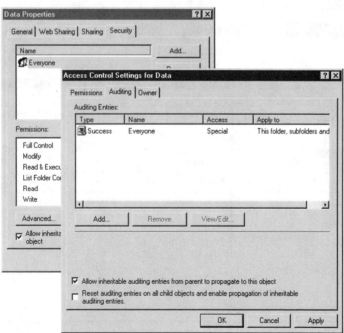

FIGURE 8-15 Auditing a resource

Finally, the audit policy settings dictate which security settings the Event Log service should log in the Security log. The Security log will identify either the failure or success of audit events. To get detailed information on the events, such as the whos and whens, simply double-click the particular event to see the Event Properties window, as shown in Figure 8-16.

It is good practice to use Local Security Policies to get familiar with some of the Group Policy settings. This is a tool that will seem overwhelming at first because of the volume of settings that can be configured. Finding exactly what you want to configure will be a matter of patience, repeated use, and trial and error. Remember that you can't make an omelet...

That being said, you will hardly ever configure Local Security settings in the real world. That's because most security settings that are important enough to set at the local level should also apply to the network as a whole. So that's what you do: set most, if not all, of your security settings at the domain level in Active Directory rather than at the local computer level. A perfect example of this would be password policies. Does it make sense to require an eight-character password on one computer and not on another? Usually not. You would set this at the domain level, so that all users of your network would need an eight-character

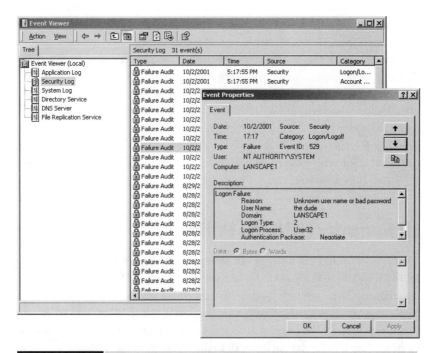

FIGURE 8-16   Examining the results of your audit

password to log on. Moreover, domain policies will by default override local policies, so that even if you set a ten-character password requirement at the local computer using the above scenario, the effective setting would still be for an eight-character password. Local settings are low man on the totem pole: local settings are overridden by site settings, which are both overridden by domain settings, which are all overridden by OU settings.

Again, while this is not crucial information for the Windows 2000 Professional exam, it is required understanding as you progress through the MCSE exam series. It can only help if you enter this test with a basic understanding of Group Policies and how they might apply to an Active Directory environment.

Travel Advisory

Local Security settings are the only GPOs that can be applied to a standalone or workgroup Windows 2000 computer. All other GPOs are domain-based.

So when might you want to change any of the local Group Policy settings? Well, it is your only Group Policy lever that is available in a workgroup setting. In this configuration, the Local Group Policies can be quite effective on securing a machine, especially one that is shared by many people.

The greater the number of GPOs that are configured for a computer, and the greater the settings within each GPO that is configured, the longer it takes for a computer to start and complete the logon process. Therefore, best practice is to minimize the number of GPOs applied to a computer in a domain, and minimize the number of settings applied to a computer in a workgroup or a domain. Configure only what you need.

IP Security (IPSec) Policies

The Internet Protocol Security policy settings allow you to configure IPSec. IPSec in Windows 2000 is designed to protect sensitive data from being intercepted and stolen on a TCP/IP network. It can be most useful when communication between two computers is not secure, such as when data needs to be exchanged using a public network, like the Internet. It provides confidentiality, integrity, and authentication of each and every packet of IP traffic crossing the network.

When using IPSec, the two communicating computers first agree on the highest common supported security policy. Each computer then handles the encryption of IP traffic at its respective end. In other words, once IPSec communication has been negotiated, each computer's IPSec driver handles the grunt work of securing traffic. Before sending data, the initiating computer transparently encrypts data by using its IPSec policy. The destination computer then transparently decrypts the data before passing it on to the receiving application or process. Because the traffic is encrypted at the IP level, the same security packages can be used for all protocols (think of the application layer protocols such as FTP, SMTP, and HTTP) in the TCP/IP stack.

The IP security policies are implemented from the IP Security Policies on the Local Machine node of the Local Security Settings snap-in. Three policy templates are preconfigured there:

- **Client (Respond Only)** Uses the default response rule to negotiate with servers that request security. This policy will communicate normally (unsecured) with untrusted servers, but will use encryption when requested by a server that requires it. Only the requested protocol and port traffic with that server is secured. This option will give you the most flexibility when negotiating security.
- **Secure Server (Require Security)** For all IP traffic, always require security using Kerberos trust. This policy does not allow unsecured communication with untrusted clients. Most traffic, because it will be unsecured, will be denied, and the number of computers you can communicate with will be limited. However, this is usually exactly the behavior you want when applying this setting.
- **Server (Request Security)** For all IP traffic, always request security using Kerberos trust. Allow unsecured communication with clients that do not respond to a request. This setting will always attempt to negotiate secure communication, but it will not prohibit data exchange with unsecured clients.

Notice that none of these policies are assigned to the computer by default. To assign a policy, right-click the policy name and choose Assign, as shown in Figure 8-17.

You can also adjust the settings of the IPSec policies by accessing the Properties dialog boxes of the given policies. For example, you can change the behavior of the IP filters for a given policy by either choosing to edit an existing IP filter rule or by adding one. An IP filter will direct action on a TCP/IP packet based on the destination of the packet. When enabled, an IP filter checks each incoming packet against the IP filter, and if a match is found, the properties of the policy are used to send the communication.

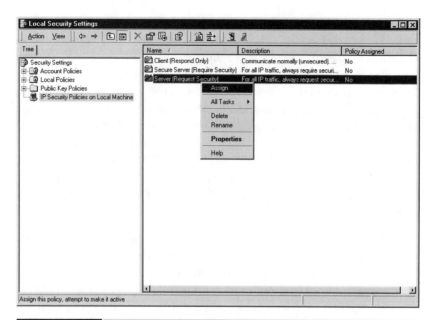

FIGURE 8-17 Assigning an IPSec Policy

CHECKPOINT

✔ **Objective 8.01** **Implement, Configure, Manage, and Troubleshoot Local User Accounts.** In this objective we dealt with the issue of who is able to access our Windows 2000 Professional installations. We configured accounts locally, in the local Security accounts database for the computer. These accounts are used to log on and gain access to local resources.

✔ **Objective 8.02** **Implement, Configure, Manage, and Troubleshoot Local User Authentication.** This objective looked at the differences between logging onto the local machine versus logging onto the domain. We also looked at some of the authentication protocols that can be implemented to keep logon credentials secure.

✔ **Objective 8.03** **Implement, Configure, Manage, and Troubleshoot A Security Configuration.** In this objective, we learned in greater detail about the security settings that are available from the Local Security Policy

MMC snap-in. We inspected the audit settings available and how they can help determine potential security threats, such as unauthorized access to files and folders. We also looked at the issue of user rights, and what rights certain users have by default. We finally looked at applying security to IP traffic through IPSec policies, which can be used to prevent certain traffic from hitting our computers.

✔ **Objective 8.04 Encrypt Data on a Hard Disk Using Encryption File System.** This objective introduced the topic of encryption, a new feature that is available with Windows 2000 on a partition that has been formatted with NTFS. We looked at the two ways in which encryption can be set on files and folders and then looked at what role the Recovery Agent plays in encrypted file recovery.

✔ **Objective 8.05 Implement, Configure, Manage, and Troubleshoot Local Security Policy.** Here we examined how to apply security templates to make many different security settings at once. We also looked at how to customize the templates that can be applied. Finally, we looked a the command-line utility for applying security settings and for refreshing security policy changes immediately.

REVIEW QUESTIONS

1. What command-line utility is used to encrypt folders and files on a computer running Windows 2000 Professional? (The files and folders reside on an NTFS partition.)

   A. efs.exe

   B. cipher.exe

   C. crypto.exe

   D. ntfsadmin.exe

2. As the administrator for your Windows 2000 domain, Frau Farbissina has set up a home folder location for all users on a network server. For additional security, the NTFS partition where these home folders are stored uses encryption. The good Frau has been doing research and stores this research in her home folder, but she is taking a three-month sabbatical. Before she leaves, she moves her files into her manager's folder, but the manager gets an access denied message when she tries to open Farbissina's files. What can be done to correct this situation?

A. Grant the manager NTFS Full Control permission to the files.

B. Grant the manager NTFS Take Ownership permission. She will then give herself access to the files.

C. Log on as the local Administrator and recover the files.

D. Log on as the domain Administrator and recover the files.

3. Beth Turner wants to prevent users from using passwords that are the same as their user account names. Which GPO should she configure to accomplish this task?

A. Enforce Password History

B. Minimum Password Age

C. Minimum Password Length

D. Passwords Must Meet Complexity Requirements

4. Paddy O'Brien is the administrator of a workgroup of Windows 2000 Professional computers called LUCKYCHARMS. Because he does not want people accessing his LUCKYCHARMS computers, he wants to configure the computers to lock out accounts after four invalid logon attempts. He has configured the Account Lockout Threshold policy setting value to 4. Paddy also wants those accounts locked out indefinitely so that he can investigate the cause of a locked out account. What should Mr. O'Brien do?

A. Set the Account Lockout Duration to 0.

B. Set the Account Lockout Threshold to 0.

C. Set the Account Lockout Duration to 99,999.

D. Take no action.

5. You are the administrator of a shared computer running Windows 2000 Professional. You notice that the system time has been changed. You reset the time, and now you want to find out who is doing this if it ever happens again. What do you need to configure?

A. Enable auditing of the Audit Logon Events policy setting.

B. Enable auditing of the Audit Privilege Use policy setting.

C. Enable auditing of the Audit Object Access policy setting.

D. Enable auditing of the Audit System Events policy setting.

6. Ash wants to implement a smart card logon process for the remote laptop users in your network. Which protocol should Ash use?

A. PAP

B. Microsoft-CHAP

    C. Microsoft-CHAP v2

    D. SPAP

    E. EAP-TLS

7. You have just installed a new software package on your server, and the software includes many components that require a user account, and further must run as a service. Your company has a Group Policy at the domain level that requires users to change passwords every 60 days, which just happens to be the time that the software application fails until you change the password of the account that the application uses. What's the best way you can alleviate this problem?

    A. Configure the account so that the password does not expire.

    B. Place a user account in the Account Operators built-in group and delegate the task of resetting the application account password to that user.

    C. Configure the application so that is uses the Administrator account.

    D. Configure a local policy on the computer where the application runs so that account passwords never expire.

8. You configure all of the Windows 2000 Servers in your network to use the highly secure template using the Security Templates snap-in. You receive calls almost immediately after you do this, saying that users of Windows 9*x* and NT 4 Workstation computers cannot connect to the 2000 Servers anymore. They can still connect to one another. How can this be corrected? (Choose all that apply.)

    A. Add the highly secure template to the Windows 9*x* and NT 4 workstations.

    B. Upgrade the Windows 9*x* and NT 4 workstations to Windows 2000 Professional.

    C. Give all users Administrator level access to the servers configured with the highly secure template.

    D. Remove the highly secure template from the Windows 2000 Servers by reapplying the basic security template.

9. Navin R. Johnson is the administrator of a network supporting a fast food chain. The Culinary department is concerned that unauthorized users might be able to access and then e-mail confidential recipes, like the one for the company's special sauce, so he is planning to place the Culinary department on its own restricted network segment. The chain's network consists mostly of Windows 98 and NT 4 Workstation computers, but he has recently purchased 10 Windows 2000 Professional computers for the Culinary department. Navin wants members of the Culinary department to communicate with each other, but does not want these computers to be accessible by any other non-Culinary computers. What should Navin do to configure this special purpose for the Culinary department users?

A. Use the Security Configuration and Analysis snap-in to apply the Securews.inf security template.

B. Use the Security Configuration and Analysis snap-in to apply the Securedc.inf security template.

C. Use the Security Configuration and Analysis snap-in to apply the Hisecws.inf security template.

D. Use the Security Configuration and Analysis snap-in to apply the Hisecdc.inf security template.

REVIEW ANSWERS

1. **B** The CIPHER command-line utility allows you to create file encryption keys and view, encrypt, and decrypt files and folders on an NTFS partition. Several switches will be used to modify this utility's behavior. None of the other command-line utilities exist.

2. **D** Here it is important to note that the computer is a part of a domain, and you should know who the default recovery agent is in a domain. As it stands, only Farbissina or the domain Administrator can access Farbissina's files. When a Windows 2000 Professional computer becomes part of the domain, the domain Administrator account becomes the recovery agent. This is so because of the Default Domain Policy GPO. **A** is incorrect because the encryption attribute is separate from NTFS permissions. Changing the ACLs on Farbissina's files will not change who is the recovery agent. **B** is incorrect for the same reason. **C** is incorrect because the local Administrator account is the recovery agent when the computer is either standalone or is part of a workgroup. This changes when the computer becomes part of a domain

3. **D** The Passwords Must Meet Complexity Requirements policy setting can be set to enforce the contents of a password by verifying that it meets a set of complexity requirements. One of the requirements is that the password cannot contain all or part of the user's account name. This policy is disabled by default in the Default Domain Policy GPO and in the Local Security Policy of a workgroup computer running Windows 2000 Professional. **A** and **B** are incorrect because these settings do not enforce the content of a password. **C** does enforce the content of a password, but not to the extent that Passwords

Must Meet Complexity Requirements does. Minimum Password Length specifies the least number of alphanumeric characters in a password.

4. **A** By setting the Account Lockout Duration setting to 0, the account will be locked out until an administrator unlocks it. This policy setting is not defined by default because account lockouts are not defined, either. It has meaning only when an account lockout policy is set. **B** is incorrect because you want to configure what happens *after* the account is locked out. This setting defines when and if an account will be locked out in the first place. Setting the Account Lockout Threshold to 0 means that the account will never be locked out. **C** is incorrect because the Account Lockout Duration of 99,999 sets the duration to about 69 days, which, while a long time, is not indefinite. **D** is incorrect because a setting of 4 invalid login attempts and an indefinite lockout duration are not defaults, so action is necessary to configure this behavior.

5. **B** Auditing privilege use allows you to capture audit events each time a user exercises a user right, like changing the system time. Success audits generate an audit entry every time a user right is successfully exercised. Failure audits generate an audit entry when the exercise of a user right fails. **A** is incorrect because Audit Logon Events allows you to audit each time a user logs on or off a computer where the computer was used to validate the account. **B** is incorrect because Object Access allows you to enable auditing of objects on an NTFS partition. **D** is also wrong because System Events allows you to audit when a user shuts down or restarts a computer or when an event has occurred that affects either the system security or the Security Log.

6. **E** EAP-TLS uses transport layer security when a PPP connection is established. Mutual authentication and encryption services are provided between client and server using certificates. All the other protocols are wrong because, while they are all authentication security protocols, they are not used in the smart card logon process.

7. **A** This is the easiest way to reach a solution for this problem. Answer **B** would work, but it requires much more effort than answer **A**. **C** is incorrect because the Administrator account would also need to change her password because of the domain policies in place. **D** is wrong because the local policy would be overridden by the domain policy.

8. **B** **D** The highly secure template configuration is only supported by Windows 2000-to-Windows 2000 communication. **B** would be a solution, albeit a potentially expensive one. **D** will also work, but of course you would then lose all the secure configuration options that were applied in the first

place. The basic security template does support communication with Windows 9x and NT 4 systems. **A** is incorrect because these computers do not support security template configurations. Answer **C** is incorrect because the user logged on does not impact the communication channel required between server and client. It is also never a good idea to give users Administrator privileges indiscriminately.

9. **C** You should use the Highly Secure security template file, hisecws.inf, to ensure that IPSec encrypts any communication over the network. After the template is applied, the Windows 2000 Professional computers will require IPSec encryption for all communication. And, because only Windows 2000 supports IPSec, no communication will be possible with pre-Windows 2000 computers. Answers **B** and **D** can be thrown out because they are templates for domain controllers, and the scenario is asking about Windows 2000 Professional computers. **A** is incorrect because the Securews.inf template increases Account Policy and Auditing security settings but does not require encrypted communications. You would know that only from spending some time exploring some of the template settings with the Security Configuration and Analysis snap-in.

About the CD-ROM

APPENDIX A

Mike Meyers' Certification Passport CD-ROM Instructions

To install the *Passport* Practice Exam software, perform these steps:

1. Insert the CD-ROM into your CD-ROM drive. An auto-run program will initiate, and a dialog box will appear indicating that you are installing the Passport setup program. If the auto-run program does not launch on your system, select Run from the Start menu and type ***d:\setup.exe*** (where ***d*** is the "name" of your CD-ROM drive).
2. Follow the installation wizard's instructions to complete the installation of the software.

You can start the program by going to your desktop and double-clicking the Passport Exam Review icon or by going to Start | Program Files | Passport | MCSE Professional.

System Requirements

- **Operating systems supported:** Windows 98, Windows NT 4.0, Windows 2000, and Windows Me
- **CPU:** 400 MHz or faster recommended
- **Memory:** 64MB of RAM
- **CD-ROM:** 4X or greater
- **Internet connection:** Required for optional exam upgrade

Technical Support

For basic *Passport* CD-ROM technical support, contact:

Hudson Technical Support

- Phone: 800-217-0059
- E-mail: mcgraw-hill@hudsonsoft.com

For content/subject matter questions concerning the book or the CD-ROM, contact:

MH Customer Service

- Phone: 800-722-4726
- E-mail: customer.service@mcgraw-hill.com

For inquiries about the available upgrade, CD-ROM, or online technology, or for in-depth technical support, contact:

ExamWeb Technical Support

- Phone: 949-566-9375
- E-mail: support@examweb.com

Career Flight Path

The Microsoft Windows certification program that you will be joining when you take the 70-210 exam includes an extensive group of exams and certification levels. Passing the Windows 2000 Professional exam is all that is required for Microsoft's baseline certification—the Microsoft Certified Professional (MCP).

Microsoft's premier certification is the Microsoft Certified System Engineer (MCSE), and the 70-210 exam is a great place to start on your path toward gaining this certification. In total, seven exams are required for obtaining the MCSE: four core exams, one core elective exam, and two elective exams.

Core Exams

Every MCSE candidate must pass four core exams. These exams test your knowledge of Windows 2000 both as a server and as a client operating system, and they also test your ability to implement a network based on Microsoft technologies. The core tests are

- **70-210** Installing, Configuring, and Administering Microsoft Windows 2000 Professional
- **70-215** Installing, Configuring, and Administering Microsoft Windows 2000 Server
- **70-216** Implementing and Administering a Microsoft Windows 2000 Network Infrastructure
- **70-217** Implementing and Administering a Microsoft Windows 2000 Directory Services Infrastructure

Core Elective Exam

The four core required exams test your ability to *do*, while the core elective exam tests your ability to *plan*. These core elective options are sometimes referred to as the "Designing" exams. Four elective exam options are available for you to choose from, and this is the first point at which you can begin to customize your MCSE certification around the topics that interest you.

- **70-219** Designing a Microsoft Windows 2000 Directory Services Infrastructure
- **70-220** Designing Security for a Microsoft Windows 2000 Network
- **70-221** Designing a Microsoft Windows 2000 Network Infrastructure
- **70-226** Designing Highly Available Web Solutions with Microsoft Windows 2000 Server Technologies

Those interested in working as an Active Directory specialist, a security specialist, a network designer, or an Internet specialist will know exactly which exam to take. For those of you not so sure, exam 70-220 may be your best bet, as knowledge of network security is always a valuable commodity.

Elective Exams

With the core elective/design exam, you are given a bit of choice, but with the last two elective exams, you can really customize your MCSE around your interests and knowledge. Microsoft lists more than 20 exams to choose from, and these can include any of the unused design exams or any of a number of exams on Microsoft server applications.

If you have a particular interest in SNA server (70-085) or SMS server (70-086), for example, then go for those exams. In most cases, though, a certification seeker who is looking to make him or herself marketable to a broad range of employers should concentrate on a core group of elective exams that relate to Microsoft's most common server applications. Probably the two best electives for MCSE candidates who are on a job hunt are these:

- **70-028** Installing, Configuring, and Administering Microsoft SQL Server 2000 Enterprise Edition
- **70-224** Installing, Configuring, and Administering Microsoft Exchange 2000 Server

Users with Windows NT 4.0 knowledge can leverage this into their Windows 2000 MCSE by taking exam 70-244, which covers support and integration of Windows NT 4.0 networks.

.NET and Beyond

One thing to remember, of course, is that computer technologies change rapidly, and most certifications therefore require you to regularly update your certifications. With the Windows 2000 MCSE, we are actually getting a reprieve, as Microsoft has declared that the .NET and 2000 exams can be used interchangeably, so recertification for XP/.NET won't be necessary. Consult the Microsoft Web site for more information on which Windows 2000 exams map to which XP/.NET exams.

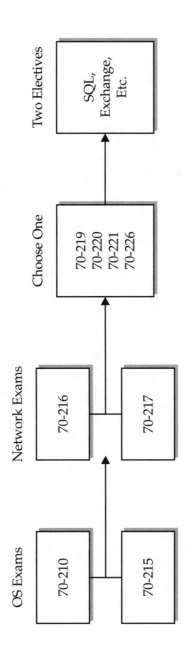

Index

ExamWeb is a leader in assessment technology. We use this technology to deliver customized online testing programs, corporate training, pre-packaged exam preparation courses, and licensed technology. ExamWeb has partnered with Osborne - McGraw-Hill to develop the CD contained in this book and its corresponding online exam simulators. Please read about our services below and contact us to see how we can help you with your own assessment needs.

www.examweb.com

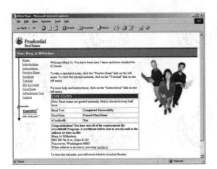

Technology Licenses and Partnerships

Publishers, exam preparation companies and schools use ExamWeb technology to offer online testing or exam preparation branded in their own style and delivered via their websites. Improve your assessment offerings by using our technology!

Check www.examweb.com for an updated list of course offerings.

Corporate Assessment

ExamWeb can customize its course and testing engines to meet your training and assessment needs as a trainer. We can provide you with stand-alone assessments and courses or can easily integrate our assessment engines with your existing courses or learning management system. Features may include:

- ✓ Corporate-level access and reporting

- ✓ Multiple question types

- ✓ Detailed strength and weakness reports by key subject area and topic

- ✓ Performance comparisons amongst groups

Coming soon:

CCNA™ Passport / A+™ Passport / Server+™ Passport / Network+™ Passport / Java™ 2 Passport
MCSE Windows 2000™ Professional Passport / MCSE Windows 2000™ Server Passport
MCSE Windows 2000™ Directory Services Passport
MCSE Windows 2000™ Network Infrastructure Passport

For more infomation, please contact corpsales@examweb.com or call 949.566.9375

INTERNATIONAL CONTACT INFORMATION

AUSTRALIA
McGraw-Hill Book Company Australia Pty. Ltd.
TEL +61-2-9417-9899
FAX +61-2-9417-5687
http://www.mcgraw-hill.com.au
books-it_sydney@mcgraw-hill.com

CANADA
McGraw-Hill Ryerson Ltd.
TEL +905-430-5000
FAX +905-430-5020
http://www.mcgrawhill.ca

**GREECE, MIDDLE EAST,
NORTHERN AFRICA**
McGraw-Hill Hellas
TEL +30-1-656-0990-3-4
FAX +30-1-654-5525

MEXICO (Also serving Latin America)
McGraw-Hill Interamericana Editores S.A. de C.V.
TEL +525-117-1583
FAX +525-117-1589
http://www.mcgraw-hill.com.mx
fernando_castellanos@mcgraw-hill.com

SINGAPORE (Serving Asia)
McGraw-Hill Book Company
TEL +65-863-1580
FAX +65-862-3354
http://www.mcgraw-hill.com.sg
mghasia@mcgraw-hill.com

SOUTH AFRICA
McGraw-Hill South Africa
TEL +27-11-622-7512
FAX +27-11-622-9045
robyn_swanepoel@mcgraw-hill.com

**UNITED KINGDOM & EUROPE
(Excluding Southern Europe)**
McGraw-Hill Education Europe
TEL +44-1-628-502500
FAX +44-1-628-770224
http://www.mcgraw-hill.co.uk
computing_neurope@mcgraw-hill.com

ALL OTHER INQUIRIES Contact:
Osborne/McGraw-Hill
TEL +1-510-549-6600
FAX +1-510-883-7600
http://www.osborne.com
omg_international@mcgraw-hill.com

LICENSE AGREEMENT

THIS PRODUCT (THE "PRODUCT") CONTAINS PROPRIETARY SOFTWARE, DATA AND INFORMATION (INCLUDING DOCUMENTATION) OWNED BY THE McGRAW-HILL COMPANIES, INC. ("McGRAW-HILL") AND ITS LICENSORS. YOUR RIGHT TO USE THE PRODUCT IS GOVERNED BY THE TERMS AND CONDITIONS OF THIS AGREEMENT.

LICENSE: Throughout this License Agreement, "you" shall mean either the individual or the entity whose agent opens this package. You are granted a non-exclusive and non-transferable license to use the Product subject to the following terms:
(i) If you have licensed a single user version of the Product, the Product may only be used on a single computer (i.e., a single CPU). If you licensed and paid the fee applicable to a local area network or wide area network version of the Product, you are subject to the terms of the following subparagraph (ii).
(ii) If you have licensed a local area network version, you may use the Product on unlimited workstations located in one single building selected by you that is served by such local area network. If you have licensed a wide area network version, you may use the Product on unlimited workstations located in multiple buildings on the same site selected by you that is served by such wide area network; provided, however, that any building will not be considered located in the same site if it is more than five (5) miles away from any building included in such site. In addition, you may only use a local area or wide area network version of the Product on one single server. If you wish to use the Product on more than one server, you must obtain written authorization from McGraw-Hill and pay additional fees.
(iii) You may make one copy of the Product for back-up purposes only and you must maintain an accurate record as to the location of the back-up at all times.

COPYRIGHT; RESTRICTIONS ON USE AND TRANSFER: All rights (including copyright) in and to the Product are owned by McGraw-Hill and its licensors. You are the owner of the enclosed disc on which the Product is recorded. You may not use, copy, decompile, disassemble, reverse engineer, modify, reproduce, create derivative works, transmit, distribute, sublicense, store in a database or retrieval system of any kind, rent or transfer the Product, or any portion thereof, in any form or by any means (including electronically or otherwise) except as expressly provided for in this License Agreement. You must reproduce the copyright notices, trademark notices, legends and logos of McGraw-Hill and its licensors that appear on the Product on the back-up copy of the Product which you are permitted to make hereunder. All rights in the Product not expressly granted herein are reserved by McGraw-Hill and its licensors.

TERM: This License Agreement is effective until terminated. It will terminate if you fail to comply with any term or condition of this License Agreement. Upon termination, you are obligated to return to McGraw-Hill the Product together with all copies thereof and to purge all copies of the Product included in any and all servers and computer facilities.

DISCLAIMER OF WARRANTY: THE PRODUCT AND THE BACK-UP COPY ARE LICENSED "AS IS." McGRAW-HILL, ITS LICENSORS AND THE AUTHORS MAKE NO WARRANTIES, EXPRESS OR IMPLIED, AS TO THE RESULTS TO BE OBTAINED BY ANY PERSON OR ENTITY FROM USE OF THE PRODUCT, ANY INFORMATION OR DATA INCLUDED THEREIN AND/OR ANY TECHNICAL SUPPORT SERVICES PROVIDED HEREUNDER, IF ANY ("TECHNICAL SUPPORT SERVICES"). McGRAW-HILL, ITS LICENSORS AND THE AUTHORS MAKE NO EXPRESS OR IMPLIED WARRANTIES OF MERCHANTABILITY OR FITNESS FOR A PARTICULAR PURPOSE OR USE WITH RESPECT TO THE PRODUCT. McGRAW-HILL, ITS LICENSORS, AND THE AUTHORS MAKE NO GUARANTEE THAT YOU WILL PASS ANY CERTIFICATION EXAM WHATSOEVER BY USING THIS PRODUCT. NEITHER McGRAW-HILL, ANY OF ITS LICENSORS NOR THE AUTHORS WARRANT THAT THE FUNCTIONS CONTAINED IN THE PRODUCT WILL MEET YOUR REQUIREMENTS OR THAT THE OPERATION OF THE PRODUCT WILL BE UNINTERRUPTED OR ERROR FREE. YOU ASSUME THE ENTIRE RISK WITH RESPECT TO THE QUALITY AND PERFORMANCE OF THE PRODUCT.

LIMITED WARRANTY FOR DISC: To the original licensee only, McGraw-Hill warrants that the enclosed disc on which the Product is recorded is free from defects in materials and workmanship under normal use and service for a period of ninety (90) days from the date of purchase. In the event of a defect in the disc covered by the foregoing warranty, McGraw-Hill will replace the disc.

LIMITATION OF LIABILITY: NEITHER McGRAW-HILL, ITS LICENSORS NOR THE AUTHORS SHALL BE LIABLE FOR ANY INDIRECT, SPECIAL OR CONSEQUENTIAL DAMAGES, SUCH AS BUT NOT LIMITED TO, LOSS OF ANTICIPATED PROFITS OR BENEFITS, RESULTING FROM THE USE OR INABILITY TO USE THE PRODUCT EVEN IF ANY OF THEM HAS BEEN ADVISED OF THE POSSIBILITY OF SUCH DAMAGES. THIS LIMITATION OF LIABILITY SHALL APPLY TO ANY CLAIM OR CAUSE WHATSOEVER WHETHER SUCH CLAIM OR CAUSE ARISES IN CONTRACT, TORT, OR OTHERWISE. Some states do not allow the exclusion or limitation of indirect, special or consequential damages, so the above limitation may not apply to you.

U.S. GOVERNMENT RESTRICTED RIGHTS: Any software included in the Product is provided with restricted rights subject to subparagraphs (c), (1) and (2) of the Commercial Computer Software-Restricted Rights clause at 48 C.F.R. 52.227-19. The terms of this Agreement applicable to the use of the data in the Product are those under which the data are generally made available to the general public by McGraw-Hill. Except as provided herein, no reproduction, use, or disclosure rights are granted with respect to the data included in the Product and no right to modify or create derivative works from any such data is hereby granted.

GENERAL: This License Agreement constitutes the entire agreement between the parties relating to the Product. The terms of any Purchase Order shall have no effect on the terms of this License Agreement. Failure of McGraw-Hill to insist at any time on strict compliance with this License Agreement shall not constitute a waiver of any rights under this License Agreement. This License Agreement shall be construed and governed in accordance with the laws of the State of New York. If any provision of this License Agreement is held to be contrary to law, that provision will be enforced to the maximum extent permissible and the remaining provisions will remain in full force and effect.